No. 1750
$19.95

# 6502 MACHINE & ASSEMBLY LANGUAGE PROGRAMMING

MIKE SMITH

TAB BOOKS Inc.
BLUE RIDGE SUMMIT, PA. 17214

To my wife Pat, and my Mother and Father.



FIRST EDITION

FIRST PRINTING



Printed in the United States of America



Library of Congress Cataloging in Publication Data

Smith, Mike, 1945-
6502 machine and assembly language programming.

Includes index.
1. 6502 (Microprocessor)—Programming.
2. Assembler language (Computer program language)
I. Title. II. Title: Six thousand five hundred two
machine and assembly language programming.
QA76.8.S63S65 1984 001.64'2 84-24032
ISBN 0-8306-0750-1
ISBN 0-8306-1750-7 (pbk.)

# Contents

# Introduction

Many people have mastered the art of BASIC programming. BASIC is a fairly simple language that enables you to develop many useful programs. It suffers from a number of disadvantages, however, some real and some imagined. Users of computers tend to become interested in learning more things about whatever computer they are using. Without their daily computer fix, these people go through the typical "cold turkey" symptoms of withdrawal, cold sweats, and irritability. As with all addicts, they often turn to harder things. Other languages appear to have what BASIC doesn't; Pascal, FORTRAN and authoring languages such as Pilot and Logo beckon for a while. However, many finally turn to machine language programming. There is something special about doing programming in the "fast lane."

Machine language programming and its close ally, assembly language programming, have a mystique all their own. The strange mixture of numbers and letters called *hexadecimal* and the funny instructions like BIT and ORA beckon and frighten. The computer user realizes that, although perhaps more difficult than BASIC, machine language programming should be within grasp. Yet where to start?

This book attempts to introduce machine language programming in rather an unusual way, by *animation*. This is animation in the computer scientist's sense and not in the cartoon way. Animation or *simulation* is a technique of making a computer model of the thing you are interested in studying, in this case a computer model of the inside workings of a microprocessor, the heart of the microcomputer. Since most people are familiar with BASIC before they become interested in machine language programming, this computer model is programmed in BASIC. In this way, you can use your current understanding of BASIC to help you understand machine code and assembly language programming.

Each chapter of the book introduces you into some aspect of how a microprocessor manages to perform its instructions. By the end of each chapter you will have built, in BASIC, a working part of a microprocessor. This breaks the BASIC programming into small, manageable steps that can be handled in less than an hour for a slow typist. By understanding what the BASIC instructions do to make the animation work, you will come to understand what the microprocessor does. This book will not attempt to explain everything about the microprocessor; it is simply intended to be an introduction. The working model that you produce, however, will enable you to animate (simulate) in slow motion all the instructions of a microprocessor if you are so inclined.

Working in slow motion can become tedious. This animation model has been designed to have two speeds. Its working speed (W) enables the programmer to watch what is happening inside the microcomputer's heart. This is the animation operating in BASIC. The second, faster speed command GO does exactly the same programs, except that they operate at full speed on the "real" heart of the computer. These two modes of operation enable the beginner to see what is happening and the advanced user to debug more extensive programs.

In addition to being a "teach-it-yourself" machine language course, this book provides the programmer with a number of useful software tools, including an *assembler* and a *disassembler*. These are designed to make machine language programming easier and more fault-free. There are discussions on when to use machine code, when to stick to BASIC, and when to mix the two—with examples.

A person who has to explain machine language programming to others will find the simulation a useful teaching tool. The program has been used for this purpose in an introductory course in machine and assembly language programming within the Department of Continuing Education at the University of Calgary, Alberta, Canada.

The BASIC program for the simulation has very few (about 10) lines of code that are machine-dependent. These are grouped and easily identified (see Appendix A). For this reason, the simulation will run on any machine that can do BASIC. The only routine that will not work is the GO command, which requires that a 6502 microprocessor be present. The book explains the lines of code needed for the Apple II/*II*e, as well as the Commodore 64, 8032, and VIC-20. The program has been tested on all of the above machines, as well as an Osborne I. The VIC-20, however, requires major modification because of its small screen size and limited memory. These changes are also detailed in Appendix A.

Be advised that each chapter of the book uses subroutines developed in earlier chapters, so you must progress from the front to the back of the book with very little jumping around. Each chapter will require about a half hour to an hour of typing to get the BASIC program typed in. Because this book is an introductory text, some of the statements about the internal operation of the 6502 microprocessor are not strictly true. They have been modified so that the apparent operation of a microprocessor and its animation in BASIC are a little easier to understand and program at the introductory level.

# Chapter 1
# What Makes a Microcomputer Tick?

A microcomputer system consists of a number of components. Most people are aware of three major ones, the *keyboard*, the *screen* and the *memory*. The keyboard allows the operator to talk to the computer. The screen allows the computer to respond. In the memory there is a program that causes a letter to be shown on the screen when a key is touched. This *echo* function is a *software tool* provided by the computer; without it, most computer operators would be lost. The computer does not do this by instinct but must be programmed to do it.

Inside the computer, stored in *read-only memory (ROM)*, there is a small program called a *monitor* that spends its time looking round the computer trying to find something to do. It is the job of the monitor program to look after everything. It must be able to see if the keyboard or disk drive needs looking after. It must know how to display letters or lines on the screen, how to make sounds, how to do BASIC. Every now and again the monitor program gets confused and gets stuck. This is when your computer *crashes*.

The monitor program is written in *machine language*. It could have more easily been written in BASIC. However, this would mean the monitor would do its job very slowly. Speed is one of the main reasons that people learn machine language programming. Games running in BASIC work, but they work so slowly that a lot of the fun is taken out of them. Games like Breakout can be made to go

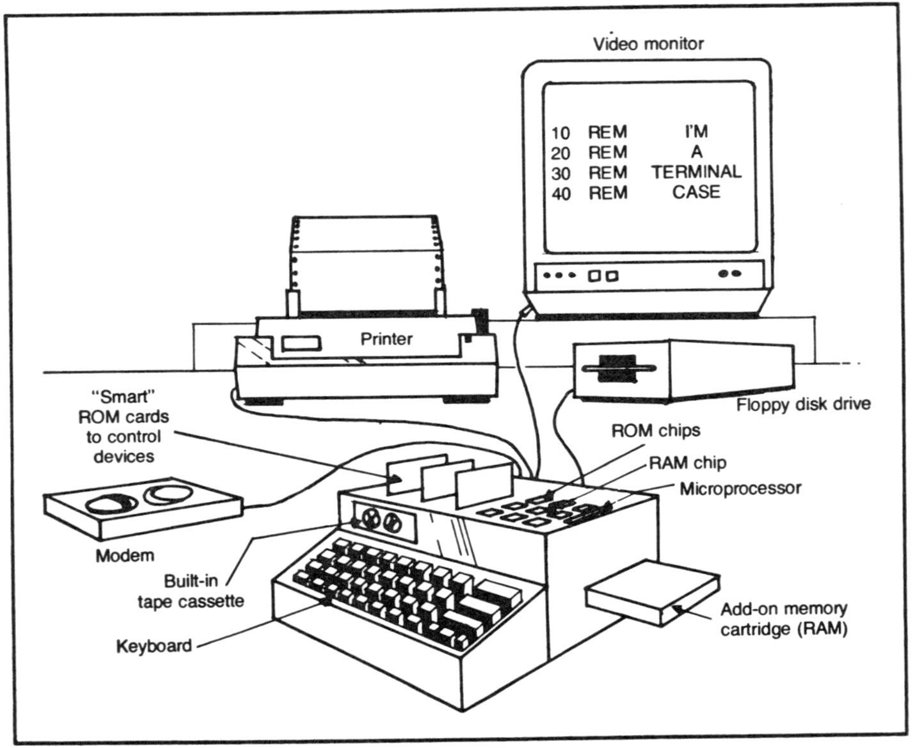


Fig. 1-1. Parts of a microcomputer system.

so fast in machine language that it is almost impossible to get a high score.

In this book, you will learn about machine language programming. Each microcomputer has its own machine language in just the same way that most machines have their own form of BASIC. However, just like the different BASICs, many things about the different machine languages are very similar. In this book, the 6502 machine language will be used. This is the language spoken by a large chip, called a *6502 microprocessor*, found inside an Apple, Commodore or ATARI microcomputer. The processor part of "microprocessor" means something that can control *processes*. Checking if the keyboard has been touched or if a letter needs to go to the screen are both examples of processes, things that need to be controlled. Other computers have different microprocessors. There are 68000, 6809, Z80 and 8080 microprocessors. There are microprocessors that, like a newborn baby, don't know a machine language and can be taught to speak any of the languages of the other microprocessors. (That sort of device is rather difficult to understand.)

In every chapter of this book, we shall develop and test many small programs that will lead us to a version of the 6502 microprocessor. We shall be using BASIC to make this working model or *animated* copy of the heart of the computer. We shall be able to see how this heart beats in slow motion. This will let us understand how each of the machine language instructions work inside a computer. Once we have entered the BASIC version of the microprocessor into our computer, we can watch the action of machine language programs. When we get tired of watching the slow animated version, we will, at the flick of a key, be able to run the same programs at full speed using the "real" heart of the microcomputer. Studying things via computer models, as we will be doing here, is a major tool used in the computer industry today.

Any microcomputer that runs BASIC will be able to get this animation to work. Those microcomputers not based on a 6502 microprocessor will get very confused if their "hearts" are asked to run 6502 machine language programs. Certain parts of the BASIC program in this book will not work in this case. However, once you see how the "6502 heart" works, a few simple changes will get the slowed-down version of your computer's heart working.

## HOW ARE PROGRAMS STORED?

Most of you know that there are two types of memory inside a computer. One is called *ROM* and the other is called *RAM*. Memory can be thought of as containers of electrical energy. This energy is our program. ROM memory is like a bathtub without a drain. Once it has been filled—by the memory manufacturer—it can't be emptied. The manufacturers even put a "lid" on the bath, so you can't add anything, even if the tub is not filled full enough. This is why ROM memory is called *read-only memory*. You can only read it; you can't change it in any way.

RAM memory gets a little upset sometimes, because RAM is not really its name. Its true name is *RWRAM* memory, but nobody ever calls it that. RWRAM means *read/write random access memory*. With RAM memory (*another type of "bathtub"*) you can read it (*see how much water there is in it*) or you can write into it and change its contents (*turn on the tap or pull the plug*). The name RAM tells about another feature of this type of memory. When you want to use it, you can use any part of it very quickly. Imagine that you have 5 songs on a cassette tape or 5 songs on a record. With the record you can choose or *access* any song. This can be done by moving the tonearm across the tracks you don't want to play and very quickly reach the one you want. A record is a *random access* song memory. If you want to hear the 5th song on a cassette type, you must run past all the other songs before getting to the one you want. This takes time. A cassette tape is a *sequential access* song memory.

In a computer you need speed. You must be able to get to any bit of a program very quickly. The computer may have over 64,000 words in it. One minute, the computer is using a program to put a letter on the screen, the next minute, another program is used to read the disk. A very short time later, a third program part is used to play a note. If the computer had to look through every bit of its memory before finding the program part it needed, it would operate excruciatingly slowly. That is why it needs random access memory. This enables the computer to jump to what ever part of memory is needed, very quickly.

The big difference between ROM and RAM memory is their use, ROM memory is used by the computer manufacturer to enable the computer to remember a program the next time it is switched on. RAM programs always disappear when you "power down" or turn the computer off. ROM memory is rather like an old dog, because "you can't teach an old ROM new tricks." If you want to change the computer's memory, by teaching it a BASIC program for example, you have to be able to *write* the new program into memory. For that you need memory that can be changed, RAM memory.

It is interesting that some computer programmers first of all use RAM to teach their computer some BASIC. They then take that program and put it into a special kind of ROM. In this way, their computers don't forget the BASIC program when they are switched off. This special kind of ROM is called *PROM* or *programmable read-only memory*. Once the information is in the PROM, it can't be changed again.

*Question: Since the monitor program can jump to whatever part of ROM it needs to use, is ROM memory also really random access memory?*

## WHAT'S STORED IN ROM?

Each ROM or RAM memory is split up into sections or *locations*. If you imagine that the computer memory is like a town, then each location, like each house, has a unique *address*. The microprocessor is the city hall for this town. In a computer controlled by a 6502 microprocessor, there can be up to 65,536 addresses. This number of locations is called *64K*. How many locations is 64K? The answer is "More than enough for the simple and fairly complex programs." Some computers have up to 2000K locations. Since every 1K means 1024 locations, this is a very large number of addresses. Figure 1-2 shows how the memory board of the computer can be divided up into *words*, *bytes*, *nybbles*, and *bits*.

At each address in our computer town there is a computer house or *word*. In the house there are a certain number of rooms, each one of which is called a *bit*. Some computers have up to 64 rooms in their houses or words, while others have as few as 4. The rooms in a 6502 town have 8 rooms or 8 *bits*. Words having 8 bits in them are called *bytes*. Words having only 4 bits in them are often called *nybbles*. You can see from the word *nybble* that early computer programmers had a rather strange sense of humor.

The interesting part of these houses/words, is their occupants. There can be one occupant per room. If the occupant is in the room, then we say that there is a 1 stored in that room or bit. If there is no occupant in the room then there is a 0 stored in that bit. Since there are 8 rooms in a 6502 word, then there can be up to 8 occupants. If the first four bits are filled and the last four are empty, then we can say that we can describe the contents of a house/word by the number 11110000. These numbers are called *machine code* or *machine language*. They are used to tell the microprocessor what to do. Tell a machine to do 11110000 and it might start to put a letter on the screen. Tell it to 00001111 and it might start to read a disk

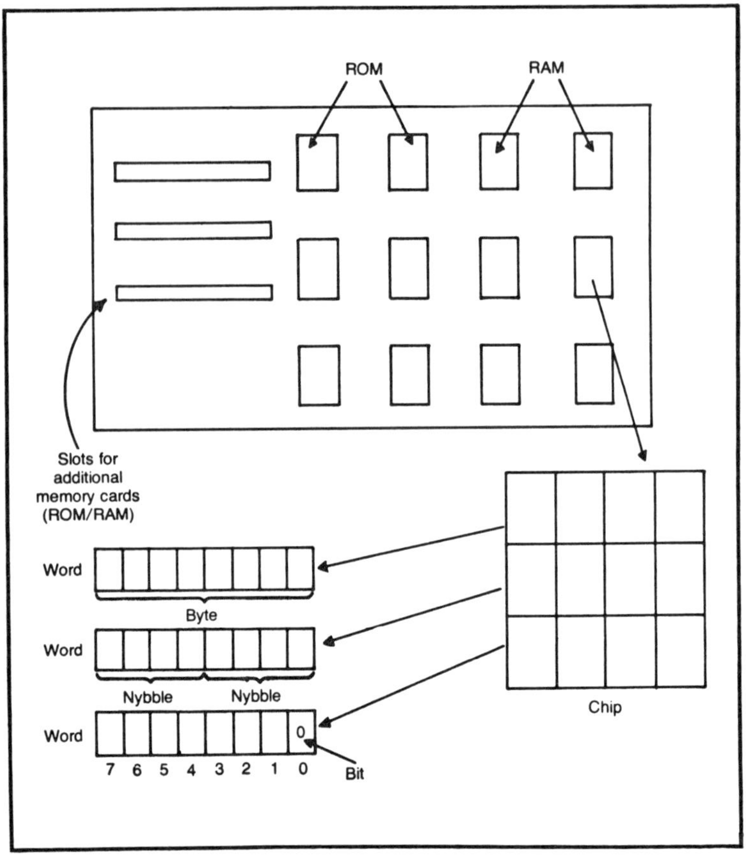


Fig. 1-2. ROM and RAM computer memory, showing how the "chip" can be broken into words, bytes, nybbles, and bits.

drive. The contents of the word written with 1s and 0s is said to be in *binary notation.*

This is all very easy for the computer. The manufacturer or any other programmer has to tell it what to do. Using numbers like 01101011 is very confusing. What would happen if you said "10110101, 10111011, 10110110" when you meant to say "10110101, 10111101, 10110110?" Mistakes like that would be difficult to find. (The difference is in the second word.) You can see this problem demonstrated in Fig. 1-3.

To try and make things easier to find mistakes computer programmers first of all split up each number into groups of 4 bits:

1011 0101   1011 1011   1011 0110

When they are grouped this way, the eye has a little less trouble handling a row of 1s and 0s. It was still rather confusing. They therefore decided to replace each of the groups of 4 bits by a single mark or symbol. If you have four numbers, then there are 16 different ways of counting them. The first four are 0000, 0001, 0010, and 0011. The computer scientists use the symbols 0, 1, 2, 3 for these. The next six ways are 0100, 0101, 0110, 0111, 1000, and 1001, which the computer scientists give the symbols 4, 5, 6, 7, 8, 9.

*Question: There is a pattern to these groups. Can you see it?*

There are six groups left; they are 1010, 1011, 1100, 1101, 1110, and 1111. Each of these groups of 1s and 0s is called by a single letter. To make things easy, the computer scientists decided to call these using a single letter starting at A. The second one was called B and so on up to F. They could have made up special symbols like $\lambda$ $\mu$ $\zeta$ $\sigma$ and $\xi$. However, that would mean that if other people used the symbols, like secretaries making up reports, they would need special typewriters. That would make things rather inconve-

```
                    BINARY FORM

 CORRECT                              WRONG

%10111110                          %10111110
%11001101                          %11010101
%10001110                          %10001110
%11011111                          %11101111
%01001100                          %01001100


                 HEXADECIMAL FORM

CORRECT                            WRONG

   $BE                               $BE
   $CD                               $D5
   $8E                               $8E
   $DF                               $EF
   $4C                               $4C
```

Fig. 1-3. Binary and hexadecimal versions of the same program, showing how hexadecimal numbers make it easier to read and debug the code.

nient and unnecessarily expensive, so the ordinary letters A to F are used.

## DISPLAYING HEXADECIMAL NUMBERS

Writing numbers with these 16 symbols is called using *hexadecimal notation,* and is a bit difficult to understand. The best way to get used to this method is to get the computer to count for us using this notation. Since displaying hexadecimal numbers is something we shall use all the time in this animation, we shall turn it into a subroutine and put it up high in our computer's memory. There it will be out of the way of the other program parts we shall develop.

Clear the memory with a NEW and enter the following program.

```
58995 REM <<set up the hexadecimal symbols>>
59000 FOR J = 0 TO 9 : SYMBOL$(J) = STR$(J) : NEXT J
59010 RETURN
```

Commodore machine users should make the following change.

```
59000 FOR J = 0 TO 9 : SYMBOL$(J) = MID$(STR$(J),2,1) : NEXT J
```

This program stores the characters 0 to 9 inside the array SYMBOL$. We should now test the subroutine to see if it can count as high as 9.

```
1000 GOSUB 59000 : REM  <<go set up the symbols>>
1010 FOR J = 0 TO 9
1020 PRINT "DECIMAL "; J; " ";
1030 PRINT "HEX $"; SYMBOL$(J)
1040 NEXT J
1050 STOP
```

If we test the program by typing RUN, we should see on the screen that for numbers 0 through 9, hexadecimal ("hex") and decimal symbols are the same.

In counting with the hexadecimal symbols we also need the letters A through F. We must add these to SYMBOL$. This makes the array SYMBOL$ too big for BASIC to generate automatically. We must *DIMension* SYMBOL$(15) to make enough room in our program. Since we are going to be doing a lot of dimensioning in making our large program, it is a good idea to put the DIM statement somewhere easy to find, in case we want to change it again. We shall therefore place a dimensioning subroutine starting at statement 60000.

```
10 GOSUB 60000 :REM <<set up our special variables>>

59990 REM <<place to set up variables>>
60000 J = 0 : REM make room
60500 DIM SYMBOL$(15)
60980 RETURN : REM leave room for other things
```

Notice that we have also *initialized* the variable J. This means that we have told the program to make room for J. In Chapter 17 we shall show that initializing all variables before using any arrays will actually make our BASIC program run faster.

Test the program using RUN again. If there are no errors then save it as CHAP.1A—just in case we do something to destroy it accidentally.

Now we want to set up the new hexadecimal symbols A to F.

```
1010  FOR J = 0 TO 15 :          REM now count up to 15

59010 FOR J = 10 TO 15
59020 TEMP = J - 10 :            REM how much bigger than 10
59030 TEMP = ASC("A") + TEMP :   REM asc turns letter into number
59040 SYMBOL$(J) = CHR$(TEMP):   REM chr$ turns a number back
59050 NEXT J :                   REM into a letter
59060 RETURN

60010 TEMP = 0 :                 REM make room for TEMP
```

If you run the program, you should see the program count up to $F in hexadecimal. Notice that 10 in decimal is $A in hexadecimal. Your screen should look like Fig. 1-4 if everything worked correctly.

Counting to 15 is not sufficient. That only uses 4 bits of our computer house or word. Counting with 8 bits requires numbers up to 255. Each number requires *two* hexadecimal symbols to show it. The animation is going to use these symbols very often when it tells us about how things are happening inside the microprocessor and memory. If we calculated what letters to print each time we wanted to use them, then the divisions that were needed would make the BASIC animation model run very slowly. We shall gain a lot of speed by precalculating the numbers and storing them in an array HEX$.

```
59095 REM store HEX numbers from decimal 0 to 255
59100 K = 0 :                   REM the number we shall change
59110 FOR I = 0 TO 15 :         REM do the 'tens' HEX digit
59120 FOR J = 0 TO 15 :         REM do the 'units' HEX digit
59130 HEX$(K) = SYMBOL$(I) + SYMBOL$(J)
59140 K = K + 1 :               REM get the next number
59150 NEXT J
59160 NEXT I
59170 RETURN :                  REM <<set-up HEX numbers>>

60020 I = 0 : K = 0 :           REM make room

60510 DIM HEX$(256) :           REM make room
60520 BELL$ = CHR$(7) :         REM used to ring a bell
60530 EH$ = BELL$ + BELL$
      : REM used when the computer doesnot understand
```

We should now test this new routine to see if it does the job. Our test program will get the computer to ask us for a decimal number between 0 and 255. It will then print out the next 10 hexadecimal numbers. Since our program only knows how to count for numbers bigger than 0 and smaller then 255, some checks must be made.

```
]RUN
DECIMAL 0 HEX $0
DECIMAL 1 HEX $1
DECIMAL 2 HEX $2
DECIMAL 3 HEX $3
DECIMAL 4 HEX $4
DECIMAL 5 HEX $5
DECIMAL 6 HEX $6
DECIMAL 7 HEX $7
DECIMAL 8 HEX $8
DECIMAL 9 HEX $9
DECIMAL 10 HEX $A
DECIMAL 11 HEX $B
DECIMAL 12 HEX $C
DECIMAL 13 HEX $D
DECIMAL 14 HEX $E
DECIMAL 15 HEX $F
```

Fig. 1-4. Screen printout showing decimal equivalents of the first 16 hexadecimal numbers.

```
TEST HEX NUMBERS

GIVE ME A DECIMAL NUMBER
BETWEEN 0 AND 255 345
<<< bell rings >>>

GIVE ME A DECIMAL NUMBER
BETWEEN 0 AND 255 34

DECIMAL NUMBER 34 HEX NUMBER $22
DECIMAL NUMBER 35 HEX NUMBER $23
DECIMAL NUMBER 36 HEX NUMBER $24
DECIMAL NUMBER 37 HEX NUMBER $25
DECIMAL NUMBER 38 HEX NUMBER $26
DECIMAL NUMBER 39 HEX NUMBER $27
DECIMAL NUMBER 40 HEX NUMBER $28
DECIMAL NUMBER 41 HEX NUMBER $29
DECIMAL NUMBER 42 HEX NUMBER $2A
DECIMAL NUMBER 43 HEX NUMBER $2B
DECIMAL NUMBER 44 HEX NUMBER $2C
```

Fig. 1-5. A range of decimal numbers converted into their hex equivalents.

When something goes wrong, the computer will say EH$, ring a bell, and try again.

(Note: strictly speaking, in line 60510 we need only dimension the array HEX$ as 255. Arrays start at 0, so that using 255 would give us 256 different storage locations. A perculiarity in the way the Commodore 64 powers up can cause the BASIC animation program to crash under certain circumstances. This occurs during the animation of one of the machine language instructions (RTS), which will be introduced in Chapter 14. Changing the size of the array HEX$ avoids this problem.)

```
1050 GOSUB 59100 :           REM  set up all the HEX symbols
1100 REM testing program
1110 PRINT : PRINT :         REM  make some room
1120 PRINT "TESTING HEX NUMBERS ": PRINT
1130 PRINT "GIVE ME A DECIMAL NUMBER "
1140 INPUT "BETWEEN 0 AND 255 "; J : REM  get a number
1150 IF (J < 0) OR (J > 255) THEN PRINT EH$: GOTO 1130
1160 TEMP = J + 10
1170 IF TEMP > 255 THEN TEMP = 255 :  REM don't count too high
```

```
1180 PRINT : FOR I = J TO TEMP : REM print out answers
1190 PRINT "DECIMAL NUMBER "; I; "  ";
1200 PRINT " HEX NUMBER $"; HEX$(I)
1210 NEXT I
1220 STOP :                        REM <<END CHAPTER 1>>
```

Test the new program and check and see if it works. Once all the syntax errors have been corrected, save it as CHAP.1. Your display should look like Fig. 1-5.

In the next chapter, we shall use these routines starting at lines 59000 and 59100 to print out the values found inside areas in the computer's ROM and RAM. Since we have saved the subroutines, they are available without having to retype them. They are also available for programs you want to develop.

**Problems:**

1) Develop a program that can count backwards in hexadecimal using the subroutines at 59000 and 59100.
2) Develop subroutines that will print things out in *binary* notation. How would you store things in the computer's memory for the greatest speed?

# Chapter 2

# Looking into Memory: The Monitor and BASIC Interpreter

As was mentioned in the last chapter, there is inside each microcomputer a monitor program that spends all its time looking for something to do. When we are using BASIC, this monitor program becomes very active. Each time we use a BASIC statement in a program, the monitor causes another machine language program to start operating. This new program also lives in ROM, just like the monitor. It is called a BASIC *interpreter*. Each time you get your computer to do a BASIC statement, the monitor program, acting like a foreman, gets the interpreter program to translate the BASIC command into a series of machine language commands. These machine language commands are something that the 6502 microprocessor can handle. This translation takes time. If the interpreter has been poorly written in the machine language of your computer then your version of BASIC will run more slowly than another version of BASIC.

While the interpreter is doing its work, the monitor program must remember which BASIC statement of your program it is doing. Since the BASIC statements keep changing, the monitor must store the information on the BASIC program somewhere that can be constantly changed. This means the storage must use RAM memory. In this chapter, we are going to create some subroutines that will enable us to look into the internal workings of the storage areas. You can also look into the ROM area and see the programs stored there. In ROM there are special areas to do the translating of

Table 2-1. BASIC Pointers for Several 6502-Based Microcomputers.

BASIC Pointers

| | Apple | | Commodore 64 | | Other Commodores | |
|---|---|---|---|---|---|---|
| | Decimal | Hex | Decimal | Hex | Decimal | Hex |
| Start BASIC | 103, 104 | $67, $68 | 43, 44 | $2B, $2C | 40, 41 | $28, $29 |
| Start variables | 105, 106 | $69, $6A | 45, 46 | $2D, $2E | 42, 43 | $2A, $2B |
| Start arrays | 107, 108 | $6B, $6C | 47, 48 | $2F, $30 | 44, 45 | $2C, $2D |
| Top of memory | 115, 116 | $73, $74 | | | 54, 55 | $36, $37 |
| Start of screen memory | 1024 | $400 | 1024 | $400 | 32768 | $8000 |
| Start of color memory | — | — | 55296 | $D800 | | |

Table 2-2. ROM Routine Starting Addresses.

| | | ROM Starting Addresses | |
|---|---|---|---|
| Apple | C64 | Other Commodore | Function |
| $D52C | $FFCF | $B4E2 | Do BASIC INPUT from keyboard |
| $D560 | $A871 | $B808 | Do BASIC RUN |
| $D648 | $A642 | $B5D2 | Do BASIC NEW |
| $FDED | $FFD2 | $E202 | Print letter on the screen |
| $FF3A | — | — | Ring Bell |
| — | $A435 | — | Print out of memory error |
| — | $B248 | — | Print illegal quantity error |
| — | — | $BB4C | Print redo from start |
| — | — | $BBF5 | Print "?" then do BASIC INPUT |

each of the BASIC commands. Table 2-1 shows the place where a number of different translations start. These are called *starting addresses*. Table 2-2 shows some of the storage areas in RAM that the monitor program uses for remembering.

Our program from the last chapter, program CHAP.1, has the subroutines we need to display hex numbers. You can either retype the program or reload the program from tape or disk. Once the program is in memory, we must make a few changes. First, we want to get the computer to make the hex numbers for us automatically. The following statements added to our program let this happen:

```
20 PRINT "SETTING UP HEX " :         REM explain the wait
30 GOSUB 59000 : GOSUB 59100 :  REM <<do the set up>>
40 GOTO 2000 :                              REM  jump round our old program

2000 STOP :                                  REM our new program
```

Test out the modifications to make sure there are no syntax errors.

In most microcomputers, most of the remembering for BASIC is done very "low" in memory. The reason for this is that some of the machine language instructions work only for memory addresses below 256, or below $100 in hex. This area is called the *zero page* of memory. If we go back to our picture on the computer as a town, then each house, or memory location, is on a certain street or *page*. The very first page in the computer is called the *zero page*. This page has all the memory locations whose addresses are between 0 and 255, or $00 and $FF in hex. You can work out the page number of a location by dividing its address by 256 and throwing away the remainder.

```
DECIMAL VALUES

LOCATION 100 VALUE 3
LOCATION 101 VALUE 0
LOCATION 102 VALUE 255
LOCATION 103 VALUE 1
LOCATION 104 VALUE 8
LOCATION 105 VALUE 80
LOCATION 106 VALUE 22
LOCATION 107 VALUE 178

HEXADECIMAL DISPLAY

LOCATION $64 VALUE $03
LOCATION $65 VALUE $00
LOCATION $66 VALUE $FF
LOCATION $67 VALUE $01
LOCATION $68 VALUE $08
LOCATION $69 VALUE $50
LOCATION $6A VALUE $16
LOCATION $6B VALUE $B2

AGAIN? Y/N
```

Fig. 2-1. Values of the BASIC pointers stored in the zero page of memory, displayed by the simulator program.

### THE ZERO PAGE DISPLAY

To start with, we shall make a program that displays the zero page and prints the answer out in decimal. We should do anything different first in the easiest way possible, just in case unexpected things happen. The BASIC statement PEEK allows us to examine memory.

```
2000 PRINT : PRINT "DISPLAYING MEMORY" : PRINT
2010 PRINT "GIVE ME A MEMORY LOCATION"
     : INPUT "BETWEEN 0 AND 255 ";J
2020 IF (J < 0) OR (J > 255) THEN PRINT EH$: GOTO 2010
2030 K = J + 7 : IF K > 255 THEN K = 255 : REM  check again !!
2040 PRINT : PRINT : PRINT "DECIMAL VALUES" : PRINT
2050 FOR I = J TO K
```

```
2060 TEMP = PEEK(I) : REM get the memory contents at location I
2070 PRINT "LOCATION "; I; " VALUE "; TEMP
2080 NEXT I
2100 STOP
```

Save this program as CHAP.2A before you run it, in case things go wrong. Take a look into memory using the value given in Table 2-2 for the BASIC *program size pointers*, once you have removed any problems with syntax. The top part of Fig. 2-1 shows what your screen might look like.

Now add the statement

```
2005 REM this is a statement to change the program size
```

and run the program again. You will notice that one or perhaps two of the values stored has been changed by the monitor program. Your screen might look something like the top part of Fig. 2-2.

```
DECIMAL VALUES

LOCATION 100 VALUE 3
LOCATION 101 VALUE 0
LOCATION 102 VALUE 255
LOCATION 103 VALUE 1
LOCATION 104 VALUE 8
LOCATION 105 VALUE 86
LOCATION 106 VALUE 22
LOCATION 107 VALUE 184

HEXADECIMAL DISPLAY

LOCATION $64 VALUE $03
LOCATION $65 VALUE $00
LOCATION $66 VALUE $FF
LOCATION $67 VALUE $01
LOCATION $68 VALUE $08
LOCATION $69 VALUE $56
LOCATION $6A VALUE $16
LOCATION $6B VALUE $B8

AGAIN? Y/N
```

Fig. 2-2. The values of the pointers change when more BASIC statements are added to a program.

Now we shall add a program to display the values stored using the hex notation.

```
2100 PRINT : PRINT "HEXADECIMAL DISPLAY" : PRINT
2110 FOR I = J TO K
2120 TEMP = PEEK(I) :REM get the memory contents
2130 PRINT "LOCATION $"; HEX$(I); " VALUE $"; HEX$(TEMP)
2140 NEXT I
```

To make it easier to look at memory a number of times, we should add a *menu*.

```
2150 PRINT : INPUT "AGAIN? Y/N "; ANS$
2160 IF MID$(ANS$,1,1) = "Y" THEN 2000 : REM  do it again
2170 IF MID$(ANS$,1,1) <> "N" THEN PRINT EH$ : GOTO 2150
2175 REM don't understand what you want!!
2200 STOP

60550 ANS$ = "" : REM make room
```

The BASIC instruction MID$(ANS$, 1, 1) takes the first letter of the answer ANS$ and looks at it. Lines 2160 and 2170 check the answer to see if it was "Yes" or "No." Since any other answer could be a mistake, we don't use it. If you now run the program with and without line 2005, your screen will look like Figs. 2-1 and 2-2.

If you use the program now, you should see that the place where the monitor stores the BASIC program size has changed once again. This happens because we have added more BASIC statements. There is another very interesting location called the *text pointer*. These memory locations actually point "inside" a BASIC line, so that the monitor can remember how far down the line it is. These locations change very rapidly, more than 2000 times a second. Why would it not seem to change when you run this program? Save your program again as CHAP.2B.

In later chapters we are going to be doing things to the memory of the computer that can quite easily destroy any program in RAM. We shall not be destroying the RAM itself. Actually we will probably not even be destroying the program in RAM. What is likely to happen is that we shall do things that so confuse the monitor program that it will not be able to remember how to read correctly what is stored in RAM. This means our computer program will crash.

## LOOKING ANYWHERE IN MEMORY

The programs in ROM have memory addresses that start from

57344 to 65535 ($E000 to $FFFF). Printing out numbers like these using decimal notation causes no problems

```
40   GOTO 2200 :                    REM  jump to new program

2200 PRINT : PRINT "GIVE ME A MEMORY LOCATION"
2210 INPUT "BETWEEN 0 AND 65535 ";J
2220 IF (J < 0) OR (J > 65535) THEN PRINT EH$: GOTO 2200
2230 K = J + 7 : IF K > 65535 THEN K = 65535
     : REM  look at next 7
2240 PRINT : PRINT "DECIMAL VALUES" : PRINT
2250 FOR I = J TO K
2260 TEMP = PEEK(I) :                         REM  get the value
2270 PRINT "LOCATION "; I; " VALUE "; TEMP
2280 NEXT I

2300 STOP
```

Check your program out by taking a look at some of the ROM routines used by the BASIC interpreter. The starting addresses were listed in Table 2-2. Save your program as CHAP.2C.

Now we need to display this same information using HEX$ symbols. As before, our program will use these numbers very often. For speed we should store them; in order to do so we should change the DIMension statement for HEX$.

```
60510 DIM  HEX$(65535) :    REM  tell the computer how many
60512 FOR J = 0 TO 65535
60514 HEX$(J) = "0000" : REM  make room for 4 HEX digits
60516 NEXT J
```

Hex numbers larger than 255 need four hex digits. In hexadecimal, the decimal number 65535 is $FFFF. Run your program again to check for syntax errors.

Did your system crash? Mine did. It crashed at statement 60510 with the message

ILLEGAL QUANTITY IN 60510

The computer does not accept numbers as large as 65535 inside a DIMension statement. There is just not enough room inside a 6502-type computer. If I made the dimension size smaller than 65535 (say 32000) then I got the message

OUT OF MEMORY ERROR IN 60510

Depending on the type of computer you are using, the message might be a little bit different. What has happened is quite simple. We have tried to get the microcomputer to store more than it could handle and gave it a "stomach ache." The effect of this illness is different for different computers. Some computers will just shake it off and keep on working. Other computers will act as though everything is all right—and then a little while later will crash for no apparent reason. Other computers will give up right now and crash completely.

The only safe way of handling errors like these is to type NEW and then reload the program CHAP.2C. When the computer crashed, all the remembered locations, called *pointers* (Table 2-2), stored in the zero page ended up pointing to the wrong things. Typing NEW resets all these pointers, making them point to the correct locations, and things become safe. This is going to be a constant problem when we do machine language programming. We are going to upset the monitor program very often. It therefore becomes very important that you save your program before trying it A slight slip can be fatal. Always save your program. I will remind you to do so when I know that it is very likely that things will go wrong. Other times you will have to do it yourself. If you forget, you'll have some retying to do.

Back to our problem of printing hexadecimal numbers up to 65535. We can't go for speed, because our computer can't handle it. We must instead somehow make the large hex numbers small enough for the computer to handle. First step is to bring back the program called CHAP.2C.

We mentioned before that all the computer houses or words were on certain streets or pages. We can make the address number easier to handle by first of all printing out the street or page number. Then we can print out the word or house number. The page number is also called the *high byte* of the address and the house number is called the *low byte*. Page and high byte are the same for our 6502 "town." (This is not true for all computers.) We can find out the high byte by taking our address and dividing by 256, throwing away the remainder. The BASIC function INT is an easy way of doing this. Again this new subroutine will be used very often by different parts of our final program. We shall put the number we want to convert to hexadecimal into the variable HEX before using the new subroutine.

```
2300 PRINT : PRINT "HEXADECIMAL PRINT" : PRINT
2310 FOR I = J TO K
```

```
2320 TEMP = PEEK (I) :REM get the value
2330 PRINT "LOCATION $";
2340 HEX = I          :REM go convert the address
2350 GOSUB 58000      :REM  the new subroutine will live here
2360 PRINT "  VALUE $";
2370 HEX = TEMP       :REM  let our sub-routine do more work
2380 GOSUB 58000      :REM  print out whats stored in HEX
2390 PRINT            :   REM  move to the next line
2400 NEXT I
2410 PRINT : INPUT "AGAIN Y/N "; ANS$
2420 IF MID$(ANS$,1,1) = "Y" THEN 2200 : REM menu again
2430 IF MID$(ANS$,1,1) <> "N" THEN PRINT EH$ : GOTO 2410
2500 STOP
57995 REM print large HEX numbers
58000 HITEMP = INT(HEX / 256)
      : REM get the page number for large numbers
58010 IF HEX > 255 THEN PRINT HEX$(HITEMP);
      : REM print only if needed
58020 LOTEMP = HEX - 256 * HITEMP
      : REM  get the 'house' or lo-byte
58030 PRINT HEX$(LOTEMP); :          REM  print it
58040 RETURN :                       REM <<END LARGE HEX PRINT>>
60030 HEX = 0 :                      REM  make room
60040 HITEMP = 0 : LOTEMP = 0
```

Once you have removed the syntax errors from the program, save it as CHAP2.D. If your program is working correctly it should display things like that in Fig. 2-3. Notice that the <<hex-print>> subroutine at 58000 is used twice. First we get it to print out the hex values for the address then we used it again for printing out the value stored at that address. To do this, we had to tell the subroutine what number we wanted to convert to hexadecimal symbols. Just before we used subroutine 58000, we put that number into the variable HEX. This is called *passing a parameter* to a subroutine. A *parameter* is the name for something being passed.

Every time you use the disk drive to save a program, you are also passing a parameter. To save a program you type something like SAVE CHAP.2D. The word SAVE is a command and the word CHAP.2D is the parameter you are passing to the SAVE subroutine in ROM. The parameter is used by your computer to provide the name for the saved program. Other computers might use more than one parameter in saving. For example on a Commodore machine you would use the command

DSAVE "CHAP.2D",D1.

The word DSAVE is a command. The first parameter is CHAP.2D, which again tells the SAVE routines in ROM what to call the saved program. The D1 is the second parameter, which tells the computer what disk drive to use when saving. Parameter passing, as you can see, is a very common thing.

## DISPLAYING A MEMORY RANGE

If we wanted to use our program to look at the SAVE subroutine in ROM we would have difficulty. This is because our program only looks at seven locations each time we use it. What we need is a program that looks at many locations at once. In this new program we ask for a starting address and then go to look for the

```
DECIMAL VALUES

LOCATION 801 VALUE 205
LOCATION 802 VALUE 0
LOCATION 803 VALUE 224
LOCATION 804 VALUE 240
LOCATION 805 VALUE 3
LOCATION 806 VALUE 44
LOCATION 807 VALUE 131
LOCATION 808 VALUE 192

HEXADECIMAL PRINT

LOCATION $0321 VALUE $CD
LOCATION $0322 VALUE $00
LOCATION $0323 VALUE $E0
LOCATION $0324 VALUE $F0
LOCATION $0325 VALUE $03
LOCATION $0326 VALUE $2C
LOCATION $0327 VALUE $83
LOCATION $0328 VALUE $C0

AGAIN? Y/N
```

Fig. 2-3. The screen printout when the simulator program displays a range of memory.

next 64 locations in memory. In hexadecimal notation decimal 64 is $40. In order to make things easier to read, we shall get our DISPLAY program to start at an address that can be divided by 8. Our new subroutine will start at statement 57000. We shall tell the subroutine where to start displaying the addresses by passing the parameter DISP to it.

```
40   GOTO 2500 :                  REM jump to our new program

2500 PRINT : PRINT "GIVE ME A STARTING ADDRESS"
2510 INPUT "BETWEEN 0 AND 65535 "; J
2520 IF (J < 0) OR (J > 65535) THEN PRINT EH$ : GOTO 2500
2530 DISP = 8 * INT(J / 8)
     : REM make the start a whole number of 8's
2540 GOSUB 57000              : REM use the new subroutine
2550 PRINT : INPUT "AGAIN? Y/N "; ANS$
2560 IF MID$(ANS$,1,1) = "Y" THEN 2500
2570 IF MID$(ANS$,1,1) <> "N" THEN PRINT EH$ : GOTO 2550
2580 STOP : REM <<end of CHAPTER 2>>

56990 REM display 64 locations starting at DISP
57000 D1TEMP = DISP + 63 : REM  find the last one to display
57010 IF D1TEMP > 65535 THEN D1TEMP = 65535
      : REM  DON'T run out of memory
57020 PRINT : PRINT "MEMORY STARTING AT $";
57030 HEX = DISP : GOSUB 58000
      : REM  use <<print-hex>> subroutine again
57040 PRINT
57050 FOR D2TEMP = DISP TO D1TEMP STEP 8
      : REM 8 locations a line
57060 HEX = D2TEMP : GOSUB 58000 : PRINT ": ";
57070 FOR D3TEMP = 0 TO 7
57080 HEX = PEEK( D2TEMP + D3TEMP) : REM  get the memory value
57090 GOSUB 58000 :              REM  use that routine again
57100 PRINT " "; :               REM  put a space between numbers
57110 NEXT D3TEMP
57120 PRINT :                    REM put out as new line
57130 NEXT D2TEMP
57140 RETURN :   REM <<end of large range memory dump>>

60050 DISP = 0 : REM make room
60060 D1TEMP = 0 : D2TEMP = 0 : D3TEMP = 0
```

Notice that we used and reused that subroutine 58000 to print many

```
]RUN
SETTING UP HEX

GIVE ME A STARTING ADDRESS
BETWEEN 0 AND 65535 800

MEMORY STARTING AT $0320

0320: 68 CD 00 E0 F0 03 2C 83
0328: C0 60 8D D2 C5 D1 D5 C9
0330: D2 C5 D3 A0 B4 B8 CB A0
0338: C4 CF D3 00 8D CE CF A0
0340: CC C1 CE C7 D5 C1 C7 C5
0348: A0 C3 C1 D2 C4 00 8D 8D
0350: A0 A0 A0 A0 A0 A0 A0 A0
0358: C7 CC CF C2 C1 CC A0 D0

AGAIN? Y/N
```

Fig. 2-4. A large range of memory in the "safe" area.

hex numbers. That's one of the advantages of developing subroutines. Each time we used the routine we had to set up the parameter HEX so that our subroutine would know what number to convert.

Once your program is working, the display should look very similar to the one in Fig. 2-4. Since your computer may be different than mine (an Apple II), the "look" will be the same but the number may be different.

## MAKING BACKUP DISKS

Once you have removed all the syntax errors, then save your program as CHAP.2. We save these programs on disk or tape so that we can reuse them. What happens if we destroy the disk by dropping coffee on it, or using it as a Frisbee? I never do this. My favorite thing is to find a new version of a program in a magazine, copy the new program, and then destroy the old one by mistake. Of course, the new version never works as well as the old. To avoid all these problems, the best way is to make a copy of all your programs on another disk. This is called a *backup copy*. For safety, you should always back up all important programs.

# Chapter 3
# Changing Memory

When we add lines to a BASIC program, we are making changes to the RAM memory in our computer. To make sure that these changes don't end up in the wrong area of memory, the built-in monitor program is working very hard. Without this monitor, the changes we make in the BASIC program could cause the computer to crash.

If we are going to start changing things in memory without the help of the built-in monitor, we must be very careful. We can't change ROM in any way, so even if things go really wrong, all we have to do is switch off the computer and start typing in our program over again. Every time we have to power down the computer to recover from a memory entry error, we waste a lot of time. It is much easier to find a safe working area in RAM memory, and do our thing there.

## WHO'S USING RAM?

In an earlier chapter we mentioned that the zero page of RAM was being used by the monitor to store pointers into the BASIC programs stored in memory. Most microcomputers use a large amount of RAM. It is used for the cassette drive subroutine, the disk drive program, the screen storage, and of course the BASIC program itself. The BASIC program, if it is small, only uses a small amount of RAM. However, the BASIC program we are writing is going to get bigger and bigger and bigger. We must therefore be

**Table 3-1. Memory Safe Areas**

| | |
|---|---|
| **Apple** | |
| $300 to $360 | |
| $2xx to $2FF | This area is safe provided no more than ($xx - 1) characters are input from the keyboard. A good starting location is $270. |
| **Commodore 64** | |
| $COOO to $CFFF | |
| **Other CBM-Computers** | |
| $27A to $339 | |
| $33A to $3F9 | This area is used by the disk commands SCRATCH and CATALOG. Avoid the first $14 (20) locations if using these commands from BASIC. |

very careful where we start storing things in memory. An area might start off being safe and then later be used by the BASIC program as it grows. Table 3-1 gives a list of the locations that are safe to use for a number of microcomputers. If yours is not given, then you'll have to look in your user's manual for a safe area. These areas might not be large enough for some of the programs given in magazines and books. Appendix B shows methods of getting a larger safe area.

Reload the program CHAP.2 and make the following changes so that we can get a safe area:

```
40  GOSUB 61000 : REM <<go and make a safe area>>
50  GOTO 3000   : REM go to our new program
3000 DISP = SAFE : REM <<Display our safe area>>
3010 GOSUB 57000
3100 STOP
60990 REM building a 'safe' area for machine language programs
60991 REM This area is 'safe' for APPLE and CBM
61000 SAFE = 0 * 4096 + 3 * 256 + 0 * 16 + 0
      : REM build your 'safe area'
61015 REM ***change 61000 for your machine***
61010 NSAFE = SAFE + 63 : REM end of 'safe' area
61020 RETURN : REM <<end safe-area-build>>
60060 SAFE = 0 : NSAFE = 0 : REM  make room
```

Test your program and look at what is already stored in the safe area of your computer. (For the Commodore 64, the safe area can be anywhere in the range $C000 to $CFFF (49152 to 53247). To be consistent with the safe area of the other machines used in this book, we shall make the safe area start at $C300).

```
61000 SAFE = 12 * 4096 + 3 * 256 + 0 * 16 + 0
```

is the line to use for the C-64.

### STORING DECIMAL NUMBERS

We now need to write a little monitor program of our own. This program will allow us to enter in values into our safe area. To make sure things are working correctly, we shall start with something simple. This means we shall enter in things using normal decimal notation or numbers.

```
3100 PRINT : PRINT "SAFE AREA FROM "; SAFE; " -> "; NSAFE
3110 INPUT "MEMORY LOCATION (IN DECIMAL) "; J
3120 IF (J < SAFE) OR (J > NSAFE) THEN PRINT EH$; "NOT SAFE"
     : GOTO 3100
3130 PRINT : INPUT "LOAD WHAT (DECIMAL) VALUE "; K
3140 IF (K < 0) OR (K > 255) THEN PRINT "CAN'T STORE"; EH$
     : GOTO 3100
3150 POKE (J), K : REM load into memory
3160 GOSUB 57000 : REM display the changes
3170 INPUT "AGAIN? Y/N "; ANS$
3180 IF MID$(ANS$,1,1) = "Y" THEN 3100
3190 IF MID$(ANS$,1,1) <> "N" THEN PRINT EH$: GOTO 3170
3200 STOP
```

Notice that we have to check if the address is somewhere in the range SAFE to NSAFE. We have to check that the value we want to store in that word is in the range 0 to 255. Try storing things into memory and show that you can change things in RAM. Your screen should look like Fig. 3-1.

Commodore 64 users: since your safe area starts at location \$C300 and not \$300, it is necessary to put the hexadecimal symbol C in front of certain numbers entered into the program. For example, if the book says ENTER \$300, you must enter \$C300. To make sure that you have no problems, extra pictures showing the correct image for a Commodore 64 screen will be given at all important stages. For the preceding example, your screen should look like Fig. 3-2.

### STORING THINGS IN HEXADECIMAL

It seems rather strange that we get a memory location in decimal and then display everything in hexadecimal. What we need to do is get a number in hexadecimal.

```
0328: 00 00 00 00 00 00 00 00
0330: 00 00 00 00 00 00 00 00
0338: 00 00 00 00 00 00 24 00

SAFE AREA FROM 768 -> 831
MEMORY LOCATION (IN DECIMAL) 840
NOT SAFE

SAFE AREA FROM 768 -> 831
MEMORY LOCATION (IN DECIMAL) 830

LOAD WHAT VALUE (IN DECIMAL) 254

MEMORY STARTING AT $0300

0300: 00 00 00 00 00 00 00 00
0308: 00 00 00 00 00 00 00 00
0310: 00 00 00 00 00 00 00 00
0318: 00 00 00 00 00 00 00 00
0320: 00 00 00 00 00 00 00 00
0328: 00 00 00 00 00 00 00 00
0330: 00 00 00 00 00 00 00 00
0338: 00 00 00 00 00 00 FE 00
AGAIN? Y/N
```

Fig. 3-1. The screen display when the simulator stores decimal numbers in memory.

```
50   GOTO 3200 : REM jump to start of new program
3200 PRINT : PRINT "HEXADECIMAL ENTRY " : PRINT
3210 DISP = SAFE : GOSUB 57000 : REM <<display the safe area>>
3220 PRINT : PRINT "SAFE FROM $";
3230 HEX = SAFE : GOSUB 58000
     : REM  use our <<HEX display>> subroutine
3240 PRINT " -> $";
3250 HEX = NSAFE : GOSUB 58000 : REM and again
3260 PRINT
3270 PRINT "WHAT MEMORY LOCATION? $";
3280 INPUT J
3290 IF (J < SAFE) OR (J > NSAFE) THEN PRINT "UNSAFE "; EH$
     : GOTO 3270
```

```
3300 PRINT "STORE WHAT VALUE? $";
3310 INPUT K
3320 IF (K < 0) OR (K > 255) THEN PRINT "CAN'T STORE"; EH$
     : GOTO 3300
3330 POKE (J), K : REM  store the value
3340 GOSUB 57000 : REM  <<display the changes>>
3350 INPUT "AGAIN? Y/N ", ANS$
3360 IF MID$(ANS$,1,1)  = "Y" THEN 3220
3370 IF MID$(ANS$,1,1) <> "N" THEN PRINT EH$: GOTO 3350
3380 STOP : REM <<end of chapter 3 >>
```

Once you have checked the program for syntax errors, try running it; you'll be surprised at the number of things that go wrong. My safe

```
C328: 00 00 00 00 00 00 00 00
C330: 00 00 00 00 00 00 00 00
C338: 00 00 00 00 00 00 24 00

SAFE AREA FROM 49920->49983
MEMORY LOCATION (IN DECIMAL) 49900
NOT SAFE

SAFE AREA FROM 49920->49983
MEMORY LOCATION (IN DECIMAL) 49982

LOAD WHAT VALUE (IN DECIMAL) 254

MEMORY STARTING AT $C300

C300: 00 00 00 00 00 00 00 00
C308: 00 00 00 00 00 00 00 00
C310: 00 00 00 00 00 00 00 00
C318: 00 00 00 00 00 00 00 00
C320: 00 00 00 00 00 00 00 00
C328: 00 00 00 00 00 00 00 00
C330: 00 00 00 00 00 00 00 00
C338: 00 00 00 00 00 00 FE 00
AGAIN? Y/N
```

Fig. 3-2. Decimal screen display for Commodore 64.

area starts at $300 and goes to $33F. When I try to type in 300, I get the message

UNSAFE

and the computer refuses to take it. If I type in a number that is 10 bigger than 300, the number 30A, the computer says to me

INVALID NUMBER, REENTER!

What is happening?

Well, it turns out we are asking the computer to accept a hexadecimal number and it does not know how. In lines 3280 and 3310, we get a number. What sort of number is it? The answer is *decimal* because that is how BASIC works. BASIC works with decimal numbers and not with hexadecimal numbers. When I type in 300, I mean hexadecimal $300. However the computer thinks I mean decimal 300, which is only $12C—far outside my safe area. That explains the UNSAFE message I kept getting.

When I type in 30A, I mean hexadecimal $30A. What does the computer think? Well first it understands the numbers 3 and 0. That means decimal 30. Then it reaches the letter A. It expects a number, *not* a letter. When it gets a letter it "knows" something is wrong. It therefore gives me a second chance and asks me to re-enter the number.

What went wrong is that the computer does not know how to get hexadecimal input. We need another subroutine which will start at 56000. It will get from the keyboard a hexadecimal number and then change it into something that BASIC can understand. It will then *pass back a parameter* for our program to use. This subroutine gives our main program a parameter rather than the other way around. The answer that BASIC can use will come back in the variable HEX.

To use this new subroutine, we make two simple changes to our main program

```
3280 GOSUB 56000 : J = HEX : REM get the memory address
3310 GOSUB 56000 : K = HEX : REM get the value to be stored
```

Notice how easy it is to change a program when we are using subroutines!

Our new routine must work like our <<print-hex>> routine in reverse. It has to take in a hexadecimal number, which includes the numbers 0 through 9 *and* the letters A through F. Then it must turn that hexadecimal number into a decimal number that BASIC can use. It had better do some other things as well. Perhaps people will by mistake enter nothing. That had better be checked. People might also use the wrong letters, like G or H. After all, the people (us) using the program have not been using hexadecimal numbers for long. We had better check for that, too. All the hexadecimal numbers that we have been printing out have had the $ sign in front of them. If people input a hexadecimal number, they might put a $ sign there sometimes and not at others. That is such a simple error and probably such a common one, the program we write should be able to ignore all $ signs if put there.

```
55990 REM get a HEXADECIMAL number
56000 INPUT ANS$ : REM  get an input of numbers AND/OR letters
56010 IF LEN(ANS$) < 1 THEN PRINT EH$ : GOTO 56000
56020 REM that checks in case there is nothing there
56030 IF MID$(ANS$,1,1) <> "$" THEN 56100 : REM  no extra '$'
56040 REM need to remove the '$'
56050 IF LEN(ANS$) < 2 THEN PRINT EH$ : GOTO 56000
56060 REM that makes sure that there wasn't just the '$'
56070 ANS$ = MID$(ANS$,2, LEN(ANS$) - 1)
56080 REM that removes the '$' at the beginning
56100 HEX = 0 : REM  we are going to return the PARAMETER HEX
56110 FOR G1TEMP = 1 TO LEN(ANS$) : REM check all the symbols
56120 TEMP$ = MID$(ANS$, G1TEMP, 1) : REM get a symbol
56130 IF (TEMP$ < "0") OR (TEMP$ > "9") THEN 56150
      : REM  not a number
56140 HEX = HEX * 16 + VAL(TEMP$) : GOTO 56200
      : REM is a number
56150 IF (TEMP$ < "A") OR (TEMP$ > "F") THEN PRINT EH$
      : GOTO 56000
56160 G2TEMP = ASC(TEMP$) - ASC("A") + 10
      : REM turn symbol ito number
56170 HEX = HEX * 16 + G2TEMP
56200 NEXT G1TEMP
56210 IF HEX > 65535 THEN PRINT EH$ : GOTO 56000 : REM too big
56220 RETURN : REM <<end HEX input>>
60070 G1TEMP = 0 : G2TEMP = 0 : REM make room
60550 TEMP$ = ""
```

Let's take a look at some of the BASIC statements we must use. The MID$ statement can be used in two ways. The first way is to pick out a particular letter. If we want to pick out the 5th letter, then we say MID$(ANS$,5,1). There is only one problem: BASIC will "bomb" if we ask MID$ to pick out a letter that does not exist. That's why we had to check that the ANS$ variable was at least one letter long before we did MID$(ANS$,1,1) (line 56010).

MID$ can also be used to pick out more than one letter for a variable. The BASIC statement MID$(ANS$,5,2) will pull out two letters from ANS$, starting at the 5th letter. If we say MID$ (ANS$,2,LEN(ANS$)−1) we are asking BASIC to

1) Start at the second character of ANS$.
2) Use all the letters in ANS$ (that's the LEN(ANS$)) but for 1 letter

```
0310: 00 00 00 00 00 00 00 00
0318: 00 00 00 00 00 00 00 00
0320: 00 00 00 00 00 00 00 00
0328: 00 00 00 00 00 00 00 00
0330: 00 00 00 00 00 00 00 00
0338: 00 00 00 00 00 00 FE 00

SAFE FROM $0300 -> $033F
WHAT MEMORY LOCATION $?33F
STORE WHAT VALUE? $?234
CAN'T STORE
STORE WHAT VALUE? $?23

MEMORY STARTING AT $0300

0300: 00 00 00 00 00 00 00 00
0308: 00 00 00 00 00 00 00 00
0310: 00 00 00 00 00 00 00 00
0318: 00 00 00 00 00 00 00 00
0320: 00 00 00 00 00 00 00 00
0328: 00 00 00 00 00 00 00 00
0330: 00 00 00 00 00 00 00 00
0338: 00 00 00 00 00 00 FE 23
AGAIN? Y/N
```

Fig. 3-3. The screen display after memory storage of hexadecimal numbers has been programmed.

```
C310: 00 00 00 00 00 00 00 00
C318: 00 00 00 00 00 00 00 00
C320: 00 00 00 00 00 00 00 00
C328: 00 00 00 00 00 00 00 00
C330: 00 00 00 00 00 00 00 00
C338: 00 00 00 00 00 00 FE 00

SAFE FROM $C300 -> $C33F
WHAT MEMORY LOCATION $?C33F
STORE WHAT VALUE? $?234
CAN'T STORE
STORE WHAT VALUE? $?23

MEMORY STARTING AT $C300

C300: 00 00 00 00 00 00 00 00
C308: 00 00 00 00 00 00 00 00
C310: 00 00 00 00 00 00 00 00
C318: 00 00 00 00 00 00 00 00
C320: 00 00 00 00 00 00 00 00
C328: 00 00 00 00 00 00 00 00
C330: 00 00 00 00 00 00 00 00
C338: 00 00 00 00 00 00 FE 23
AGAIN? Y/N
```

Fig. 3-4. Hexadecimal memory storage on the Commodore 64.

Since we use all the letters but one and start at the second letter, we are removing one letter, the first one. This way we can get rid of the $ if it is at the beginning of our answer. We could have used the BASIC instruction RIGHT$. A number of BASICs have different forms of this instruction, however, but MID$ is nearly universal.

In the next part of the subroutine, MID$ is used to get a single letter TEMP$ from the input. This letter is stored inside the computer in a way that depends on the computer in use. Statement 56130 checks to see if TEMP$ is between the *characters* 0 through 9. If it is in this range, then it is turned into a *number* between 0 and 9 and the result is added to HEX. If the contents of TEMP$ is not in this character range, then line 56150 checks to see if it is between the letters A through F—which are valid hex characters. If it is the letter A then it is turned into the number 10. If it is B then it becomes 11, and so on. Any other letter is invalid.

Once you have your new subroutine working save it as CHAP.3. When your program is working correctly then the display should look something like Fig. 3-3, or Fig. 3-4 for the Commodore 64.

In this chapter, we have been able to find a safe working area; then, using a simple BASIC program, we entered things into RAM memory. If you change the SAFE line (61000) so that SAFE is $FF00 or decimal 65280, you can try writing into ROM. As should be expected, you can't change ROM. Don't forget to change line 61000 back to its correct value.

We are now getting to a stage where we can enter simple machine language programs into memory. The routines we have now will do it, but they work slowly. In the next chapter, we shall improve our BASIC program so that it allows us to quickly enter in a large range of memory and quickly change anything we enter in incorrectly. We are building our own customized BOS or *basic operating system*.

# Chapter 4

# Making Computing Easier: Software Tools

Computer programmers like you and me are like the pilot of a plane that has just crashed in the mountains. The pilot, at the beginning, is just interested in staying alive. You and I, with our new computers, are just interested in programming. After a while, the pilot decides that surviving is not enough, he wants an easier life. To do this, he takes parts of his plane and turns them into tools. Using these tools, he can build things more easily and enjoy life, rather than just surviving.

Computer programmers are also beginning to make computer tools. Many of these tools are easy to use. I am writing this book using a computing tool called an *editor.* This tool, a special program, enables me to enter words, find words, correct words and even move paragraphs around. Once the book has been entered into the computer's memory, another computing tool called a *text formatter* takes what I have written and arranges the words to fit on a line with just enough lines on each page. It lets me use big or small letters, and remembers to put extra spaces into lines that are at the beginning of paragraphs. If I want to, I can even buy a program that will take my writing and check that I have spelled every word correctly. That program is very specialized and would find many mistakes with my spelling. I was born in England and my spelling is rather inconsistent. In one line I use the English spelling, the next line Canadian, and the line after that American. A SPELL program would point out all these errors.

All these computing tools are programs. I am also using other tools. My disk drive helps me to quickly save things. I use an 80-column card that gives me 80 letters on my screen instead of the normal 40 the Apple would give me. I use a modem to help me talk to other computers. These computer tools help me in the same way that the programs do, but they are different. They are built-in *hardware.* Tools like a disk drive are hardware and are rather difficult to change. The program tools are *software* tools because they are themselves programs. The nice feature about software tools is that, if they don't do the job exactly the way you want them to, you can change them. Changing a program is an easy thing to do if the program is written in BASIC and you have written it yourself. Many of the software tools, like the editor I am using, were written in machine language, and are more difficult to change. Unfortunately, many software tools are written on *protected disks.* When a program is written on a protected disk, it becomes almost impossible to change.

Software tools can be very useful. They can also take a lot of time to make. Software firms spend a lot of money getting them to work; they are frightened of losing money by people copying the programs illegally. It is understandable but a shame. Many of these programs are good, but a few changes to *personalize* them would make them better. Lately, many of these firms have decided to trust people more and are putting the programs onto unlocked disks. If you refuse to copy disks for your friends, you will help many other programmers, because more firms will start leaving their programs unlocked.

In the last chapter, we had a small software tool called a *BOS.* This program enabled us to enter things into memory. However it was very slow and clumsy to use. In this chapter, we want to personalize this BOS and make it easier to use. This new version must let us do a number of things:

1) Quickly enter machine language programs.
2) Allow us to check our machine language programs.
3) Allow us to correct or change our machine programs.
4) Allow us to RUN our machine language programs.
5) Allow us to do all the above in the order we want.

Thing number 5 is rather important. Many software tools lock you in. You can enter a program into memory and then change it, but the program then locks you in or forces you to run the program before you can do anything else. Our program must be a bit more helpful than that.

We are going to start our software tool using a *menu*. This will allow us to choose what we want. Menus should be *useful*. This means that they must be neat. Our programs so far have not looked very tidy on the screen. We need to add a number of subroutines to help things look better. We need to *clear the screen* and *move down the screen* so that things can be set up more easily.

Every microcomputer has its own BASIC. One way that most BASICs are different is in the way that they clear the screen or move the cursor down the screen. We shall put machine-dependent commands in subroutines. Inside our main program, when we want to clear the screen, we shall call that special subroutine. That way our main program will work on any machine. With all the computer-dependent subroutines in one location, it is very easy to make changes to a program to let it run on another computer. This program can be very easily transferred between computers via a modem.

## ADDING THE MENU

Reload your program CHAP.3.

```
61095 REM <<clear-the-screen subroutine>>
61100 HOME : REM xxx change for your machine xxx
61110 RETURN

61195 REM <<move-down-the-screen>>
61196 REM <<parameter DOWN tells how much to move>>
61200 VTAB(DOWN) : REM xxx change for your machine xxx
61210 RETURN
```

For the 80-column Apple version, line 61100 should read:

```
61100 PRINT CHR$(12);
```

and for Commodore machines substitute the following:

```
61100 PRINT CHR$(147);

61200 PRINT CHR$(19);:FOR J = 1 TO DOWN : PRINT CHR$(17);
      : NEXT J
```

In our menu, we are going to run a machine language program after we have entered it into memory. If I want to run a machine language program on a Commodore machine, I have to use the BASIC command SYS. On an Apple the command is CALL. Once again, the command is different for each type of machine.

```
61295 REM <<run-a-machine-language-program>>
61300 PRINT "START ADDRESS $";
      : REM get a HEX number to use as the START
61310 GOSUB 56000 : BEGIN = HEX
      : REM use our special <<get-hex>> routine
61320 IF (BEGIN < SAFE) OR (BEGIN > NSAFE) THEN PRINT EH$
      : GOTO 61300
61330 REM need to check that BEGIN in SAFE area
61340 CALL BEGIN : REM xxx change for your machine xxx
61350 RETURN
60080 BEGIN = 0 : REM make room
```

For Commodore machines line 61340 should read:

```
61340 SYS (BEGIN)
```

We now need to build our menu program. Since we are going to use the menu to enter the machine language programs into the safe area, it makes sense to display the safe area each time.

```
54995 REM <<display-the-safe-area>>
55000 GOSUB 61100 : REM <<clear-the-screen>>
55010 DOWN = 6 : GOSUB 61200 : REM <<move-down-the-screen>>
55020 DISP = SAFE : GOSUB 57000 : REM <<display-any-memory>>
55030 RETURN
```

Our BOS program should have the following commands:

| | |
|---|---|
| ST | Stop the program. |
| CL | Clear the memory area so we can use it. |
| GO | Go and run the machine language program. |
| CH | Change a location in the memory area. |
| LOAD | Bring in a large machine language program. |

In our menus in previous chapters, we used commands like YES or NO and checked the first letter of the command. This time we have two commands that have the same letter at the start. We must be careful. One of our commands will actually go and run a program in memory. Although we are writing things in a safe area, we must watch out. Machine language programs that start in a safe area might, by mistake or intention, jump out of that safe area. This can cause the computer's monitor program to get confused and crash the system. Before you try any of this new program, make sure you have SAVEd a version of the BASIC program.

First we should test that our clear-the-screen and move-down-the-screen subroutines work.

```
50 GOTO 4000 : REM jump to our new menu

4000 GOSUB 55000 : REM <<display-safe-area>>
4010 DOWN = 20 : GOSUB 61200 : REM <<move-down-the-screen>>
4100 PRINT "MENU WILL START HERE"
4110 STOP
```

Test this program out to see if things are placed nicely on the screen. If you have a lot of room on the screen and things look cramped, change line 4010 to suit yourself. Save this program as CHAP.4A.

Now we need to check out the menu control. We want to get a command and then check it out to make sure it is valid. There will probably be other commands we shall add later on, so we should not cramp ourselves for line numbers. In our next bit of programs we just check out whether we can find a command and then go to the correct place in memory to do the command. We shall later build a full subroutine for each command.

```
4100 PRINT "YOUR WISH, MASTER! "; BELL$;
     : REM I like polite computers
4110 INPUT ANS$ : REM  make sure there is an answer there
4120 IF LEN(ANS$) < 1 THEN PRINT EH$ : GOTO 4010
4190 REM  check for commands that have 1 letter important
4200 REM  for each command jump to a subroutine
4210 TEMP$ = MID$(ANS$,1,1) : REM  get first letter
4220 IF TEMP$ = "L" THEN GOSUB 40000 : GOTO 4000 : REM <<load>>

4490 REM  check for commands with 2 letters important
4500 IF LEN(ANS$) < 2 THEN PRINT EH$ : GOTO 4010 : REM invalid!
4510 TEMP = MID$(ANS$,1,2) : REM get first two letters
4520 IF TEMP$ = "CH" THEN GOSUB 43000 : GOTO 4000
     : REM <<change>>
4530 IF TEMP$ = "CL" THEN GOSUB 42000 : GOTO 4000
     : REM <<clear>>
4540 IF TEMP$ = "GO" THEN GOSUB 44000 : GOTO 4000 : REM <<go>>
```

```
4550 IF TEMP$ = "ST" THEN GOSUB 41000 : GOTO 4000
     : REM <<stop>>
4890 PRINT EH$ : GOTO 4010 : REM everything else is wrong
4900 STOP : REM <<end chapter 4>>
```

Because we want to make sure our BASIC syntax is good, we want to put a very small program at each subroutine, just to make sure we get to the correct place. First we shall add the STOP command:

```
41000 PRINT "STOP FOUND"
41010 RETURN
```

Try this out and see if your program can find the STOP command.

If you had no syntax errors anywhere, you will have noticed that the program went through the place where it printed STOP so quickly that you could not see anything. We need to add a WAIT. Since each command needs a WAIT, it is quicker to make the WAIT a subroutine. Using a single subroutine WAIT rather than many different ones also saves memory space. Later, if we find the WAIT is too long, we only have to change one line in our program.

```
55490 REM <<wait>>
55500 FOR WTEMP = 1 TO 300
55510 NEXT WTEMP
55520 RETURN
60070 WTEMP = 0 : REM make room
39990 REM <<menu commands>>
40000 PRINT "LOAD "
40010 GOSUB 55500 : REM <<wait>>
40020 RETURN
41000 PRINT "STOP"
41010 GOSUB 55500 : REM <<wait>>
41020 RETURN
42000 PRINT "CLEAR"
42010 GOSUB 55500 : REM <<wait>>
42020 RETURN
43000 PRINT "CHANGE"
43010 GOSUB 55500 : REM <<wait>>
43020 RETURN
44000 PRINT "GO"
44010 GOSUB 55500 : REM <<wait>>
44020 RETURN
```

Test out your program and save it as CHAP.4B.

**THE HELP COMMAND**

We have one problem. We now have many commands. Today, because we are using the commands a lot, we can remember them, but what happens when we try to use the program in a month's time? Then we might not remember the commands. We need a HELP command. This command will give us a list of the valid commands.

```
4230 IF TEMP$ = "H" THEN GOSUB 45000 : GOTO 4000 : REM <<help>>
```

```
45000 PRINT "HELP"
45010 GOSUB 55500 : REM <<wait>>
45020 RETURN
```

Test your syntax again.

Why are we adding only a little bit of the program at a time? It is so slow! The answer is simple. We know that we are going to make mistakes as we enter in any large program. By adding a small amount at a time, we will know exactly where the mistake is. Since we are adding only small bits, I bet you are making fewer mistakes than normal, *and* finding the mistakes more quickly. I find that when things go very smoothly, I *think* that they are also going slowly. It is not so! Only poor programmers have to use a lot of time making mistakes.

The first command we should add is the HELP command. This should clear the screen and then list the commands

```
44990 REM <<help>>
45000 GOSUB 61100 : REM <<clear-the-screen>>
45010 PRINT "VALID COMMANDS"
45020 PRINT "xxxxxxxxxxxxxx" : REM underline
45030 PRINT
45040 PRINT "CH - CHANGE ONE MEMORY LOCATION"
45050 PRINT "CL - CLEAR THE SAFE MEMORY AREA"
45060 PRINT "GO - GO DO MACHINE PROGRAM"
45070 PRINT "L  - LOAD MACHINE PROGRAM"
45080 PRINT "ST - STOP THE PROGRAM"
45200 DOWN = 20 : GOSUB 61200
      : REM jump past menu and all future commands
45210 PRINT "PRESS  ANY KEY TO CONTINUE ";
45220 GET ANS$ : IF ANS$ = "" THEN 45220
45230 RETURN : REM <<end help>>
```

```
VALID COMMANDS
**************

CH - CHANGE ONE MEMORY LOCATION
CL - CLEAR THE SAFE MEMORY AREA
GO - GO DO MACHINE PROGRAM
L  - LOAD MACHINE PROGRAM
ST - STOP THIS PROGRAM









PRESS RETURN TO CONTINUE
```

Fig. 4-1. Display produced by the HELP command.

Try out the program and see if the HELP command works. Your HELP command should leave the screen looking like Fig. 4-1.

Notice a problem? We have this wonderful HELP command, but when anybody starts to use the program, we don't tell them about it. A few changes will fix that.

```
4100 PRINT "TYPE 'HELP' FOR COMMANDS "; BELL$
4110 INPUT "YOUR WISH, MASTER? "; ANS$
```

Now when you start up the program, you should get a picture like Fig. 4-2 on the Apple and like Fig. 4-3 on the C-64.

### THE STOP COMMAND

This command should let us leave the animation gracefully. Sometimes we might try to STOP by mistake. By the end of Chapter 12, we shall be able to save the machine language programs we have developed. If we use ST by mistake, we could lose our machine

```
MEMORY STARTING AT $0300
0300: 00 00 00 00 00 00 00 00
0308: 00 00 00 00 00 00 00 00
0310: 00 00 00 00 00 00 00 00
0318: 00 00 00 00 00 00 00 00
0320: 00 00 00 00 00 00 00 00
0328: 00 00 00 00 00 00 00 00
0330: 00 00 00 00 00 00 00 00
0338: 00 00 00 00 00 00 FE 23

TYPE HELP FOR COMMANDS
YOUR WISH, MASTER
```

Fig. 4-2. Screen display as the simulator waits for a command.

language program and have to retype it. Putting in a check avoids this problem.

```
40990 REM <<stop>>
41000 GOSUB 61100 : REM <<clear-the-screen>>
41010 DOWN = 10 : GOSUB 61200 : REM <<move-down-the-screen>>
41020 PRINT "PROGRAM STOPPING" ; EH$; EH$
41030 INPUT "ARE YOU SURE? "; ANS$
41040 IF LEN(ANS$) < 1 THEN PRINT EH$ : GOTO 41020
41050 IF MID$(ANS$,1,1) = "Y" THEN STOP
41060 IF MID$(ANS$,1,1) <> "N" THEN PRINT EH$ : GOTO 41020
41070 RETURN : REM didn't mean it! <<end stop>>
```

```
MEMORY STARTING AT $C300
C300: 00 00 00 00 00 00 00 00
C308: 00 00 00 00 00 00 00 00
C310: 00 00 00 00 00 00 00 00
C318: 00 00 00 00 00 00 00 00
C320: 00 00 00 00 00 00 00 00
C328: 00 00 00 00 00 00 00 00
C330: 00 00 00 00 00 00 00 00
C338: 00 00 00 00 00 00 FE 23

TYPE HELP FOR COMMANDS
YOUR WISH, MASTER
```

Fig. 4-3. Commodore 64 version of Fig. 4-2.

Save this program as CHAP.4D.

### THE CLEAR COMMAND

This command will set all of our safe area of memory to zero. Its like getting a new, clean sheet of paper before writing a letter. In BASIC, the equivalent command is NEW. There is one problem; however, the CLEAR and CHANGE commands are very similar when they are typed in. We would not want to spend time typing in a program—only to erase it by mistake. More checks need building in:

```
41990 REM <<clear>>
42000 GOSUB 61100 : REM <<clear-the-screen>>
42010 DOWN = 10 : GOSUB 61200 : REM <<move-down-the-screen>>
42020 PRINT "CLEARING MEMORY" ; EH$; EH$
42030 INPUT "ARE YOU SURE? "; ANS$
42040 IF MID$(ANS$,1,1) = "N" THEN RETURN : REM mistakes happen
42050 IF MID$(ANS$,1,1) <> "Y" THEN PRINT EH$ : GOTO 42020

42100 FOR G1TEMP = SAFE TO NSAFE
42110 POKE (G1TEMP), 0 : REM clear a location
42120 NEXT G1TEMP
42130 RETURN : REM <<end clear>>
```

### THE CHANGE COMMAND

We seem to have two commands that are very similar in what they appear to do. There is L, the LOAD memory command and CH, the CHANGE memory command. They seem very similar. The difference is very small and we don't really need two different commands. The LOAD command will let us load a large number of memory locations, but we could, if we wanted to, use it to change only one location. As you see when we write the LOAD command, it is much easier to have another command, CHANGE, to allow us to alter only a few locations. We don't really need CHANGE if we have LOAD. But then you don't really need 25 flavors of ice cream if you have vanilla!

Our CHANGE command will simply let us change one location of memory. It will ask us for the memory location (in hex) and then the value to be loaded (also in hex).

```
42990 REM <<change>>
43000 PRINT "WHAT LOCATION $";
43010 GOSUB 56000 : I = HEX : REM <<get-a-hex-number>>
43020 IF (I >= SAFE) AND (I <= NSAFE) THEN 43100
```

```
43030 PRINT "UNSAFE"; EH$ : REM bad location
43040 GOSUB 55500 : REM <<wait>>
43050 RETURN
43100 PRINT "WHAT VALUE $";
43110 GOSUB 56000 : J = HEX : REM <<get-a-hex-number>>
43120 IF (J < 0) OR (J > 255) THEN PRINT EH$: GOTO 43100
43130 POKE (I), J
43140 RETURN : REM <<end change>>
```

**THE GO COMMAND**

Our next command is GO, which runs our machine language programs. Here we have to be careful. First, we want to keep our memory display on the screen. This allows us to be sure where the machine language program starts. Second, the running of the program can do nasty things to BASIC. We should therefore remind the user to save the current BASIC program before running.

```
43990 REM <<go>>
44000 PRINT : PRINT "RUNNING MACHINE LANGUAGE PROGRAMS"
44010 PRINT "IS DANGEROUS FOR YOUR BASIC" ; EH$; EH$
44020 PRINT: INPUT "ARE YOU SURE? "; ANS$
44030 IF MID$(ANS$,1,1) = "N" THEN RETURN : REM mistake
44040 IF MID$(ANS$,1,1) <> "Y" THEN PRINT EH$ : GOTO 44020
44050 GOSUB 61300 : REM <<go-run-a-machine-language-program>>
44060 PRINT BELL$;: "FINISHED MACHINE LANGUAGE PROGRAM"
44070 FOR J = 1 TO 1000 : NEXT J : REM a fixed wait
44080 RETURN : REM <<end go>>
```

Be careful that you save your program before testing this one out. Before you use it, you should put a very simple machine language program into the safe area. This is the command to return to BASIC. Using the CHANGE command of the menu, change location $300 to $60. If you do this, then your screen should look like Fig. 4-4 or 4-5. Now when you test the GO command, nothing dangerous *should* happen.

As before, the *starting address* for our GO instruction is $300, or $C300 for the Commodore 64. Non-6502 machines can't actually perform real 6502 programs using their microprocessor. We need to change a few lines to make sure we don't try to do it:

```
44000 PRINT "UNABLE TO DO 6502 CODE"
44010 PRINT BELL$; BELL$
```

```
MEMORY STARTING AT $0300
0300: 60 00 00 00 00 00 00 00
0308: 00 00 00 00 00 00 00 00
0310: 00 00 00 00 00 00 00 00
0318: 00 00 00 00 00 00 00 00
0320: 00 00 00 00 00 00 00 00
0328: 00 00 00 00 00 00 00 00
0330: 00 00 00 00 00 00 00 00
0338: 00 00 00 00 00 00 00 00

TYPE HELP FOR COMMANDS
YOUR WISH, MASTER
```

Fig. 4-4. The screen display required before the GO command can be used.

```
44020 FOR J = 1 TO 1000: NEXT J
44030 RETURN : REM <<end go>>
```

**THE LOAD COMMAND**

We are finally at the last command of our BOS. Although each part of the program we have developed is quite simple, you can see that it has taken a long time. You can understand why some software tool makers try to stop people from giving their program away free.

Our last command is LOAD. This should allow us to add easily many machine language instructions. To make it easy, the program

```
MEMORY STARTING AT $C300
C300: 60 00 00 00 00 00 00 00
C308: 00 00 00 00 00 00 00 00
C310: 00 00 00 00 00 00 00 00
C318: 00 00 00 00 00 00 00 00
C320: 00 00 00 00 00 00 00 00
C328: 00 00 00 00 00 00 00 00
C330: 00 00 00 00 00 00 00 00
C338: 00 00 00 00 00 00 00 00

TYPE HELP FOR COMMANDS
YOUR WISH, MASTER
```

Fig. 4-5. Commodore 64 screen required before using the GO command.

should ask us for a starting address. It should then allow us to type in as many instructions as we want. When we have typed in enough, then we should be able to type END and it should quit. In addition, it should *automatically* put things into the next memory location *without* being told.

```
39990 REM <<load>>
40000 PRINT : PRINT "WHAT STARTING ADDRESS $";
40010 GOSUB 56000 : BEGIN = HEX : REM <<get-a-hex-number>>
40020 IF (BEGIN >= SAFE) AND (BEGIN <= NSAFE) THEN 40100
40030 PRINT "UNSAFE "; EH$
40040 GOSUB 55500 : REM <<wait>>
40050 RETURN : REM bad address - exit

40100 PRINT : PRINT "TYPE 'END' TO QUIT "
40110 FOR I = (BEGIN) TO NSAFE : REM do all allowed things
40120 HEX = I : GOSUB 58000 : REM <<print-large-hex-number>>
40130 PRINT ": ";
40140 INPUT ANS$ : REM  get the answer
40150 IF ANS$ = "END" THEN RETURN
40160 GOSUB 56010 : REM use part of <<get-hex-number>>
40170 IF HEX > 255 THEN PRINT "TOO LARGE"; EH$ : GOTO 40120
40180 POKE (I), HEX : REM store in memory
40190 NEXT I
40200 PRINT : PRINT "CAN'T ADD MORE "; EH$
40210 GOSUB 55500 : REM <<wait>>
40220 RETURN : REM <<end load>>
```

Once you have gotten rid of all the syntax errors, save the program as CHAP.4. If everything is running correctly, your screen should look similar to Fig. 4-6 or Fig. 4-7 for the Commodore 64.

Notice the brackets around BEGIN in line 40110. Try removing them and you will get an unexpected syntax error. Why? If you type

FOR I = BEGIN TO NSAFE

BASIC thinks you have typed

FOR I = BEG INT ONSAFE

which is complete nonsense. I got around this problem on the Apple by using the variable name START instead of BEGIN. However,

```
MEMORY STARTING AT $0300
0300: 60 00 00 00 00 00 00 00
0308: 00 00 00 00 00 00 00 00
0310: 00 00 00 00 00 00 00 00
0318: 00 00 00 00 00 00 00 00
0320: 00 00 00 00 00 00 00 00
0328: 00 00 00 00 00 00 00 00
0330: 00 00 00 00 00 00 00 00
0338: 00 00 00 00 00 00 00 00

TYPE HELP FOR COMMANDS
YOUR WISH, MASTER LOAD

WHAT STARTING ADDRESS? $?300

TYPE 'END' TO QUIT
0300: ?EA
0301: ?EA
0302: ?EA
0303: ?60
0304: ?END
```

Fig. 4-6. Using the LOAD command.

the Commodore machines use the variable ST (STATUS) for telling if things are going correctly. It took me a long time to find out why things were going strangely when I was testing the animation on a Commodore 8032.

## MENU IMPROVEMENTS

We have spent a large amount of time getting our menu program working. We have done this because we will use the menu a lot in the rest of the book. The menu is not perfect; there are still a large number of things that could be checked. For example, in our LOAD subroutine, what would happen if we typed in ENDD by mistake? Can you add some more checks to correct this? Is it worthwhile checking all mistakes?

A nice and simple thing would be to modify the CH command. What would happen if you wanted to make these three changes?

$300 –> $EA

$310 –> $EA
$320 –> $EA

Each time we made one change, we would have to wait until the screen was redrawn before making another change. Although this does not take a very long time, it *seems* to take forever if we have more than one thing to change. It would be much nicer if this command automatically asked us for another address until we typed END. That would make the thing look like Fig. 4-8 or Fig. 4-9. It is a small and simple change that makes things very user-friendly.

In Chapter 12 we shall add a few more menu commands. You might want to jump to Chapter 12 and enter the BASIC needed for those commands now. If you wait until you have read Chapters 5 through 11 before adding those commands, you will better be able to understand how the commands work and why it is nice to have them. If you get those commands working now, however, they will be there to help you through the next few chapters.

```
MEMORY STARTING AT $C300
C300: 60 00 00 00 00 00 00 00
C308: 00 00 00 00 00 00 00 00
C310: 00 00 00 00 00 00 00 00
C318: 00 00 00 00 00 00 00 00
C320: 00 00 00 00 00 00 00 00
C328: 00 00 00 00 00 00 00 00
C330: 00 00 00 00 00 00 00 00
C338: 00 00 00 00 00 00 00 00

TYPE HELP FOR COMMANDS
YOUR WISH, MASTER LOAD

WHAT STARTING ADDRESS? $?C300

TYPE 'END' TO QUIT
C300: ?EA
C301: ?EA
C302: ?EA
C303: ?60
C304: ?END
```

Fig. 4-7. Using LOAD with the Commodore 64.

```
MEMORY STARTING AT $0300
0300: AC 20 03 E8 E8 E8 88 D0
0308: FA 8E 21 03 00 00 00 00
0310: 00 00 00 00 00 00 00 00
0318: 00 00 00 00 00 00 00 00
0320: 00 00 00 00 00 00 00 00
0328: 00 00 00 00 00 00 00 00
0330: 00 00 00 00 00 00 00 00
0338: 00 00 00 00 00 00 00 00


TYPE 'HELP' FOR COMMANDS
YOUR WISH, MASTER? CHANGE
WHAT LOCATION $?320
WHAT VALUE $?01
WHAT LOCATION $?326
WHAT VALUE $?03
WHAT LOCATION $?END
```

Fig. 4-8. The improved CHANGE command at work.

```
MEMORY STARTING AT $C300
C300: AC 20 03 E8 E8 E8 88 D0
C308: FA 8E 21 03 00 00 00 00
C310: 00 00 00 00 00 00 00 00
C318: 00 00 00 00 00 00 00 00
C320: 00 00 00 00 00 00 00 00
C328: 00 00 00 00 00 00 00 00
C330: 00 00 00 00 00 00 00 00
C338: 00 00 00 00 00 00 00 00

TYPE 'HELP' FOR COMMANDS
YOUR WISH, MASTER? CHANGE
WHAT LOCATION $?C300
WHAT VALUE $?01
WHAT LOCATION $?C326
WHAT VALUE $?03
WHAT LOCATION $?END
```

Fig. 4-9. The improved CHANGE command on the Commodore 64.

**DISASSEMBLE (D).** This command will take the machine language program stored in memory and turn the commands into a more English-like form called *assembly language mnemonics.* (A *mnemonic,* by the way, is an easily remembered phrase that helps us recall something more complex. The old "Thirty days hath September . . ." rhyme is a mnemonic almost everyone uses.) A disassembler program is a very convenient tool for checking whether you have loaded your machine language program correctly.

**ASSEMBLE (A).** This command works the other way around from DISASSEMBLE. It takes the more English-like assembly language mnemonics and changes them into the machine code that the microprocessor can understand. This will be a much better way of entering large machine code programs than the LOAD command.

**SAVE (S).** This command saves a machine language program from memory to the disk.

**GET (GE).** This command loads a machine language program from the disk into memory.

**CATALOG (CA).** This command allows us to determine what files are saved on the disk drive.

# Chapter 5

# Using Built-in ROM Routines

As was explained in previous chapters, there is a very busy machine language program called the monitor. The monitor provides many help functions to the computer programmer. It reads the letters from the keyboard when a key is pressed. It echos or repeats that key on the screen. The monitor reads and writes to the disk. All of these instructions must be hidden somewhere in ROM or RAM. We can make these programs work for us. Table 2-2 listed the starting addresses for a number of ROM routines.

To be able to use these subroutines, we must learn our first machine language instruction. This is the machine language instruction called

*JUMP and do the program starting at a certain address*

The computer does not understand this; it sees only the hexadecimal instruction $20. This instruction works the same way as the BASIC instruction GOSUB.

The name "jump and do the program starting at a certain starting address" is too long for us to remember. When the name gets too long, computer scientists introduce a mnemonic or memory aid. Instead of using that very long name, the scientists use *JSR* and call this a *jump to subroutine* instruction.

The JSR instruction needs a parameter. This parameter is, of course, the starting address. The starting address is a number between $0000 and $FFFF (or between 0 and 65535 for those who still like decimal). The JSR instruction takes up three locations in memory. First there is the instruction $20. Next there are *two* locations needed for the starting address.

*Question: Why are two locations needed for the starting address of a routine in ROM?*

Like the JBR instruction, many machine language instructions that don't have parameters only need one location saved for them in memory. Some instructions only use the numbers between $00 and $FF (0 and 255 decimal) and these need only two locations, one for the instruction and one for the number.

Let us suppose that we want to make our computer use a machine language program that gets a character from the keyboard. This ROM routine built into its memory. Look at Fig. 5-1, for the starting address of that program. For an Apple it is $D52C, for the C64 it is $FFCF, and for the other Commodore machines it is $B4E2.

We can use the LOAD command to make these special routines work. Load and run the program CHAP.4.

```
MEMORY STARTING AT $0300
0300: 20 2C D5 60 00 00 00 00
0308: 00 00 00 00 00 00 00 00
0310: 00 00 00 00 00 00 00 00
0318: 00 00 00 00 00 00 00 00
0320: 00 00 00 00 00 00 00 00
0328: 00 00 00 00 00 00 00 00
0330: 00 00 00 00 00 00 00 00
0338: 00 00 00 00 00 00 00 00




TYPE 'HELP' FOR COMMANDS
YOUR WISH, MASTER?
```

Fig. 5-1. The screen display when a machine language "read from the keyboard" program has been loaded into the animation program (Apple II version).

1) Choose the menu function for clearing the safe area of memory. If you can't remember what it is then type HELP!
2) Type in LOAD to start loading a machine language program.
3) Enter in the start of your safe area. For the Commodore 64 it is $C300. For the other CBMs and the Apple it is $300.
4) Type in the hexadecimal number for the JSR instruction $20 and press Return. The next number of the safe area should automatically appear.
5) Type in the low byte of the starting address of the INPUT routine (Apple is $2C, C64 is $CF, and the other CBMs are $E2).
6) Type in the high byte of the starting address (Apple is $D5, C64 is $FF and other CBMs are $B4).
7) Type in $60, which is the "return to BASIC" command.
8) Type END to show that all the program has been entered.
9) VERY IMPORTANT! Check that the machine language program has been entered correctly. If you have either the high byte or the low byte of the starting address wrong—by even 1—you could do a machine language program you did not want to do. (When I am working with a machine language program, I even open the disk drive doors just to make sure that I don't delete my files. All you have to do is jump to the DELETE DISK FILES routine in ROM instead of the INPUT routine and bingo, no more disk files.) Don't forget, that helpful little monitor program that normally protects us is not going to be working.
10) Check again! Your screen should look like Fig. 5-1, 5-2, or 5-3, depending on whether your computer is an Apple, C-64, or other Commodore machine.
11) Type GO to get your program to run. You will be reminded that "Machine language programs are dangerous for your BASIC." Look at your machine language program again. Is it all right? Check it against Figs. 5-1, 5-2, or 5-3. Then type YES to get past that check. Now type in the starting address ($300 or $C300). Your computer is now expecting input, not from a BASIC program but from a machine language program. Type in a letter (or a letter plus a carriage return) and the BASIC animation program will restart.

You have just run your first "real" machine language program. Congratulations!

Try some of the other routines whose starting addresses are

```
MEMORY STARTING AT $C300
C300:  20 CF FF 60 00 00 00 00
C308:  00 00 00 00 00 00 00 00
C310:  00 00 00 00 00 00 00 00
C318:  00 00 00 00 00 00 00 00
C320:  00 00 00 00 00 00 00 00
C328:  00 00 00 00 00 00 00 00
C330:  00 00 00 00 00 00 00 00
C338:  00 00 00 00 00 00 00 00




TYPE 'HELP' FOR COMMANDS
YOUR WISH, MASTER?
```

Fig. 5-2. "Read the keyboard" program for the Commodore 64.

```
MEMORY STARTING AT $0300
0300:  20 E2 B4 60 00 00 00 00
0308:  00 00 00 00 00 00 00 00
0310:  00 00 00 00 00 00 00 00
0318:  00 00 00 00 00 00 00 00
0320:  00 00 00 00 00 00 00 00
0328:  00 00 00 00 00 00 00 00
0330:  00 00 00 00 00 00 00 00
0338:  00 00 00 00 00 00 00 00




TYPE 'HELP' FOR COMMANDS
YOUR WISH, MASTER?
```

Fig. 5-3. Machine language "read the keyboard" program for other Commodore computers.

listed in Table 2-2. Don't forget to load the low byte first into memory and then the high byte. Some of the ROM programs don't always give exactly the result you expect. This is because some of the *registers* of the microprocessor have not had the correct parameters put into them. Registers will be explained in Chapter 6.

Some of the machine language programs stored in the computer's ROM will cause your system to crash. Don't worry about this. To get the animation program to restart, try the following:

**Apple** Type CTRL C
Press Return
Type RUN

**C64** Type RUN

**Other CBMs** Type X
Press Return
Type RUN

A number of computers have a special software tool already built into the computer. This is a tool that works in reverse to what we have done in the first part of this chapter. We have been turning assembly language instructions into machine language instructions and storing them into the computers memory. A number of computers, the Apple II for one, have built into them a program that takes machine language instructions in hexadecimal notation and turns them into assembly language instructions. This special program is called a *disassembler*. In Chapter 12, we shall build a BASIC disassembler to help us understand what is being stored in memory. Until that time, those lucky users who have an Apple (or another machine that has a built-in disassembler) will have one more command on their menu than the rest of us.

When the disassembler works, it will turn the machine code of the first three figures into what you see in Fig. 5-4. You can see that is very useful for checking that you have entered the machine code correctly. You should make a habit of using the disassembler to do this checking for you.

First we should add the disassembler command to the menu and check that we can understand it when it is typed.

```
4240 IF TEMP$ = 'D' THEN GOSUB 46000 :  GOTO 4000 :
     REM <<DISASSEMBLER>>
45055 PRINT "D  - DISASSEMBLE MEMORY INSTRUCTIONS"
```

```
0300-   20 2C D5    JSR   $D52C
0303-   60          RTS
0304-   00          BRK
0305-   00          BRK
0306-   00          BRK
0307-   00          BRK
0308-   00          BRK
0309-   00          BRK
030A-   00          BRK
030B-   00          BRK
030C-   00          BRK
030D-   00          BRK
030E-   00          BRK
030F-   00          BRK
0310-   00          BRK
0311-   00          BRK
0312-   00          BRK
0313-   00          BRK
0314-   00          BRK
0315-   00          BRK
PRESS RETURN TO STOP
ANYTHING ELSE CONTINUES
```

Fig. 5-4. Screen display after using the built-in Apple disassembler.

```
46000 PRINT "DISASSEMBLE"
46010 GOSUB 55500 : REM <<wait>>
46020 RETURN
```

Check your syntax and save as program CHAP.5.

The Apple disassembler lives in ROM at location 65121. This ROM subroutine looks into the *zero page* of the Apple at locations 58 and 59. Using the values it finds in these locations as a starting address, it disassembles programs. Once you have the new instruction working, go and look at the ROM subroutines starting at 65121 ($FE61) and see how it is done.

```
45995 REM <<disassemble>>  xxxBUILT IN DISASSEMBLERS  ONLYxxx
46000 DISASSEMBLE = 65121
46010 PRINT : PRINT "STARTING AT WHAT ADDRESS $";
46020 GOSUB 56000 : START = HEX : REM <<get-hex-number>>
```

```
46030 SPECIAL = 58
46040 POKE (SPECIAL), START - 256 * INT(START / 256)
      : REM lo-byte
46050 POKE (SPECIAL + 1), START / 256 : REM hi-byte
46060 GOSUB 61100 : REM <<clear-the-screen>>
46070 CALL DISASSEMBLE
46080 PRINT : PRINT "PRESS RETURN TO STOP "
46090 PRINT "ANYTHING ELSE CONTINUES ";
46100 GET ANS$ : IF ANS$ = "" THEN 46100
46110 IF ANS$ <> CHR$(13) THEN 46060 : REM do it again
46120 RETURN : REM <<end disassemble>>
60100 DISASSEMBLE = 0 : SPECIAL = 0 : REM make room
```

Once the syntax mistakes are out, save your program as CHAP.5. Test it, and your screen should look like Fig. 5-4.

# Chapter 6

# Introducing the Registers

When we run a BASIC program, how does the monitor know which part to do next? The answer is *line numbers*. Every one of our BASIC statements has a line number. Once a statement has been translated by the built-in interpreter subroutines, the monitor goes and finds the BASIC statement having the next higher line number. Things get a bit more difficult when we put a GOTO statement in our program. When this happens, many monitors jump to the beginning of the program and look at *every* line number of *all* the statements in the program. When it finds the line number that is the same as the one we want, the monitor uses it. This jumping to the beginning and searching is one of the reasons that BASIC runs rather slowly and inefficiently for long programs.

We understand how the monitor uses line numbers to find the next BASIC statement to do. The question is "How does the monitor know what to do?" We know that there is a machine language program that controls what the monitor does. But *how* does it happen? In the last chapter we used the JSR or *jump to subroutine* instruction. But *what* is doing the jumping?

## THE INSTRUCTION REGISTER AND THE PROGRAM COUNTER

In order for a microprocessor to know what instruction to do next, it has to remember what instruction it did last. To do this it must store the information somewhere. Since this information must be stored and then changed very often, it must be stored in special, fast-acting RAM. There are a few special RAM locations built *inside* the microprocessor. Yes, inside! Since these are very special locations, they are called by a special name: *registers*.

Most microprocessors have registers inside them, the registers come in different sizes, styles, and numbers. In this chapter we shall introduce two of the more important registers of the 6502 microprocessor. One is called the *Program Counter* register (or PC for short); the other is the *Instruction Register*, or IR. These registers are shown in Fig. 6-1. You may already know about some of the other registers inside a microprocessor. There is an X Register, a Y Register, an A Register, and a Flag Register—to name but four. These will be explained in later chapters.

The registers inside a microprocessor come in two sorts, those you can change by programming and those that change automatically. The program counter is an example of the first sort, while the Instruction Register is of the other kind. The micro-

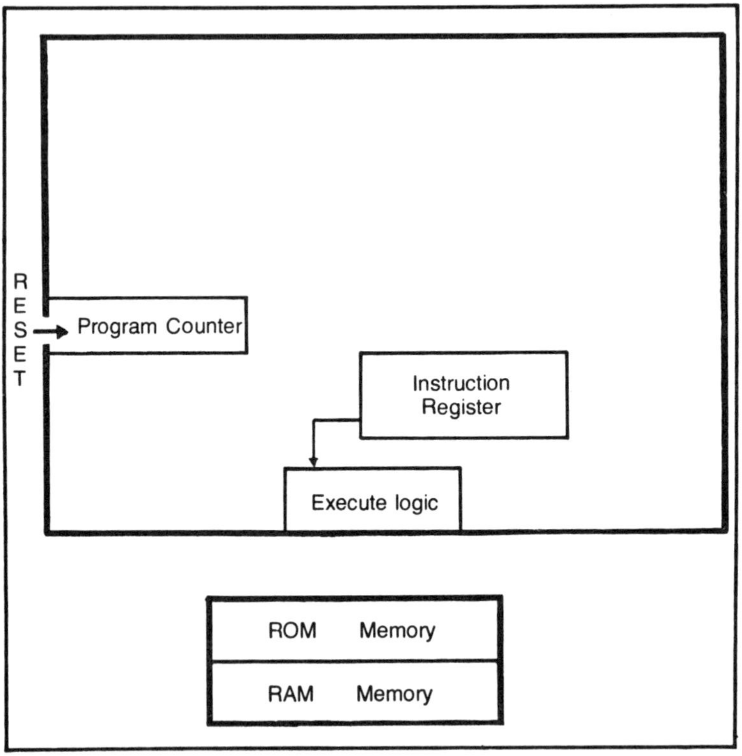


Fig. 6-1. Internal structure of a microprocessor, showing the Program Counter, Instruction Register, and EXECUTE logic.

processor inside your computer is rather like your body. Some things happen because you want them to, such as raising your arm to eat blueberry pie. Digesting the pie in your stomach, for example, happens automatically.

The Instruction Register, IR, is used to store whatever instruction the microprocessor is about to do. The Program Counter, PC, is used to remember what instruction to bring into the microprocessor. When you used the JSR instruction to fetch a character in Chapter 5, what you made happen was this:

1) First the starting address was placed into the Program Counter (PC).
2) Then, acting like a waiter in a restaurant, the Program Counter went and *fetched* the next instruction (JSR) from that starting address.
3) This instruction was then put automatically into the Instruction Register (IR) so that the microprocessor could know what to do next.
4) Once the microprocessor knew what to do, it would then *execute* or do the next instruction.

That's how the monitor works. The Program Counter register is used to remember where the next instruction to be done is stored. That next instruction is then fetched and stored in the Instruction Register. Once in the Instruction Register, the instruction is executed. When the instruction has finished executing, the Program Counter is used to fetch the next instruction. And so it goes on until you turn the power off. Figure 6-2 is a diagram of how this, the ultimate computer program, is always occurring inside your computer.

Choosing which instruction to fetch is done by the Program Counter. It can be done when you want to, like raising an arm to bring blueberry pie to your mouth. It can also be done automatically, just like you can automatically find your mouth when you eat popcorn in a dark cinema. Executing an instruction stored in the Instruction Register is rather like your body digesting your food. It always happens automatically and you have no real control over how it happens. To change what happens, you'll have to buy a different microprocessor.

Since it is impossible to see the fetching and execution of an instruction occurring inside your computer, this is an excellent thing to animate or show on the screen. To make this model of the

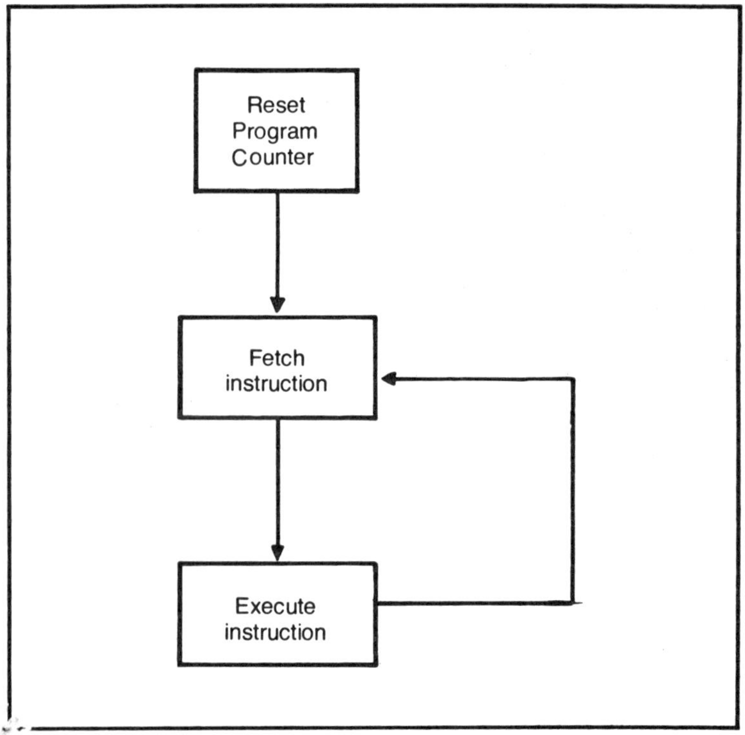


Fig. 6-2. The fetch-execute loop that occurs inside every microprocessor.

computer work, we need a number of subroutines:

1) A routine to display the registers and their values or contents.
2) A routine to make a fetch happen.
3) A routine to make an execute happen.
4) A new command in our menu to enable our working model to be chosen.

A good place to show the registers is at the top of the screen; Fig. 6-3 shows what we will be doing on the Apple; Fig. 6-4 shows the Commodore 64.

In order to display the registers at the top and to the right of the screen, we need to be able to HOME the cursor to the top of the screen without erasing the memory display and then horizontal TAB over to the column we want.

```
                         ! IR $00 PC $00
                         !--------------------

MEMORY STARTING AT $0300
0300: 4C 3A FF 60 00 00 00 00
0308: 00 00 00 00 00 00 00 00
0310: 00 00 00 00 00 00 00 00
0318: 00 00 00 00 00 00 00 00
0320: 00 00 00 00 00 00 00 00
0328: 00 00 00 00 00 00 00 00
0330: 00 00 00 00 00 00 00 00
0338: 00 00 00 00 00 00 00 00

TYPE 'HELP' FOR COMMANDS
YOUR WISH, MASTER?
```

Fig. 6-3. Simulator screen display with the Program Counter and Instruction Register added.

```
                 ! IR $00 PC $00
                 !--------------------

MEMORY STARTING AT $C300
C300: 4C 3A FF 60 00 00 00 00
C308: 00 00 00 00 00 00 00 00
C310: 00 00 00 00 00 00 00 00
C318: 00 00 00 00 00 00 00 00
C320: 00 00 00 00 00 00 00 00
C328: 00 00 00 00 00 00 00 00
C330: 00 00 00 00 00 00 00 00
C338: 00 00 00 00 00 00 00 00

TYPE 'HELP' FOR COMMANDS
YOUR WISH, MASTER?
```

Fig. 6-4. Adding the Program Counter and Instruction Register to the Commodore 64.

```
61390 REM <<home-the-cursor-to-the-top-of-the-screen>>
61400 VTAB(1) : REM xxxchange for your machinexxx
61410 RETURN :  REM make sure that you DON'T clear the screen

61490 REM <<tab-over>> move across to the 'OVER' column
61500 HTAB(OVER) : REM xxxchange for your machinexxx
61510 RETURN
```

The Commodore machine version substitutes these two lines:

```
61400 PRINT CHR$(19);
61500 PRINT TAB (OVER - 1);
```

**REGISTER ANIMATION**

Now we add the display of the registers:

```
53990 REM <<display-registers>>
54000 GOSUB 61400 : REM <<home-the-cursor>>
54010 OVER = 20 : REM xxxadjust for your machinexxx
54020 GOSUB 61500 : REM <<horizontal-tab-over>>
54030 PRINT "! IR $"; : REM display the INSTRUCTION REGISTER
54040 HEX = IR : GOSUB 58000
      : REM <<display-hex-value>> of the IR
54050 PRINT " PC $"; : REM display the PROGRAM COUNTER
54060 HEX = PC : GOSUB 58000
      : REM <<display-hex-value>> of the PC
54070 PRINT : REM xxxxx WATCH LINE NUMBERS xxxx

54800 GOSUB 61500 : REM <<horizontal-tab-over>>
54810 PRINT "!----------------"
      : REM puts BOX around registers
54990 RETURN : REM  <<end reg-display>>
```

A call to test the new display looks like this:

```
50    GOTO 5000 : REM get to our new program

5000  DISP = SAFE : GOSUB 55000 : REM <<display-safe-memory>>
5010  GOSUB 54000 : REM <<display-registers>>
5100  DOWN = 20 : GOSUB 61200 : STOP

60110 OVER = 0 : IR = 0 : PC = 0 : REM make room
```

Once you have your display looking like Figs. 6-3 or 6-4, save your program as CHAP.6A.

Now we need to make the fetches and executes happen. The easiest thing to do is the execution. Since we don't yet know what is going to be needed, let us make a "do nothing" or *no operation* (NOP) machine language instruction.

```
29995 REM <<execution-of-instructions>>
30000 GOSUB 61400 : REM <<home-the-cursor>>
30010 PRINT "EXECUTING "; BELL$; : REM explain what is happening
30020 PRINT "NOP"
30030 RETURN
```

This may seem like a strange instruction to use, but it is very useful when you use machine language programming. As you will see later, machine language programmers use the NOP or no operation instruction like an eraser over all their programming mistakes. It is also used to make WAIT loops exactly the correct time length. A NOP is really an instruction that does nothing except use up time and memory space.

How does a machine language program work? After the last instruction has been done or executed, the next instruction has to be fetched. The address of the next instruction is stored inside the Program Counter. The microprocessor fetches the instruction and puts it into the Instruction Register. Now comes the important part. *Before* going and executing the instruction, the microprocessor *automatically* adds 1 to the Program Counter and makes it point to the *next* instruction to do. This is just like the monitor program and BASIC. The monitor program automatically gets ready for the next BASIC statement by finding the next higher line number. For machine language programs, the people who designed the microprocessor have made it so that it automatically points to the next machine language instruction.

*Question: How does 1 get added to the Program Counter?*

The answer? More logic. Inside the microprocessor there is logic which can add, subtract, divide by 2, multiply by 2, and make things equal to 0 or $-1$. These things happen quickly and automatically.

In our fetch instruction in BASIC we have to do add 1 to the Program Counter to make it point to the next instruction.

```
38990 REM <<fetch-next-instruction>>
39000 GOSUB 61400 : REM <<home-cursor>>
39010 PRINT "FETCH       " : REM explain what's happening
```

```
39020 IR = PEEK(PC) : REM get the next instruction using the PC
39030 PC = PC + 1
      : REM PROGRAM COUNTER points to the next instruction
39040 RETURN : REM <<end fetch>>
```

Now everything is ready for our "working" model of the microprocessor. All we need is to get the Program Counter pointing to the instruction we want to fetch first. When we power up the computer, the Program Counter inside the real microprocessor is automatically made to point to a special set of instructions called the *RESET* instructions. These make the computer get ready to run a BASIC program.

In our BASIC version of a microprocessor we want to be able to choose our own RESET instruction, so we can watch what happens. If you remember from before, nasty things can happen if the machine language instructions get out of the safe area of memory. We can now control things to make sure that that never happens. The Program Counter always stores the place where the next instruction will be fetched from. If we check that this never goes outside the safe area then nothing nasty can happen (touch wood).

```
5100 DOWN = 22 : GOSUB 61200 : REM <<move-down-the-screen>>
5110 PRINT "WHAT STARTING ADDRESS $"; BELL$;
5120 GOSUB 56000 : BEGIN = HEX
     : REM <<get-hex-number>> for BEGIN
5130 IF (BEGIN < SAFE) OR (BEGIN > NSAFE) THEN PRINT EH$
     : GOTO 5100
5140 PC = BEGIN : REM 'RESET' PROGRAMME COUNTER
5150 GOSUB 39000 :  REM <<FETCH>> an instruction
5160 GOSUB 54000 : REM <<display-registers>> to show change
5170 GOSUB 30000 : REM <<EXECUTE>> an instruction
5180 GOSUB 54000 : REM <<display-registers>> to show change
5190 GOSUB 55500 : REM <<wait>>
5200 IF (PC >= SAFE) AND (PC <= NSAFE) THEN 5150
5210 REM go and 'FETCH' and 'EXECUTE' the next instruction
5300 DOWN = 22 : GOSUB 61200 : STOP
```

Once you have entered the program, get it to run. Type in a starting address near the end of your safe area, around $338. You should see the animation first go and fetch an instruction and store it in the Instruction Register. Next the Program Counter will be increased by 1 to make it ready for the next instruction. Once the instruction is in the Instruction Register, then you should see the display go through the next stage of execution. You now have a working "heart" of a microprocessor. In the next chapter, we shall get it to execute two machine language instructions. When the Program Counter reaches an instruction outside the safe area, the animation will stop.

Before saving our program, we need to add this animation as a new command. This WORK (W) command in our menu will let us use it as needed.

```
50     GOTO 4000 : REM jump to our MENU
4005   GOSUB 54000 : REM <<display registers>>
4250   IF TEMP$ = "W" THEN GOSUB 5100 : GOTO 4000
45090 PRINT "W  - WORKING MODEL OF MICRO-PROCESSOR"
5300   RETURN : REM <<end CHAPTER 6>>
```

Save this program as CHAP.6. Test out the menu and make sure that you can get the WORK command to work.

I hope you noticed that we did not have to do very much programming in this chapter. Most of the things we needed to use we had already built in earlier chapters. For our full working model of the 6502 microprocessor, there is not much more to do. We must add a few more registers to the <<display-registers>> subroutine. Finally, we must get the instructions to work. There are about 200 different instructions that the 6502 microprocessor understands. We shall only be dealing with the most important ones. If you want to add more, then you'll find it rather easy.

## WHAT IS EXECUTE LOGIC?

In the last section we talked about fetching an instruction using the Program Counter and putting it in the Instruction Register. Once there, the *EXECUTE logic* built into the microprocessor took over and did the instruction.

Memory ROM and RAM are built of a number of transistors and wires. The wires allow electrical signals to pass between the transistors. Once the electrical signal is on a wire, it can't be stopped from moving down the wire to the next transistor. The transistors are made to do two things. First, they can be used to store electrical signals. When they are storing a signal, we say there is a 1 stored in memory. When there is no energy stored, we say that there is a 0 in memory.

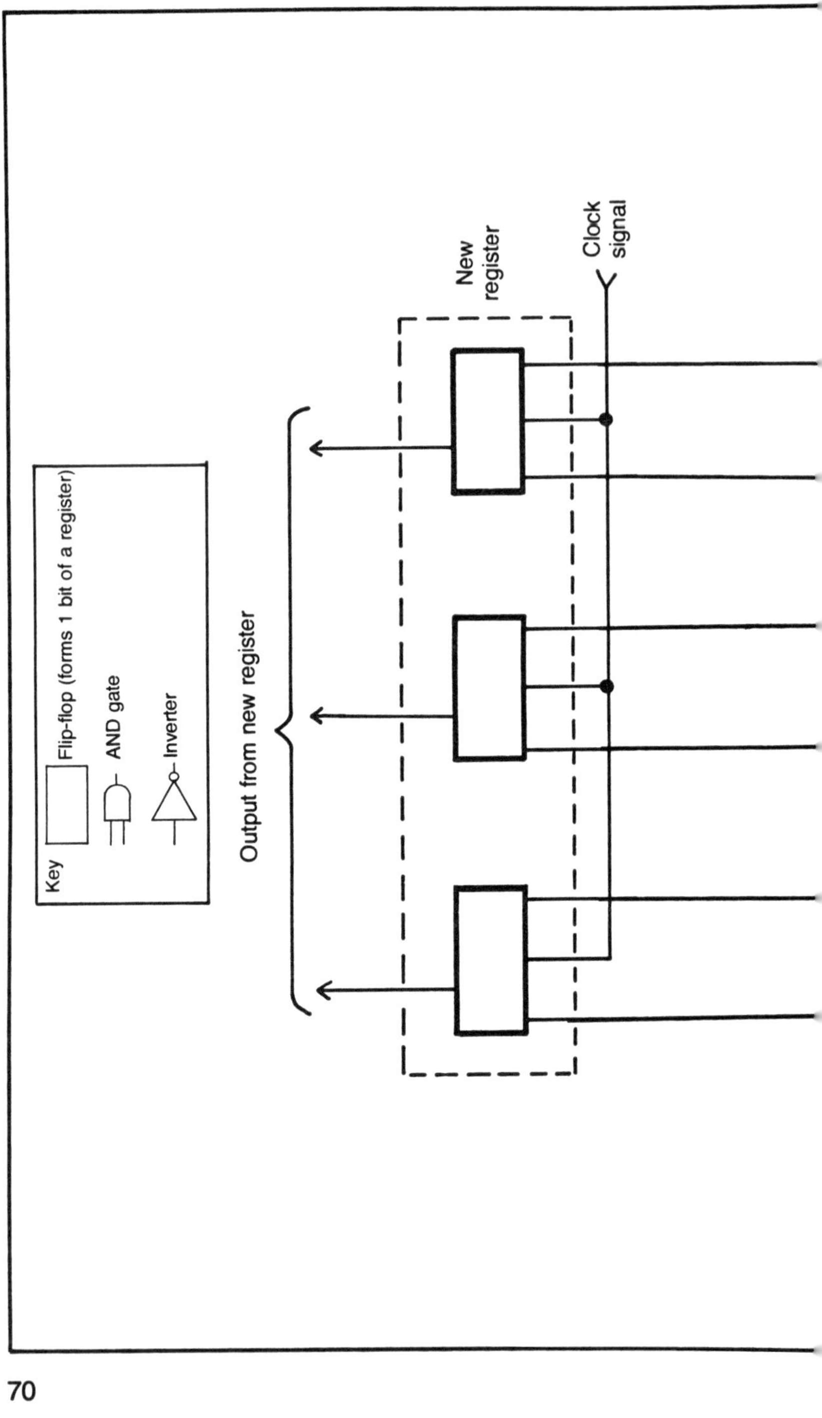
Key
Flip-flop (forms 1 bit of a register)
AND gate
Inverter
Output from new register
New register
Clock signal

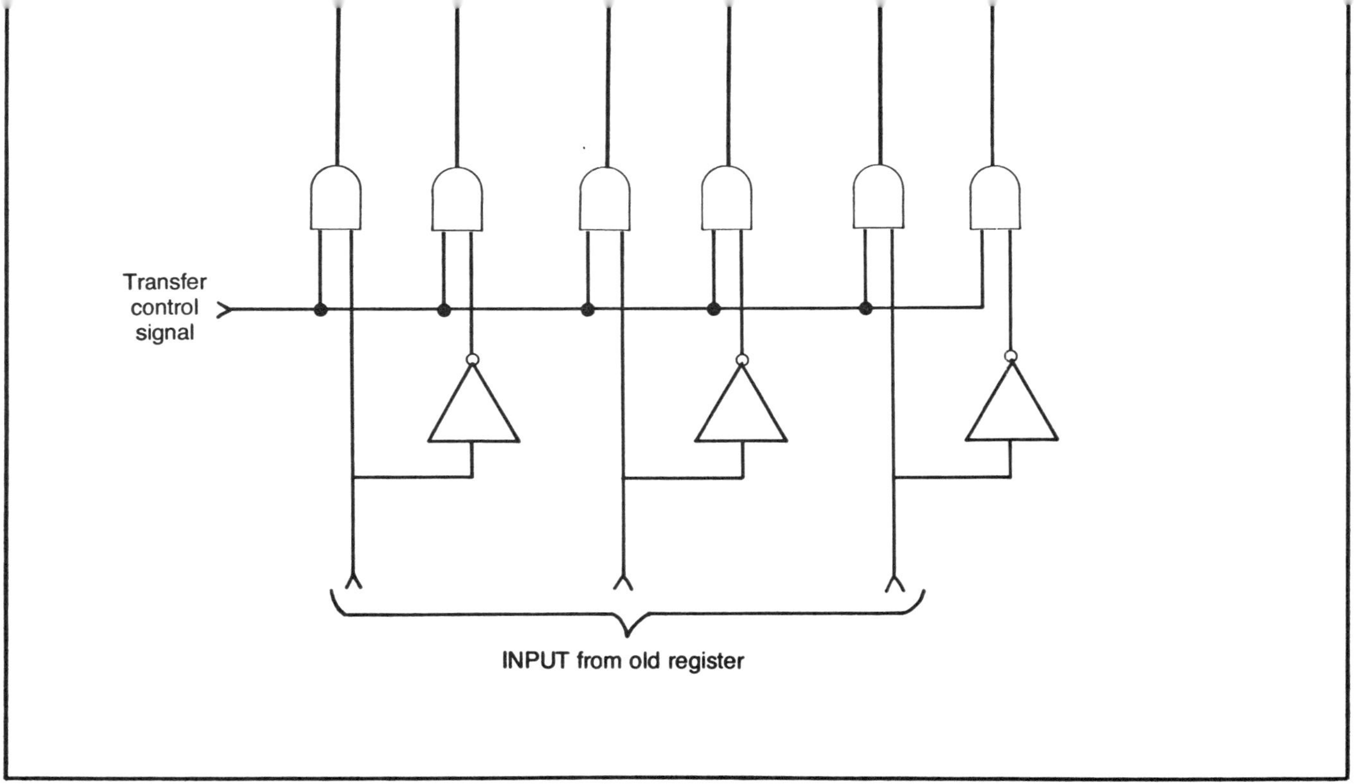


Fig. 6-5. The logic components needed to create part of a register.

The second job of transistors is also very important. They act like electrical switches. Have you ever thought what stops a piece of information in one piece of memory moving into another memory location? If nothing was there to stop this, we could never store any information. It would always be changing. The movement of electricity is controlled by other transistors acting as switches. In fact the transistors that store the 1s and 0s can also be thought of as switches. Figure 6-5 shows some of the logic necessary to make up a register. You'll have to find a more advanced textbook if you want more information on this aspect of computers.

Inside the microprocessor itself, there is more RAM. These were called *registers*. The Program Counter, the Arithmetic Logic Unit (ALU), and the Instruction Register were examples. For a machine language instruction to work, there must be wires and more transistors to control the passing of electrical signals between the registers. The EXECUTE logic is another special lot of transistors and wires that control the working or *execution* of all the other wires and transistors. What is special about the EXECUTE logic is that the gates and transistors in it control themselves. (That's not easy.)

Let's look at something not too complicated, but just the same something that happens with every single machine language instruction. After the Program Counter is used to fetch an instruction for the Instruction Register, the Program Counter must be made ready to fetch the next instruction. This is done by increasing the value of the Program Counter by 1 using the *arithmetic registers*. This takes five steps:

1) The EXECUTE logic sends a signal to open a gate between the Program Counter and one of the arithmetic registers. This allows the value in the PC to move into some sort of arithmetic register.
2) The EXECUTE logic sends a signal to close the gate.
3) The EXECUTE logic sends a signal to the logic unit that controls the arithmetic registers. The EXECUTE logic sends a signal that says "Increase by 1." The logic unit then opens and closes gates, does this and that, and finally the value stored in the Arithmetic Register is increased by 1.
4) The EXECUTE logic sends a signal to open the gate from the Arithmetic Register to the Program Counter to let the increased value move back into the Program Counter.

5) The EXECUTE logic sends a signal to close the gate and the microprocessor has managed to increment the Program Counter. Figure 6-6 shows this happening via diagrams.

Remember, those five steps happen with *every* machine language instruction. It is very fortunate that the microprocessor manufacturers have managed to make this happen automatically.

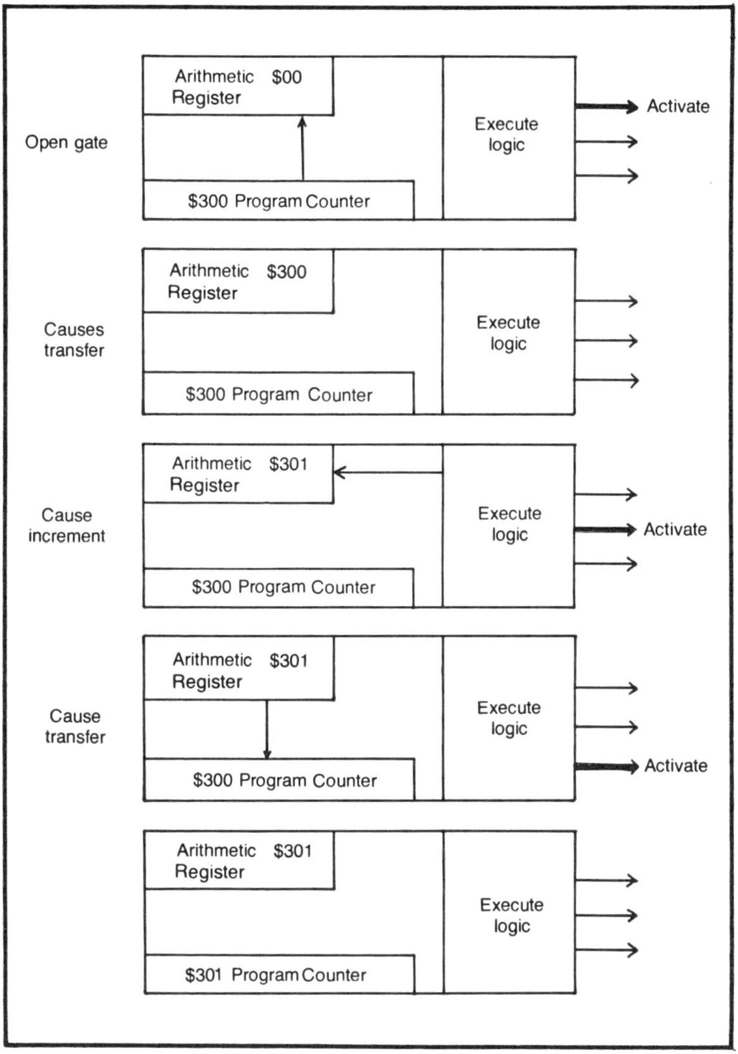


Fig. 6-6. When the control logic activates different control signals, the Program Counter can be incremented.

Every one of the other machine language instructions needs a slightly different set of signals to open and close gates. If we tried to show everything happening in our animated model using BASIC, then the model would work very slowly.

## WHAT HAPPENS IN A FETCH?

The way that a fetch was described in the last section is sufficient and reasonably accurate. In Fig. 6-1, there were no connections between the Program Counter, the memory, and the Instruction Register. In "real life" there are more wires and more registers. The more real-life picture of what it looks like inside a microprocessor is shown in Fig. 6-7.

Notice that there are wires going from the Program Counter to a register called the *Address Register*. The Address Register is a register that controls the getting of information from the memory (ROM and RAM). When something needs to be fetched, the address of the information is put into the Address Register. Then a signal

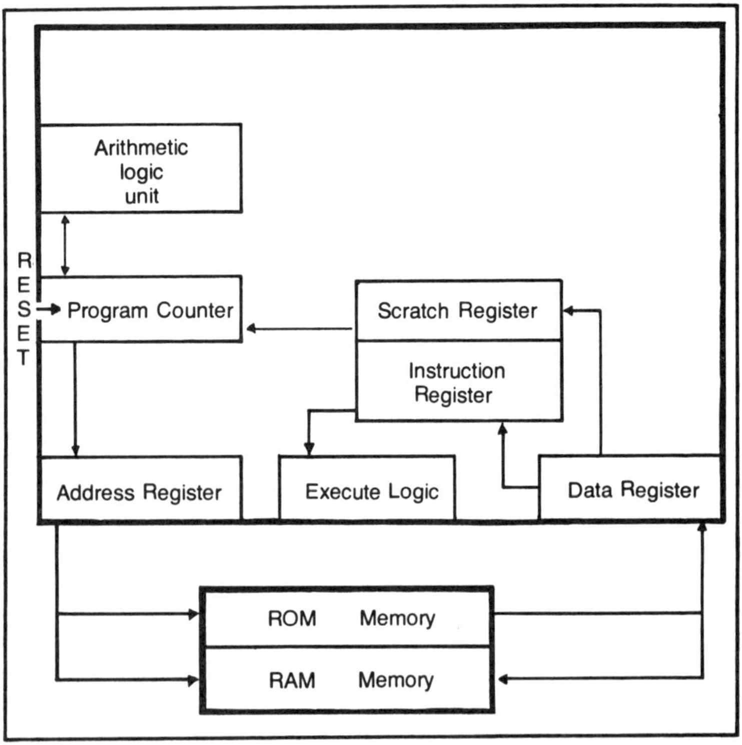


Fig. 6-7. All the internal microprocessor components we have discussed.

from the EXECUTE logic causes the address stored in the Address Register to move down the wires to the memory.

Once the signal reaches the right memory location, that location puts its contents—that means the bits—onto another set of wires that lead to the *Data Register*. It is the job of the Data Register to store all information that comes from, or goes to, the memory. The Address Register is used to say which bit of memory is to be used, and the Data Register stores the value that comes from the memory. The set of wires is called a *bus*.

Once the data or bits are in the Data Register, there are more wires that go from the Data Register up to the Instruction Register. All the wires need to have gates on them to make sure that the information moves at the right time. These gates are controlled by the EXECUTE logic.

*Question: We showed all the signals that were needed to increment the Program Counter. Can you give the series of signals needed to fetch a value from memory and store it into the instruction register?*

We can improve our animation of a working microprocessor to show some of these gates opening and closing. If we did this for everything the EXECUTE logic does, the animation would become too slow. Since the animation now fetches the correct value, we don't need to go any further now if we don't want to.

For those who do, here are the BASIC instructions that are needed to add the two new registers used in fetching an instruction to the <<register-display>> subroutine:

```
54080 GOSUB 61500 :  REM <<move-over>>
54090 PRINT "!  DR $";
54100 HEX = DRREG :  GOSUB 58000 :  REM <<print-hex-number>>
54110 PRINT "  AR $";
54120 HEX = AADDREG : GOSUB 58000
      : REM <<print-hex-number>> **watch name**
54130 PRINT
60120 DRREG = 0 : AADDREG = 0 : REM make room
```

Now we need to change the fetch instruction to show the gates opening and closing. First the gate from the Program Counter to the Address Register must be opened:

```
39000 AADDREG = PC : REM gate opened **watch the name**
39010 GOSUB 54000 : REM <<display-registers>>
39020 GOSUB 61400 : REM <<home-cursor>>
```

```
39030 PRINT "FETCH PART 1 " : REM  explain
39040 GOSUB 55500 : REM <<wait>>
```

The gate from the Address Register to the memory must be used to allow the value stored in the memory to be put into the Data Register:

```
39100 DREG = PEEK(AADDREG)
      : REM get information into the DATA REGISTER
39110 GOSUB 54000 : REM <<display-registers>>
39120 GOSUB 61400 : REM <<home-cursor>>
39130 PRINT "FETCH PART 2 " : REM explain
39140 GOSUB 55500 : REM <<wait>>
```

Finally, the gate from the Data Register to the Instruction Register must be opened:

```
FETCH PART 1           ! IR $00 PC $0306
                       ! DR $00 AR $0306
                       !-----------------




MEMORY STARTING AT $0300
0300: 4C 3A FF 60 00 00 00 00
0308: 00 00 00 00 00 00 00 00
0310: 00 00 00 00 00 00 00 00
0318: 00 00 00 00 00 00 00 00
0320: 00 00 00 00 00 00 00 00
0328: 00 00 00 00 00 00 00 00
0330: 00 00 00 00 00 00 00 00
0338: 00 00 00 00 00 00 00 00



TYPE 'HELP' FOR COMMANDS
YOUR WISH, MASTER? W
WHAT STARTING ADDRESS $?300
```

Fig. 6-8. Screen display with the Data Register and Address Register added.

```
FETCH PART 1                ! IR $00 PC $C306
                            ! DR $00 AR $C306
                            !-----------------





MEMORY STARTING AT $C300
C300: 4C 3A FF 60 00 00 00 00
C308: 00 00 00 00 00 00 00 00
C310: 00 00 00 00 00 00 00 00
C318: 00 00 00 00 00 00 00 00
C320: 00 00 00 00 00 00 00 00
C328: 00 00 00 00 00 00 00 00
C330: 00 00 00 00 00 00 00 00
C338: 00 00 00 00 00 00 00 00



TYPE 'HELP' FOR COMMANDS
YOUR WISH, MASTER? W
WHAT STARTING ADDRESS $?C300
```

Fig. 6-9. Data and Address Registers added to the Commodore 64.

```
39200 IRREG = DREG : REM move the information over
39210 GOSUB 54000 : REM <<display-registers>>
39220 GOSUB 61400 : REM <<home-cursor>>
39230 PRINT "FETCH PART 3 " : REM explain
39240 GOSUB 55500 : REM <<wait>>
39250 PC = PC + 1 : REM get ready for the next instruction
39260 RETURN : REM <<end fetch>>
```

Now delete line 5160 because it puts an unnecessary wait into the program. Run the program and check for syntax errors. Save it as CHAP.6.

When you choose the menu command W ("working model"), you should get a picture that looks like Fig. 6-8 for the Apple and Fig. 6-9 for the C-64. The model works very slowly because of the <<wait>> used. It is a bit too long. If you want to remove the <<wait>> entirely you could do this by removing the <<wait>>

subroutine. This can be done in one line, since all statements using the <<wait>> come to only one place in our very large program.

```
55500 RETURN : REM  <<wait>> subroutine is not used
```

A better way is to just make the <<wait>> less long. This can be done by changing line 55500 a different way.

```
55500 FOR WTEMP = 1 TO 30 : REM short wait
```

If you find that 30 has become too short or is still too long, then change it to a value you like.

This chapter has showed you that there are things going on deep inside the microprocessor. All these things happen automatically. Without them, we could not have a computer. It is only in the last couple of years that manufacturers have been able to put all the wires and gates together in a cheap enough way that we can afford microcomputers in our home and school.

## STILL DEEPER INTO THE EXECUTE LOGIC

As you can see, the EXECUTE logic has a lot of things to do. All that it does is controlled by the gates and wires inside the EXECUTE logic itself. In some microprocessors, there is a program built into a ROM inside the EXECUTE area of the microprocessor. This ROM controls what has to happen so that a machine language instruction works. The machine language instructions control how BASIC works. Finally BASIC controls how your program works. There are many levels of things happening inside your computer and they are shown in Fig. 6-10.

In Chapter 1 we mentioned that there were some microprocessors that could be made to understand the machine language of other machines. You can now see how that can be made to happen. The EXECUTE logic controls how machine language instructions are done. If you change what controls the EXECUTE logic, then you change the machine language instructions that the microprocessor can do. This means that these specialized microprocessors have a RAM or changeable memory to control the EXECUTE logic. This is a very advanced topic; for more information see the "other books" section of the Appendices.

With these special microprocessors, you just change the program stored in the RAM used to control the EXECUTE logic and you've changed the way the microprocessor "thinks." You can go

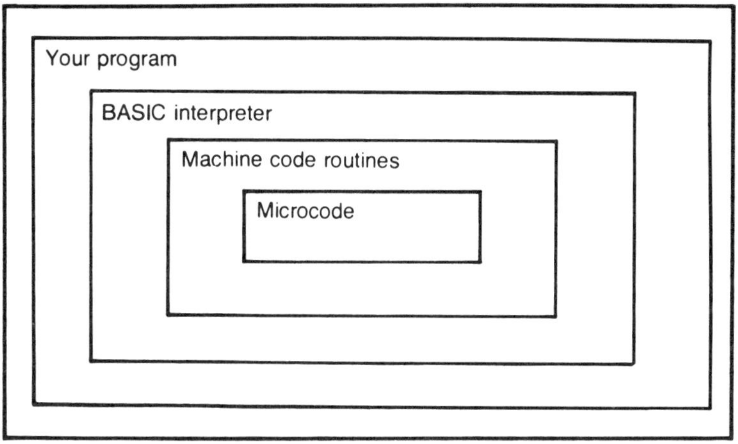

Fig. 6-10. Different program levels available inside a sophisticated microcomputer.

from an XYZ microprocessor to a 6502 to a 68000 and back again. You can even do all of this while you are running a program. These special microprocessors are called *microprogrammable* microprocessors, and the special program is called a *microprogram*. The instructions inside the microprogram are called *microcode*.

Why would computer manufacturers want to do these things? You write programs in such a way that when you have a program that does something useful, you want to be able to use it in other programs. The computer designers decide that when they have found a useful idea, they also want to be able to reuse it in other computers. Microcode is a method of doing this.

# Chapter 7

# NOP, BAK, and JMP Instructions

In the last chapter, we made our "animated" microprocessor go and fetch an instruction. Then the instruction was loaded into the Instrument Register and "executed." The only trouble was, every single instruction was treated as an NOP or No operation instruction. Real microprocessors have about 200 or more machine language instructions. We must modify the execute part of our program so that it can deal with these different instructions. In each of the next chapters, a number of machine language instructions and their meaning will be introduced. Once these instructions have been loaded into the safe area using the load instruction of our menu, we can do one of two things:

1) Use the W (work) instruction and watch the animated version of the microprocessor do the instruction.
2) Use the GO instruction and have the real microprocessor actually do the instructions.

Don't think that animating a microprocessor is just for beginners. It is not. Computer scientists do a lot of animating, which they call *simulation.* People spend all their time making simulations of things from real life so that they can better study and test that thing.

Imagine that you think you have a technique for building a high speed car. Your car will go better if it is streamlined. Is it or is it not important to make sure that the headlights on the car are streamlined? I know that it will be better if they are streamlined, but is it really *important* that they be streamlined? Does it make enough difference that it becomes worthwhile to spend the money to do it? It might seem strange, with cars being so expensive, that the manufacturers would worry about the extra $20 needed to streamline the headlights. If however, 20 million cars of one kind might be sold, then $20 per car becomes a lot of money.

One way of finding out whether it is worth worrying about the headlights is to build 10 or 20 cars. Each one will have to be custom-made, of course, and you know that is expensive. Each one will be slightly different; some will have streamlined headlights, some square headlights, and so on. Then each one of these cars can be put into a wind tunnel and tested.

Another way of finding out is to write a computer program that animates or simulates the way that cars behave in the wind. Then we can do all our testing of the headlights using a program. This approach *might* be a lot cheaper than building all those special cars. (Computer programs are not cheap either. People in industry estimate that by the time they take into account things like wages, buildings, computers, secretaries, and other costs, *each line* of a computer program costs $100.)

Inside a microwave oven there is probably a small microprocessor to control the heat and the timing of the cooking. Testing the program used by that chip would be rather difficult. The oven manufacturers may have built an animation or simulation of the workings of that particular microprocessor, in just the same way that we are doing for the 6502. They might even have tested it in the same microcomputer that you are using. So animation or simulation is not "chicken-feed," but a very important part of the computer industry.

In this chapter we are going to simulate three machine language instructions. The three instructions we are going to simulate have the assembly language mnemonics NOP, BRK, and JMP. The *only* big difference how one microprocessor does these instructions is how the instruction is stored in memory: that means the HEX codes needed for the instructions. They are:

| ASSEMBLY LANGUAGE MNEMONIC | MACHINE LANGUAGE (6502) | NEAREST BASIC EQUIVALENT |
|---|---|---|
| NOP | $EA | REM |
| BRK | $00 | STOP |
| JMP | $4C | GOTO |

In response to the NOP or no operation instructions, which we have already discussed, the microprocessor does nothing. This instruction is often used to create gaps in a program so that things can be added later. It is used to write over the top of unwanted parts of the program so that the program can be changed without having to be rewritten.

The BRK (break) instruction causes the microprocessor to stop what it is doing. Any instruction that the microprocessor does not understand automatically becomes a break. It is used when you want the microprocessor to stop. In a program you often want to check if something has happened properly. If you put in a BRK instruction, the microprocessor will stop, and you will be able to check most—but not all—conditions. You are very often interested to see what has been put into a register. With a simulation, however, you don't have to use the break instruction to do this because the values in the registers are always displayed.

The JMP (jump) instruction diverts the microprocessor from its usual sequence of execution. Normally, the microprocessor will pick up the next instruction from a memory location next to that used for the last instruction. Jump, just like a BASIC GOTO, allows you to change this. If you think back, the Program Counter is used to remember what instruction should be done next. The JMP construction has to do things to the Program Counter to make it jump to the instruction we want, rather than to the instruction stored in memory beside the instruction just used. Now let's add these three instructions to our simulator.

### The BREAK Instruction

The easiest instruction to animate is the break or BRK instruction. To do this we need to modify the decision and execution logic stored in line numbers 30000 on. The first thing we need to find out is what instruction is to be done. Then we explain it and finally do it.

```
DEL 30000, 35000 : REM delete old EXECUTE instructions.
```

Now we can add decision logic.

```
30000 GOSUB 61400 : REM <<home-cursor>>
30010 PRINT "EXECUTING "; BELL$;
30020 PRINT "BRK" : REM explain
30030 IF IR = 0 THEN 31000
      : REM IR describes what instruction to do
```

```
30900 PRINT EH$ : REM don't know this instruction
30910 RETURN : REM <<end execute>>
```

We need two BASIC statements for the BRK instruction animation. One statement must be the execution logic part of the animation, and the other must cause the simulation itself to stop the work command and return us to the menu.

```
5185 IF IR = 0 THEN RETURN : REM stops the 'W'ork instruction

31000 RETURN : REM <<BRK>>
```

Save the program as CHAP.7A *before* checking the syntax. Remember, we are working with machine language instructions; if something accidentally goes wrong, we can lose the program. To test the program, do the following steps:

```
                         ! IR $00 PC $0304
                         ! DR $00 AR $0303
                         !-----------------




MEMORY STARTING AT $0300
0300: EA EA EA 00 00 00 00 00
0308: 00 00 00 00 00 00 00 00
0310: 00 00 00 00 00 00 00 00
0318: 00 00 00 00 00 00 00 00
0320: 00 00 00 00 00 00 00 00
0328: 00 00 00 00 00 00 00 00
0330: 00 00 00 00 00 00 00 00
0338: 00 00 00 00 00 00 00 00



TYPE 'HELP' FOR COMMANDS
YOUR WISH, MASTER? WORK
```

Fig. 7-1. The screen display after three NOP instructions have been loaded into the simulator program. The W (work) command may be used to show them in operation.

```
                           ! IR $00 PC $C304
                           ! DR $00 AR $C303
                           !-----------------

MEMORY STARTING AT $C300
C300:  EA EA EA 00 00 00 00 00
C308:  00 00 00 00 00 00 00 00
C310:  00 00 00 00 00 00 00 00
C318:  00 00 00 00 00 00 00 00
C320:  00 00 00 00 00 00 00 00
C328:  00 00 00 00 00 00 00 00
C330:  00 00 00 00 00 00 00 00
C338:  00 00 00 00 00 00 00 00


TYPE 'HELP' FOR COMMANDS
YOUR WISH, MASTER? WORK
```

Fig. 7-2. Three NOP instructions loaded into the Commodore 64.

1) Use the CL (clear) instruction. Notice that all of the safe area is turned into break ($00) instructions.
2) Use the L load instruction to place some NOPs at the start of the safe area. For a 6502 the NOP's are $EA. Load about three NOPs.
3) Use the W (work) instruction to get the program to operate.

Your screen should look like Fig. 7-1 or Fig. 7-2, depending on your machine.

When you use the W instruction with a starting address of $300, you should hear bells each time the simulation trys to do a NOP. At the moment, it does not know how to do that instruction. The simulation from the last chapter just kept on going until the Program Counter tried to fetch instructions out of the safe area. This time the simulation should stop long before that—just as soon as it reaches the first BRK instruction. Figure 7-1 shows what your program should look like if everything went right. I am using $300 as my safe area so my Program Counter might look a little different from yours.

Once everything is working resave the program as CHAP.7A. Now that everything is saved on disk, take a deep breath and use the GO menu instruction and really get the program to work using the real microprocessor inside the computer.

What happened? My system did exactly what I told it to do. I said, "Break. Stop everything you are doing." That meant stop BASIC, stop reading the keyboard, stop using the disk drive. When you say "stop," your microprocessor runs into a brick wall. Your system crashes.

Nastier things can happen. With some 6502-based microcomputers, you must have three break instructions, one after the other, if you use BRK in machine code called from BASIC. This means three $00 hex values next to each other in memory. That's why I got you to use the CL instruction. You *did* use the CL instruction, didn't you? If you did not then I can't say what your computer did. You may even have found yourself back in an unexpected part of your program.

To recover from a break instruction back into BASIC, try hitting the RESET key; that often works. Try hitting the CTRL and the C keys at the same time; that works on an Apple. When a Commodore machine acts like this, an X followed by a carriage return is often helpful. If none of those work, then you'll have to use the "extra special works-every-time technique." Move your finger to the computer OFF switch and kill the power. Then turn it back on again. That *always* works. Now reload the program CHAP.7A. (You did save it, didn't you?)

### The NOP Instruction

Let's add the NOP instruction to our simulation:

```
30020 PRINT "NOP"
30040 IF IR = $EA THEN 31100 : REM use IR to check
31100 RETURN : REM <<nop>> do nothing
```

Try it using the W(work) instruction. It does not work. There is a message of

SYNTAX ERROR IN 30040

The table shows that the NOP instruction is $EA. If you check the screen, you'll see that the value $EA is in the instruction register as it should be. So what's wrong?

The answer is, once again, that BASIC can't understand hexadecimal numbers. Some programming languages can, but not BASIC. We need to turn hex numbers into decimal numbers in all BASIC statements. Since this is something we will be doing often in our animation, it is worthwhile making a software tool to do it.

```
52990 REM <<HEX-TO-DECIMAL>>
53000 PRINT "WHAT NUMBER TO CONVERT? $";
53010 GOSUB 56000 : REM <<get-a-hexadecimal-number>>
53020 PRINT HEX
53040 STOP
```

That was pretty painless. Save this program as CHAP.7B. To find out what $EA is in decimal, type

GOTO 53000

and type in $EA.

If you have just reloaded CHAP.7B, then the new program will not work. If you had just run the main program, then the new program will work. Try it both ways and see what I mean. How can it be corrected?

The problem is that our new program does not know what should be stored in the arrays HEX$ and SYMBOL$ unless the main program has made them and placed them in memory. We have to make sure that it does. That means *initialization* should occur.

```
53000 IF HEX$(0) = "00" THEN 53008
      : REM no need to re-initialize
53004 GOSUB 60000 : GOSUB 59000 : GOSUB 59100
      : REM do initialization
53008 PRINT "CONVERT WHAT NUMBER $";
```

Now try it. What is the decimal number for $EA? It is decimal 234. One change to our program and everything should be great.

```
30040 IF IR = 234 THEN 31100 : REM <<nop>>
```

If you try the simulation now the program should run. All the bells should have disappeared because now the simulation understands how to do an NOP instruction. The program now works well for both instructions, but the explanations do not. The explanation for the break instruction has vanished. We need an array that will store the explanation and print the correct one as needed. This array must be large enough to put all possible mnemonics in it. We will use the array MN$. We also need an array TYPE% to save the type of instruction we are doing. (What an instruction *type* means will be explained in later chapters. Both arrays MN$ and TYPE% will be used later by the software tools programmed Chapter 12). We are using an integer array TYPE% rather than a decimal array TYPE to store numbers because integer arrays only need 40 percent of the memory decimal arrays require for storage.

```
30015 IF MN$(IR) = "" THEN MN$(IR) = "EH?"
      : REM in case not known
30020 PRINT MN$(IR) : REM explain the instruction we are doing
60490 DIM TYPE%(255) : REM make room
60500 DIM SYMBOL$(15) : DIM MN$(255)
      : REM watch the line numbers
60560 MN$(0) = "BRK" : TYPE%(0) = 5
60570 MN$(234) = "NOP" : TYPE%(234) = 5
```

If you are using a small computer such as a VIC-20, then the MN$ array may be too large for it. In that case you'll have to go without the explanations. You'll have to add the following statement.

```
30020 PRINT
```

and nothing else.

Save the program as CHAP.7B. Try running the machine language program using the W command and check that the correct explanation is displayed for each instruction.

### The JMP Instruction

The final instruction we need to add is the jump instruction. This is quite a bit different than either the NOP or BRK instructions. The jump instruction is three bytes long; the NOP and BRK each only used one byte of memory. It also changes the Program Counter in a special way. The NOP and BRK instruction simply incremented the Program Counter by one.

This is how the jump instruction works:

1) Just as with any other instruction, the Program Counter is used to fetch the next instruction and put it in the Instruction Register.
2) The EXECUTE logic says, "Aha! A JMP instruction needs doing!"
3) The Program Counter is used again to get another value from memory. This time, the value does not go into the Instruction Register but into another register called a *Scratch Register.* This is used by the EXECUTE logic to hold things that don't need to be remembered for a long period of time.
4) The Program Counter is again increased by 1.
5) The Program Counter is used a third time to get another value from memory. This value is first multiplied by 256 and then added to the value stored in the Scratch Register. The answer is put back into the Scratch Register.
6) The value stored into Scratch Register is pushed into the Program Counter, changing its value.
7) Now, when the Program Counter is used to fetch a new instruction, it does so from somewhere that is not next to the old instruction. The program has jumped to a new place in memory, a place depending on what numbers were pulled out of memory and put into the Scratch Register.

All of these seven steps happened by the opening and closing of gates controlled by the EXECUTE logic.

To get the JUMP simulation to work we must first add the JMP instruction ($4C) to the decision and execution logic, using the program at 53000 to turn hexadecimal into decimal notation.

```
30050 IF IR = 76 THEN 31200 : REM <<jmp>>
31200 SC = PEEK(PC) : REM get the new value
31210 GOSUB 54000 : REM <<display-registers>>
31220 PC = PC + 1 : REM increment the PROGRAMME COUNTER
31230 GOSUB 55500 : REM <<wait>>
31240 SC = PEEK(PC) * 256 + SC : REM use the new value
31250 PC = PC + 1 : REM increment
31260 GOSUB 54000 : REM <<display-registers>>
31270 GOSUB 55500 : REM <<wait>>
31280 PC = SC
      : REM push SCRATCH PAD REGISTER into the PROGRAMME COUNTER
31290 RETURN : REM <<end jmp>>
```

```
                              ! IR $00 PC $00
                              ! DR $00 AR $00
                              ! SC $0000
                              !-----------------

MEMORY STARTING AT $0300
0300: EA EA EA EA EA EA EA EA
0308: 4C 00 03 00 00 00 00 00
0310: 00 00 00 00 00 00 00 00
0318: 00 00 00 00 00 00 00 00
0320: 00 00 00 00 00 00 00 00
0328: 00 00 00 00 00 00 00 00
0330: 00 00 00 00 00 00 00 00
0338: 00 00 00 00 00 00 00 00


TYPE 'HELP' FOR COMMANDS
YOUR WISH, MASTER?
```

Fig. 7-3. Eight NOP and one JMP instruction loaded into memory.

Then we add the Scratch Register to the <<register-display>> subroutine

```
54200 GOSUB 61500 : REM <<move-over>>
54210 PRINT "!           SC $"; : REM show SCRATCH PAD REGISTER
54220 IF SC < 256 THEN PRINT "00";
54230 HEX = SC : GOSUB 58000 : REM <<print-hex-number>>
54240 PRINT
60130 SC = 0 : REM make room
60590 MN$(76) = "JMP" : TYPE%(76) = 2
```

Save your program as CHAP.7C. To test it, use the CL and the L instructions. Starting at the beginning of the safe area, put in six NOPs ($EA) followed by the JMP instruction ($4C). Now we need to tell the JMP where to jump. Load the low byte of the start of the safe area. Next load the high byte of the address for the start of the safe area. Your program in memory should look like Fig. 7-3 or 7-4.

The microprocessor's internal wiring with the new register looks like Fig. 7-5.

Now use the W menu instruction and watch the Program Counter slowly increase as the simulation does all those NOPs. Then the PC should jump back to the start of the safe area and start over again . . . and again, and again, and again. The only way to stop it is to hit RUN/STOP or CTRL-C. I did say to save it, didn't I?

The way this program goes on forever is obviously no good. What we need is a machine language instruction that is like a BASIC IF. With such an instruction, we could decide whether we did want to jump or whether we wanted to stop. We need to be able to do the same as the following BASIC statements:

```
##30  IF X > 0 THEN GOTO ##00 : REM  do the jump
##40  STOP : REM  don't do the jump
```

There are eight machine language IF statements; we shall learn about four of them (the most common ones) in the next chapter.

```
                               ! IR $00 PC $00
                               ! DR $00 AR $00
                               ! SC $0000
                               !-----------------


MEMORY STARTING AT $C300
C300: EA EA EA EA EA EA EA EA
C308: 4C 00 C3 00 00 00 00 00
C310: 00 00 00 00 00 00 00 00
C318: 00 00 00 00 00 00 00 00
C320: 00 00 00 00 00 00 00 00
C328: 00 00 00 00 00 00 00 00
C330: 00 00 00 00 00 00 00 00
C338: 00 00 00 00 00 00 00 00


TYPE 'HELP' FOR COMMANDS
YOUR WISH, MASTER?
```

Fig. 7-4. Commodore 64 version of Fig. 7-3.

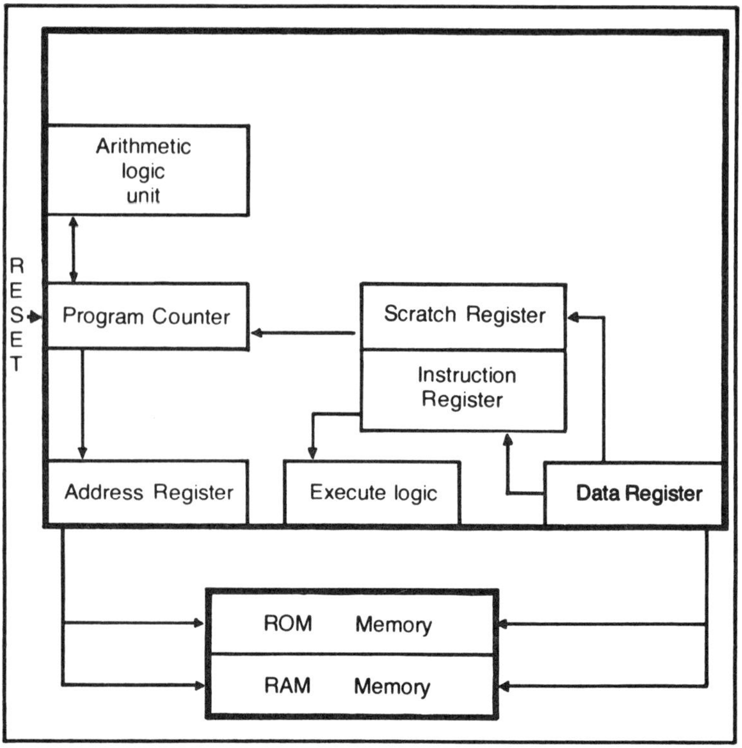


Fig. 7-5. Internal architecture of the microprocessor with the new Scratch Register connections.

Reload the program CHAP.7C. If you look at your disk directory, you will find that the program is getting rather large. There are many BASIC statements that we will never use again. They can be deleted.

```
DEL 990, 3900
```

will remove them. Now save the program as CHAP.7 and you will be using much less disk space. You can also delete all the files you have saved that have a letter in them. Delete CHAP.7A, CHAP.7B for example, but keep those programs that just end in a number, like CHAP.7. I hope you are also keeping backup disks.

One last thing: try the GO command on this machine language program. Before you try it, what do you think will happen?

# Chapter 8

# The X, Y, and Flag Registers

In the last chapter we animated or simulated three machine language instructions. They were NOP, the do-nothing instruction; BRK, the stop-everything instruction; and the JMP instruction, which changed the Program Counter. The series of instructions we are going to add introduce us to three new registers inside the microprocessor. These are:

1) The X Index Register or X Register.
2) The Y Index Register or Y Register.
3) The Condition Flag Register or Flags.

The *X and Y Registers* are used for counting and pointing. In a BASIC program, you can use the FOR. . . NEXT instruction. The X and Y Registers can be used in the machine language equivalent of such FOR. . . NEXT loops. In a BASIC program you can have arrays and pick out one particular thing from the array using a statement like

K$ = HEX$(M)

The X and Y Registers can be used in the machine language equivalent of doing that.

The *Condition Flag Register* is used to remember certain things about what the microprocessor has just done. If a person has been eating blueberry pie, then you can tell by looking at their T-shirt front. (But not with you and me, of course.) If you look at the T-shirt front of the microprocessor, you can tell a number of things. Figure 8-1 shows what I mean. We can find the answers to questions such as these:

1) Has the microprocessor just used a zero number? If so, part of the Condition Flag Register is set to 1. This part is called the *Z flag* or *zero flag*.
2) Has the microprocessor just used a number that was *not* zero? If so, the Z flag is *cleared* or set to 0.
3) Has the microprocessor just used a number that was negative? If so, the *N flag* or *negative flag* of the Flag Register is set to 1.
4) Has the microprocessor just used a number that was *not* negative? If so, the N flag is cleared or made to 0.

```
                               ! IR $00  PC $00
                               ! DR $00  AR $00
C I N V Z                      !         SC $0000
? ? ? ? ?                      ! X  $00  Y  $00
                               !-----------------

MEMORY STARTING AT $0300
0300: EA EA EA 00 00 00 00 00
0308: 00 00 00 00 00 00 00 00
0310: 00 00 00 00 00 00 00 00
0318: 00 00 00 00 00 00 00 00
0320: 00 00 00 00 00 00 00 00
0328: 00 00 00 00 00 00 00 00
0330: 00 00 00 00 00 00 00 00
0338: 00 00 00 00 00 00 00 00


TYPE 'HELP' FOR COMMANDS
YOUR WISH, MASTER?
```

Fig. 8-1. Screen display showing the new X and Y Registers, together with the flags.

The Flag Register has both an N (negative) flag and a Z (zero) flag which are used very often. There are also other flags, which will be explained in greater detail in other chapters. These flags are

C or carry flag.
V or overflow flag.
D or decimal flag.
I or interrupt flag.

The C, V, and D flags are special things that help the computer handle very large numbers and numbers that have a decimal point in them—numbers such as 60,000 and 6.71. Remember that normally the memory can only store whole numbers between 0 and 255. The I flag is used by the computer so that it can do the correct thing when you press the RESET button, or if other unexpected things occur.

We need to add these new flags and register to our <<display-register>> subroutine:

```
                        ! IR  $00  PC  $00
                        ! DR  $00  AR  $00
C I N V Z               !          SC  $0000
? ? ? ? ?               ! X   $00  Y   $00
                        ! ----------------------



MEMORY STARTING AT $C300
C300:  EA EA EA 00 00 00 00 00
C308:  00 00 00 00 00 00 00 00
C310:  00 00 00 00 00 00 00 00
C318:  00 00 00 00 00 00 00 00
C320:  00 00 00 00 00 00 00 00
C328:  00 00 00 00 00 00 00 00
C330:  00 00 00 00 00 00 00 00
C338:  00 00 00 00 00 00 00 00



TYPE 'HELP' FOR COMMANDS
YOUR WISH, MASTER?
```

Fig. 8-2. Commodore 64 screen display showing the X, Y, and Flag registers.

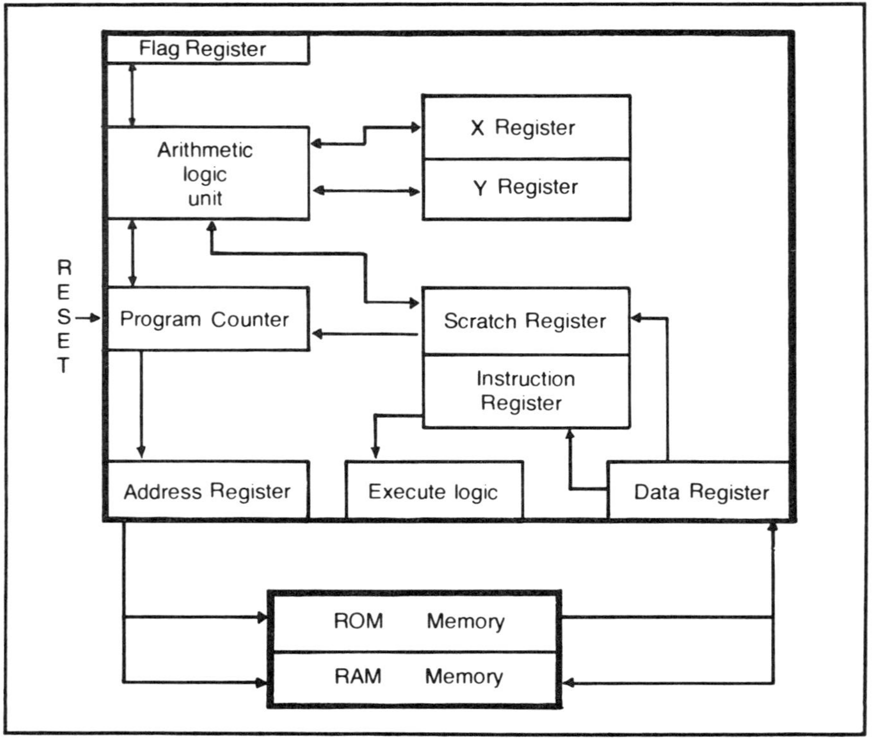


Fig. 8-3. Microprocessor architecture with the X, Y, and Flag Registers.

```
54300 GOSUB 61500 : REM <<move-over>>
54310 PRINT "! X  $"; : REM show X-REGISTER
54320 HEX = XREG : GOSUB 58000 : REM <<print-hex-number>>
54330 PRINT " Y  $"; : REM show Y-REGISTER
54340 HEX = YREG : GOSUB 58000 : REM <<print-hex-number>>
54350 PRINT
      : REM xxx Watch the line numbers. We are leaving room xxx
54900 GOSUB 61400 : REM <<home-cursor>>
54910 DOWN = 3 : GOSUB 61200 : REM <<move-down>>
54920 PRINT "C I N V Z"
54930 PRINT C$; " "; I$; " "; N$; " "; V$; " "; Z$
60160 XREG = 0 : YREG = 0 : REM make room
60600 N$ = "?" : Z$ = "?" : REM make room
60610 C$ = "?" : I$ = "?" : V$ = "?"
```

Run the program and check that the new display is like Fig. 8-1 (Fig. 8-2 for the C-64). With the three new registers, the interconnections inside the microprocessor are getting more complex. They now look like Fig. 8-3.

## FOUR NEW INSTRUCTIONS

The four new machine language instructions we are going to introduce are:

| ASSEMBLY MNEMONIC | HEX CODE | WHAT IT DOES |
|---|---|---|
| INX | $E8 | INcrease X Register by 1 |
| INY | $C8 | INcrease Y Register by 1 |
| DEX | $CA | DEcrease X Register by 1 |
| DEY | $88 | DEcrease Y Register by 1 |

The instructions themselves are very easy, but there is a problem. Numbers inside the X and Y Registers and inside the memory can't exceed 255 or be smaller than 0. There is simply no room to store the number 256 with 8 bits.

This is rather difficult to believe. Try this small program and see that it is true.

```
1 INPUT "GIVE ME A NUMBER "; J
2 POKE 0, J : REM try to put the number into memory
3 PRINT PEEK(0): REM get it out of memory
4 GOTO 1
```

Try the program using numbers like 0, 127, or 255 and you will have no problems. Numbers like 1.2, 2.5, or 234.5 will go into memory, but will not come out correctly. Numbers like 256, 300, and −1 give

ILLEGAL QUANTITY IN 2

*Don't* forget to delete the lines after testing, using

DEL 1,4

Handling numbers outside the range 0 to 255 happens all the time when we make programs. The computer manufacturers had to do something, and what they did was this:

1) If the number gets bigger than 255, subtract 256 from it.
2) If the number gets smaller than 0 then add 256 to it.

That way the numbers are always between 0 and 255 and will always fit into the memory.

Other manufacturers did something different. They decided that 8 bits is too small a word, so they decided to use 16 bits. This helps a little. Now the computer can store all the whole numbers from 0 to 65,535 inside one word instead of only 0 to 255. However, if the number gets bigger than 65,535, the problem happens all over again. How computers can handle numbers containing a decimal point is something for a more advanced book than this.

If our simulation is going to work, then we must adjust all our numbers to get remain in the correct range, $00 to $FF (0 to 255). This will be done by passing a parameter called ADJUST to a new subroutine. This subroutine will adjust the number and then pass back the parameter. When it comes back, the number will be adjusted correctly to fit into memory.

The next few BASIC statements have a few things that don't seem correct. For the moment, you'll just have to trust me. Once the animation is working, you'll be able to see why these unexpected things are needed. The problem will be in the N flag, which checks to see if a number is negative. What the program does just does not seem correct!

The decision logic:

```
30060 IF IR = 232 THEN 31300 : REM <<inx>>
30070 IF IR = 200 THEN 31400 : REM <<iny>>
```

```
30080 IF IR = 202 THEN 31500 : REM <<dex>>
30090 IF IR = 136 THEN 31600 : REM <<dey>>
```

The execute logic:

```
31300 ADJUST = XREG + 1 : REM <<inx>>
31310 GOSUB 52000 : REM <<go-adjust>>
31320 XREG = ADJUST
31330 RETURN : REM <<end inx>>
31400 You add what is needed for the
31410 INcrement Y register by 1
31420 instruction
31430
31500 ADJUST = XREG - 1 : REM <<dex>>
31510 GOSUB 52000 : REM <<go-adjust>>
31520 XREG = ADJUST
31530 RETURN : REM <<end dex>>
31610 DEcrement Y register by 1
31620 Instruction
31630
```

The logic needed for keeping the numbers in the correct range is as follows:

```
51990 REM <<adjust>> Also set the N and Z flags
52000 IF ADJUST < 0 THEN ADJUST = ADJUST + 256 : GOTO 52000
52010 IF ADJUST > 255 THEN ADJUST = ADJUST - 256 : GOTO 52010
52020 Z$ = "C" : REM  clear the Z flag
52030 IF ADJUST = 0 THEN Z$ = "S" : REM  set if needed
52040 N$ = "C" : REM clear the N flag
52050 IF ADJUST > 127 THEN N$ = "S" : REM  set if needed
52060 RETURN : REM <<end adjust>>
60620 MN$(232) = "INX" : TYPE%(232) = 5
60630 MN$(200) = "INY" : TYPE%(200) = 5
60640 MN$(202) = "DEX" : TYPE%(202) = 5
60650 MN$(136) = "DEY" : TYPE%(136) = 5
```

Yes, line 52050 really says "If a number is bigger than 127 then it is negative." Believe it or not! You'll understand why when you have run the next program.

## USING INX AND DEX INSTRUCTIONS

Let's us use the clear CL and the load L menu instruction to

```
                                ! IR  $00  PC  $00
                                ! DR  $00  AR  $00
C  I  N  V  Z                   !          SC  $0000
?  ?  C  ?  C                   ! X   $00  Y   $00
                                !-------------------


MEMORY STARTING AT $0300
0300:  E8  E8  E8  E8  E8  E8  CA  CA
0308:  CA  CA  CA  CA  CA  CA  00  00
0310:  00  00  00  00  00  00  00  00
0318:  00  00  00  00  00  00  00  00
0320:  00  00  00  00  00  00  00  00
0328:  00  00  00  00  00  00  00  00
0330:  00  00  00  00  00  00  00  00
0338:  00  00  00  00  00  00  00  00


TYPE 'HELP' FOR COMMANDS
YOUR WISH, MASTER?
```

Fig. 8-4. Six INX and eight DEX instructions loaded into memory.

load a program of six INcrement X Register and eight DEcrement X Register instructions. That means we need 6 $E8s followed by 8 $CAs. At the end of the program put a BRK $00 so that the animation stops. If you have the disassembler command already working, then use it to check that you have loaded the machine language program correctly. Before you run your BASIC program, just in case, save it as CHAP.8A.

Now what should happen is this:

1) When we start, the X Register will be 0.
2) When we do the INX instructions the X Register should get bigger until it becomes 6.
3) When we do the DEX instructions the X Register should start to become smaller.
4) When the X Register becomes zero the Z flag should change from Clear to Set, showing that the computer is using a zero number.
5) Then the X Register should become −1. When this happens the N flag should change from Clear to Set to show that the computer is using a negative number. Also, the Z

flag should change from Set to Clear because the computer is using a nonzero number.

6) Finally, the X Register should become −2 and the program should break or stop.

When your program works, your screen should look like Figs. 8-4 or 8-5. Now RUN the program. What does the Z flag say? Is it Clear or Set? Does it make sense? What does the N flag say? Is it Clear or Set? Does it make sense? What does the X Register say? That certainly is not −2 . . . or is it?

The Z flag is clear, which makes sense because the expected −2 is not a zero number. The N flag is set because the expected −2 is a zero number. The X Register does not say the negative, nonzero number −2, but instead says the positive, nonzero number $FE. When it should have said −1 while the program was running, you might have noticed that it said $FF instead of −1. Why?

It actually makes sense. The computer is unable to store

```
                          ! IR $00 PC $00
                          ! DR $00 AR $00
C I N V Z                 !           SC $0000
? ? C ? C                 ! X  $00 Y  $00
                          !------------------

MEMORY STARTING AT $C300
C300:  E8 E8 E8 E8 E8 E8 CA CA
C308:  CA CA CA CA CA CA 00 00
C310:  00 00 00 00 00 00 00 00
C318:  00 00 00 00 00 00 00 00
C320:  00 00 00 00 00 00 00 00
C328:  00 00 00 00 00 00 00 00
C330:  00 00 00 00 00 00 00 00
C338:  00 00 00 00 00 00 00 00


TYPE 'HELP' FOR COMMANDS
YOUR WISH, MASTER?
```

Fig. 8-5. Six INX and eight DEX instructions loaded into the Commodore 64.

numbers smaller than 0 or bigger than 255. When it reaches the number −1, what does it do? It adds 256 to it! What is −1 + 256? The answer is 255 or $FF. If it were trying to store −2, what would it do? It adds 256 to it. What is −2 + 256? The answer is 254 or $FE. That is exactly what was in the X Register. Everything is correct.

## STORING NEGATIVE NUMBERS IN MEMORY

Table 8-1 shows how some negative numbers are stored inside the computer. The strange way of storing negative numbers in a computer is not so strange if you have ever owned a bicycle with a speedometer on it. Those meters tell how fast you are going and how far you have gone. Have you tried to run one backwards? One of two things would have happened.

1) It would have broken.
2) The numbers counted backwards like this:

| SPEEDOMETER | MILES TRAVELED |
|---|---|
| 00005 | 5 |
| 00004 | 4 |
| 00003 | 3 |
| 00002 | 2 |
| 00001 | 1 |
| 00000 | 0 |
| 99999 | −1 |
| 99998 | −2 |
| 99997 | −3 |

When the speedometer tried to show a negative distance all the 0s were turned into the highest number that the speedometer could store, 9s. Memory works in a similar way, except that since mem-

**Table 8-1. Setting the N and Z Flags.**

| Decimal | Hex | Binary | Z Flag | N Flag |
|---|---|---|---|---|
| 0 | $00 | %00000000 | Set | Clear |
| 10 | $0A | %00001010 | Clear | Clear |
| 31 | $1F | %00011111 | Clear | Clear |
| 126 | $7D | %01111110 | Clear | Clear |
| −1 | $FF | %11111111 | Clear | Set |
| −6 | $FA | %11111010 | Clear | Set |
| −10 | $F6 | %11110110 | Clear | Set |
| −31 | $E1 | %11100001 | Clear | Set |
| −128 | $80 | %10000000 | Clear | Set |

ory works in binary (or base-two) arithmetic, instead of all 9s coming up, all 1s come up.

| BINARY NUMBER | HEX NUMBER | DECIMAL NUMBER |
|---|---|---|
| BIT 76543210 | | |
| 00000100 | $04 | 4 |
| 00000011 | $03 | 3 |
| 00000010 | $02 | 2 |
| 00000001 | $01 | 1 |
| 00000000 | $00 | 0 |
| 11111111 | $FF | −1 |
| 11111110 | $FE | −2 |
| 11111101 | $FD | −3 |
| 11111011 | $FC | −4 |

If you look at Table 8-1, all the negative numbers start with a hexadecimal number bigger than $8. If you look at numbers written out in binary, then they all start with the high (7th) bit a 1. Since all negative numbers start with the high bit a 1, this bit is often called the *sign bit.*

The largest negative number that the computer can store is

%1000000 (binary) or $80 (hexadecimal) or −128 (decimal)

To find out how −128 is stored in the computer you must add 256. This gives 128. This means that all negative numbers are stored in the computer as numbers between 128 and 255. That is why line 52050 checked to see if ADJUST was *bigger than 127,* rather than *less than 0.* That had to be done because of the way negative numbers are stored in a computer's memory locations.

There are many different ways of storing negative numbers in a computer. The way I have described is one of the more common ones. This method is called *two's complement binary numbers.* Don't worry too much about it. Just remember that numbers between $80 and $FF, when stored in a computer's memory, can actually be thought of as being a way of writing negative numbers.

## THE *IF* INSTRUCTIONS—MACHINE LANGUAGE STYLE

In BASIC we can use the GOTO statement if we *always* want to go to that statement. If we might want to use a GOTO only under certain circumstances, then we use an IF along with the GOTO. The following program is another example of the use of an IF. It would print out "positive number" if you gave it a positive number.

```
INPUT "GIVE ME A POSITIVE NUMBER"; J
IF J >= 0 THEN PRINT "POSITIVE NUMBER"
```

If you gave it a negative number then it would not do anything.

In machine language instructions we have a number of IFs. The four most common ones are:

1) BEQ If the last number was *zero* then go to or branch to another memory location.
2) BNE If the last number was *not zero* then go to or branch to another memory location.
3) BMI If the last number was *negative* then go to or branch to another memory location.
4) BPL If the last number was *positive* then go to or branch to another memory location.

Machine language programmers use the word branch when they jump or branch to a memory location that is not too far away. "Too far" means more than 127 locations higher than the memory location now in use, or more than 128 locations lower. The JMP instruction (another type of "GOTO") does not have this restriction.

The microprocessor can make decisions like, "If the last number was zero do this" if it uses the flags. Remember, the flags can tell us such things as whether or not the last number used by the computer was zero. There are two flags and each of them can help us make one of two decisions. The new machine language instructions are

| WORKS WHEN FLAG IS | ASSEMBLY LANGUAGE | HEX CODE | MEANING |
|---|---|---|---|
| Z = S | BEQ | $F0 | Branch if equal to zero |
| Z = C | BNE | $D0 | Branch if not equal to zero |
| N = C | BPL | $10 | Branch if plus or positive |
| N = S | BMI | $30 | Branch if minus or negative |

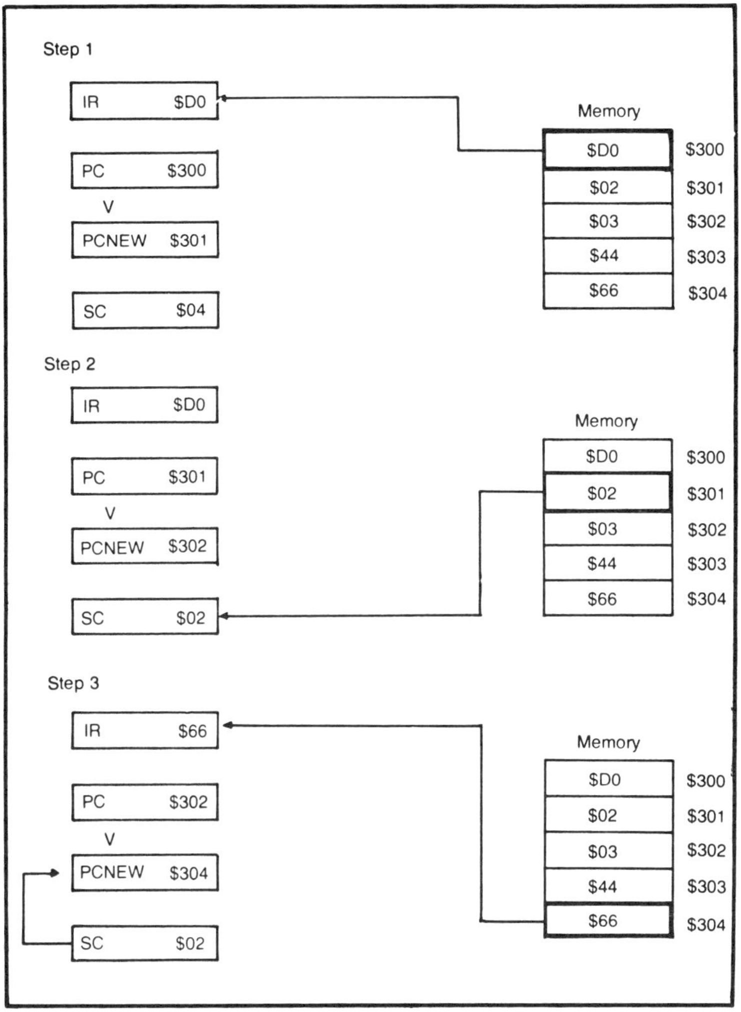


**Fig. 8-6. Executing a BNE instruction. When the Z flag is clear, the branch occurs.**

Let us add the code of these instructions to our animation and then we can see what happens. Remember, branch means the same as jump, except that branching normally does not jump very far. In addition, the branch instructions work in conjunction with the flags. Just like the JMP instructions, these branch instructions change the Program Counter.

The JMP instruction used the next two locations in memory and put them in the Scratch Register. Then the whole of the Scratch

Register was put into the Program Counter. The branch instructions are quite a bit different.

1) First the branch instructions only use the next one location in memory and put it into the Scratch Register.
2) Then the Program Counter is changed *if* and *only if* the branch has to happen.
3) If the branch is not needed, then the value stored in the

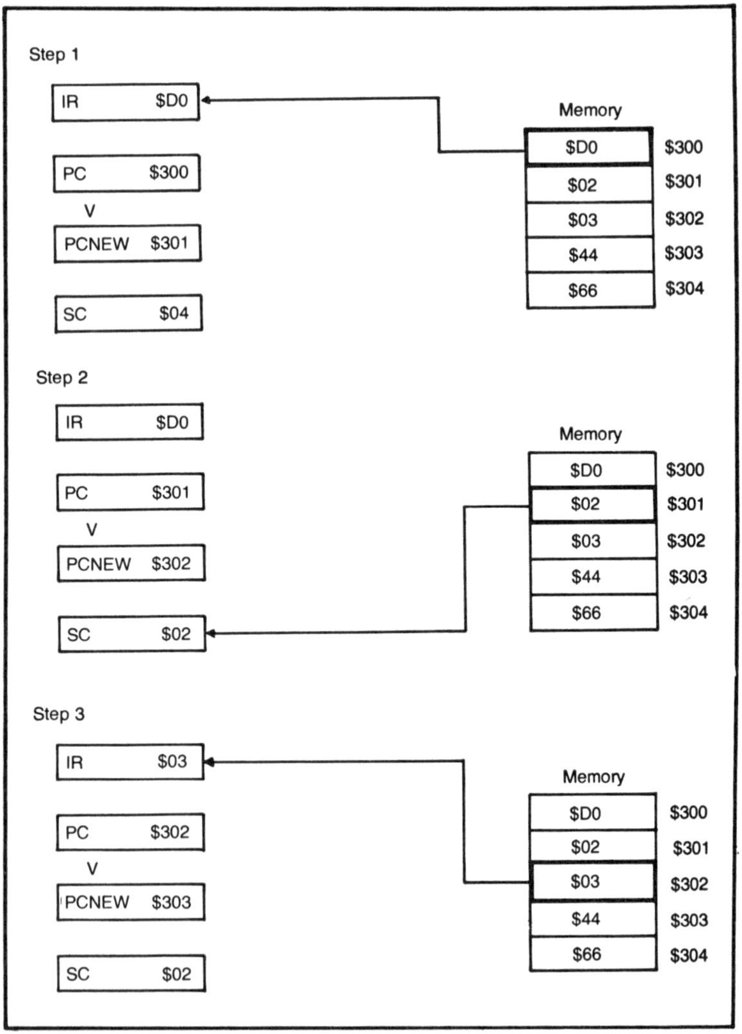


Fig. 8-7. The BNE instruction is not executed if the Z flag is not clear.

Scratch Register is not used and the Program Counter is not changed.

The JMP instruction *always* changed the Program Counter. Figure 8-6 shows the changes that happen to the registers when the computer does a BNE instruction when the branch occurs. Figure 8-7 shows what happens when the branch does not occur.

The branch instruction differs in another way from JMP. With the JMP instruction, the Program Counter was completely changed. With the branch instruction, the Program Counter and the Scratch Register are added together. If the Scratch Register is negative, then the program jumps or branches backwards. If the Scratch Register is positive, then the program jumps forwards. This is like the following BASIC program:

```
1000 IF J < 0 THEN 100 : REM backward branch
1010 IF J >= 0 THEN 2000 : REM forward branch
```

The branching works using the flags. Let us write the BASIC code and you will see how the flags are used. First is the execution code:

```
30100 IF IR = 240 THEN 31700 : REM <<beq>>
30110 IF IR = 208 THEN 31800 : REM <<bne>>
30120 IF IR = 16  THEN 31900 : REM <<bpl>>
30130 IF IR = 48  THEN 32000 : REM <<bmi>>
```

Now the branching logic:

```
31700 GOSUB 51000 : REM <<get-the-next-memory-location>>
31710 IF Z$ <> "S" THEN RETURN
31720 GOSUB 50000 : REM <<change-programme-counter>>
31730 RETURN : REM <<end beq>>
31800 GOSUB 51000 : REM <<get-the-next-memory-location>>
31810 IF Z$ <> "C" THEN RETURN
31820 GOSUB 50000 : REM <<change-programme-counter>>
31830 RETURN : REM <<end bne>>
31900 GOSUB 51000 : REM <<get-the-next-memory-location>>
31910 IF N$ <> "C" THEN RETURN
31920 GOSUB 50000 : REM <<change-programme-counter>>
31930 RETURN : REM <<end bpl>>
32000 You put in the code for
32010 the machine language instruction
32020 BRanch on MInus or negative
32030
```

The explanation codes to add are:

```
60660 MN$(240) = "BEQ" : TYPE%(240) = 11
60670 MN$(208) = "BNE" : TYPE%(208) = 11
60680 MN$(16)  = "BPL" : TYPE%(16)  = 11
60690 MN$(48)  = "BMI" : TYPE%(48)  = 11
```

You can see that the branching occurs depending on whether the flag is set or "unset."

Now we need to write the subroutine that puts the next memory location value into the Scratch Register.

```
50990 REM <<fetch-another-next-memory>>
51000 SC = PEEK(PC) : REM get the next location
51010 PC = PC + 1
      : REM PROGRAMME COUNTER must point to next instruction
51020 RETURN : REM <<end fetch-another>>
```

Finally, we must be able to use the Scratch Register to change the Program Counter. Remember, things are stored in memory using hexadecimal while BASIC can only use decimal. That means that if the number in memory is between \$80 (128) and \$FF (255) then we must turn it into a negative number.

```
49990 REM <<relative-adjust-program-counter>>
50000 IF SC > 127 THEN SC = SC - 256
      : REM adjustment to decimal
50010 PC = PC + SC : REM PROGRAMME COUNTER adjustment
50020 RETURN : REM <<end adjust-pc>>
```

Store the program as CHAP.8 and then try it out with the BNE instruction. Clear the memory with the clear instruction and use the LOAD instruction to load in five INX (\$E8) and then one DEX (\$CA) instruction. What we want to do is write a program that increments X to 5 using five INX and then decreases X back to zero and then stops automatically. To do that we need to add a Branch if Not Equal instruction (BNE=\$D0) after the DEX instruction. Then we must tell the program how far to jump back. Our program looks like this?

```
$300:   INX  $E8
$301:   INX  $E8
$302:   INX  $E8
$303:   INX  $E8
$304:   INX  $E8
```

```
$305:  DEX  $CA  Must make PC come to here
$306:  BNE  $D0
$307:  ??   $??
$308:  BRK  $00  Normally PC goes to here
```

(For the Commodore 64, all the addresses will start with $C3 and not $3.)

If you look at the program, you can see that we need to make the Program Counter jump backwards by three steps compared to where it would normally want to go. That means we must put a −3 in the place where the ?? currently is. What is −3 in two's complement binary numbers? It is hexadecimal $FD. Your screen should look like Figs. 8-8 or 8-9.

Just before you try it, get your watch out. We want to time how long this animation takes. Use the W (work) menu command.

```
                              ! IR  $00  PC  $00
                              ! DR  $00  AR  $00
C I N V Z                     !          SC  $0000
? ? C ? C                     ! X   $00  Y   $00
                              !-----------------------

MEMORY STARTING AT $0300
0300: E8 E8 E8 E8 E8 CA D0 FD
0308: 00 00 00 00 00 00 00 00
0310: 00 00 00 00 00 00 00 00
0318: 00 00 00 00 00 00 00 00
0320: 00 00 00 00 00 00 00 00
0328: 00 00 00 00 00 00 00 00
0330: 00 00 00 00 00 00 00 00
0338: 00 00 00 00 00 00 00 00


TYPE 'HELP' FOR COMMANDS
YOUR WISH, MASTER?
```

Fig. 8-8. Five INX and one DEX instruction used in a loop with the BNE instruction. This program does the same thing as the one shown in Fig. 8-5.

```
                         ! IR $00 PC $00
                         ! DR $00 AR $00
C I N V Z                !         SC $0000
? ? C ? C                ! X  $00 Y  $00
                         !------------------

MEMORY STARTING AT $C300
C300: E8 E8 E8 E8 E8 CA D0 FD
C308: 00 00 00 00 00 00 00 00
C310: 00 00 00 00 00 00 00 00
C318: 00 00 00 00 00 00 00 00
C320: 00 00 00 00 00 00 00 00
C328: 00 00 00 00 00 00 00 00
C330: 00 00 00 00 00 00 00 00
C338: 00 00 00 00 00 00 00 00

TYPE 'HELP' FOR COMMANDS
YOUR WISH, MASTER?
```

**Fig. 8-9. Commodore 64 version of a loop with five INX and one DEX instructions.**

You should see the X Register increase by 1s to 5. Then it will decrease to 4. At this point the Branch if Not Equal (to zero) instruction gets into the Instruction Register. Since 4 is not zero, the program jumps back. You can see that this happens because the Program Counter gets smaller. Now the 4 becomes 3. Since 3 is also not equal to zero, we branch again. Now the 3 becomes 2, which means another branch. Now the 2 becomes a 1, causing another branch. Finally the 1 becomes a 0. Since 0 is equal to zero, the branch does not happen and the break instruction gets put into the Instruction Register. The program stops.

How long did that take? My computer took 40 seconds.

Now let us see how long the "real" microprocessor can do it. Use your watch and the GO instruction. Mine goes so quickly that it was impossible to time. Now you can really see that machine language programs work fast. In the next chapter, we shall be able to load the X and Y Registers with large numbers without having to use INX instruction a large number of times. That way, we shall be able to get some machine language programs that use numbers large enough that we can time properly to see how fast machine language programs really work.

# Chapter 9

# Getting Things from Memory With Machine Language

In the last chapter we were introduced to two new registers. They were the X Register and the Y Register. These registers, together with the branch instructions, enabled us to do IF statements. The following machine language, assembly language, and BASIC programs do the same thing.

```
    PROGRAM 1

      BASIC              ASSEMBLY            MACHINE
    LANGUAGE             LANGUAGE            LANGUAGE

0   X = X + 1            $300: INX             $E8
1   X = X + 1            $301: INX             $E8
2   X = X + 1            $302: INX             $E8
3   X = X + 1            $303: INX             $E8
4   X = X + 1            $304: INX             $E8
5   X = X - 1            $305: DEX             $CA
6   IF X > 0 THEN 5      $306: BNE $305        $D0
                                               $FD
8   STOP                 $308: BRK             $00
```

Suppose that we want to have a machine language or assembly language program do the same as the following BASIC program:

PROGRAM 2

```
0 X = 126
1 X = X - 1
2 J = X
3 IF X > 0 THEN 1
4 X = J
5 STOP
```

We could do this program using the machine or assembly language instructions we already know. That would mean that we would have to put 126 INX ($E8) instructions into memory. There must be an easier way!

There is—if we use a couple of new instructions. To do the same in machine code as in BASIC Program 2, we need to be able to do three things:

1) To be able to store the value inside the X Register anywhere in memory. This is the same as the BASIC statement

   J = X

2) To be able to put a number into the X Register. This is the same as the BASIC statement

   X = 126

3) To be able to put a number stored anywhere in memory into the X Register. This is the same as the BASIC statement

   X = J

Of course, anything we want to do with the X Register we should be able to do with the Y Register. This gives us six new instructions:

| BASIC LANGUAGE | ASSEMBLY MNEMONIC | MACHINE INSTRUCTIONS | WHAT THE MACHINE LANGUAGE EXPRESSION DOES |
|---|---|---|---|
| J = X | STX $600 | $8E $00 $06 | Store X-register in location $600 |

| | | | |
|---|---|---|---|
| X = 6 | LDX #$6 | $A2 $06 | Load X-register with 6 |
| X = J | LDX $600 | $AE $00 $06 | Load X-register with what is stored in location $600 |
| J = Y | STY $1234 | $8C $34 $12 | Store Y-register in location $1234 |
| Y = 32 | LDY #$20 | $A0 $20 | Load Y-register with decimal 32 ($20) |
| Y = J | LDY $1234 | $AC $34 $12 | Load Y-register with what is stored in location $1234 |

You will notice a number of things:

1) In loading Y with a number like 32, we must remember that BASIC uses decimal numbers but machine language and assembly language use hexadecimal numbers.
2) LDX and LDY are used twice in two different ways. The only thing that seems to be different in the way that things are written for these two instructions is the # sign that is present in the "load a number" instructions.

## TWO TYPES OF *LOAD* INSTRUCTIONS

As you can well expect, the fact that there are two types of LOAD instructions is *very* confusing until you get used to it. It is at this point that many people stop bothering with machine language programs because they feel it becomes difficult. Actually it makes a lot of sense if you know what the # means. The # means, in English, "immediately with."

The instruction to load the X Register with the number 5 is

```
LDX #$5
```

which means, "Load the X Register *immediately with* the number $5." What does LDY #$20 mean?

On the other hand what does LDX $600 mean? It means "Load the X Register *using* the number $600." Notice that the # sign is not present in the mnemonic.

One word *using* means just that. The computer must use the number $600 to get another number. The instruction looks into memory location $600 for a second number. It is the second number that is put into the X Register. This is known as a *deferred instruction*. Figure 9-1 shows the action of the immediate and absolute instruction on the X Register.

You should already be used to the idea of deferred and immediate instructions if you have been using BASIC. When you type

PRINT "HELLO"

the computer *immediately* replies HELLO. However when you type

1 PRINT "HELLO"

the computer just sits there. The instruction is *deferred* until you run your BASIC program. The immediate and deferred machine language instructions are similar but different. The immediate instruction LDX #$5 says, "Load the X Register now with the number

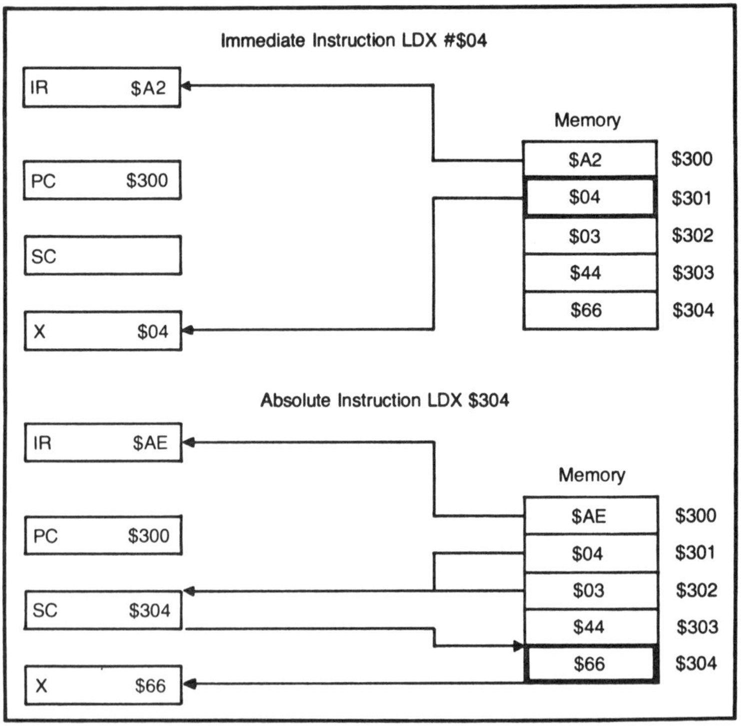


Fig. 9-1. Differences in the use of the X Register for LDX immediate and LDX absolute instructions.

$5." The instruction LDX $5 says, "Load the X Register with the number that is stored in memory location $5."

You can see why people get confused. The instructions look very similar but they act so very differently. Let's put the two immediate instructions into the animation program first.

What does the LDX immediate instruction do? Well, it is very like a branch instruction in parts. In the branch instruction, the Program Counter was used to fetch a number and store it in the Scratch Register. The LDX immediate instruction has to do exactly the same. (That is good because then we can use the same <<fetch-another-next-memory>> subroutine already in our animation program.)

The next bit is different. In the branch instructions, the number in the Scratch Register was added to the Program Counter. In the LDX instruction, the number in the Scratch Register is put into the X Register. It can't be added. It turns out that you can't do adding or subtracting using the X and Y Registers. You can only make them bigger or smaller by 1. Finally, since the computer is handling numbers, we must make sure that the N and Z flags are set correctly. Figure 9-2 shows the internal wiring of the microprocessor that allows the X and Y Registers to get their information from the Scratch Register.

Now that we know what has to happen, let's add the action to the simulation and then test out these new instructions. The decision logic:

```
30140 IF IR = 162 THEN 32100 : REM <<ldx #>>
30150 IF IR = 160 THEN 32200 : REM <<ldy #>>
```

The execution logic:

```
32100 GOSUB 51000 : REM <<fetch-another>>
32110 ADJUST = SC : GOSUB 52000 : REM <<adjust-N-and-Z-flags>>
32120 XREG = ADJUST : REM load the X-register
32130 RETURN : REM <<end ldx #>>

32200 GOSUB 51000 : REM <<FETCH-ANOTHER>>
32210 ADJUST = SC : GOSUB 52000 : REM <<adjust-N-and-Z-flags>>
32220 YREG = ADJUST : REM load the Y-register
32230 RETURN : REM <<end ldy #>>

60700 MN$(162) = "LDX" : TYPE%(162) = 1
60710 MN$(160) = "LDY" : TYPE%(160) = 1
```

Save this program as CHAP.9A.

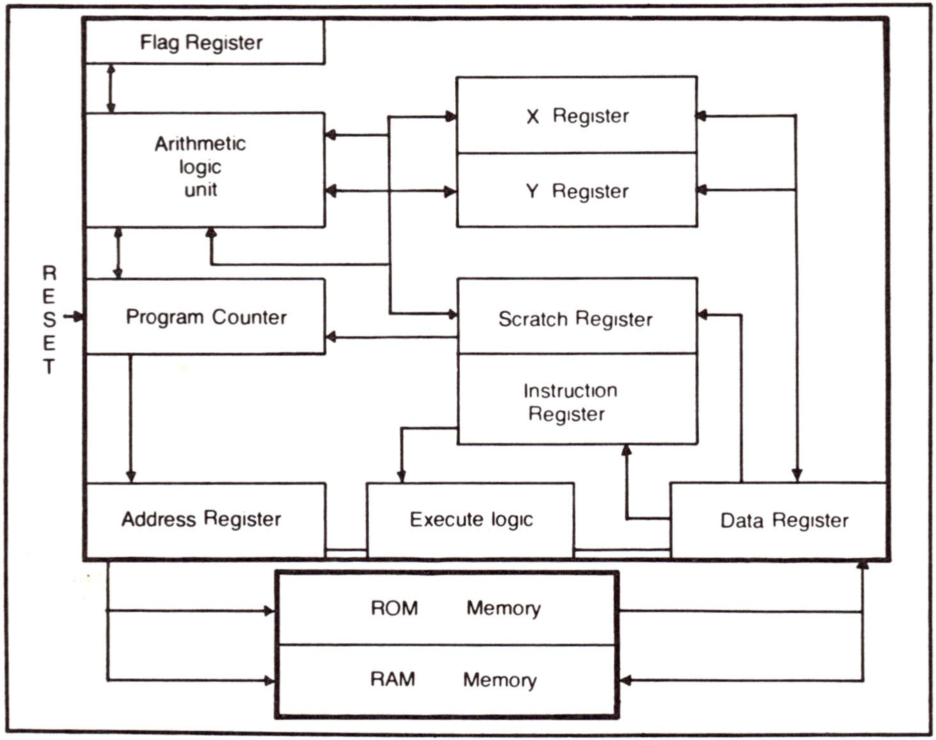


Fig. 9-2. Data paths needed to store the contents of the X and Y Registers in memory.

We shall test the animation by writing the machine language equivalent to a BASIC program with two loops:

```
1 FOR Y = 1 TO 126
2 FOR X = 1 TO 126
3 NEXT X
4 NEXT Y
5 STOP
```

Before trying the machine language program that follows, time the two-loop BASIC program to see how long it takes. Don't forget to remove it after you have used it.

The machine and assembler language programs to do the same loops are given below. We shall now show how machine and assembly language programs are normally written down. This way you will get used to reading machine and assembly language programs. Many magazines and books give very useful machine language programs that you can change to suit your own needs.

The programs are written out in four columns:

1) The first column is the starting address of each instruction.
2) The second column is the machine language instruction (the hex code that needs to be stored in memory).
3) The third column is the assembly language mnemonic.
4) The final column is the comment. Comments are like BASIC REM statements. They help explain what is happening but don't actually do anything.

Here are the programs:

```
START  MACHINE    ASSEMBLY    COMMENTS
       LANGUAGE   LANGUAGE

$300:  $A0 $7E    LDY #$7E   ; Load Y register with decimal 126
$302:  $A2 $7E    LDX #$7E   ; Load X register with decimal 126
$304:  $CA        DEX        ; Make X register smaller by 1
$305:  $D0 $FD    BNE $304   ; Branch back if not end of loop
$307:  $88        DEY        ; Make Y register smaller by 1
$308:  $D0 $F8    BNE $302   ; Branch back if not end of loop
$310:  $00        BRK        ; QUIT!!!!
```

For Commodore 64 users:

```
Start   Machine    Assembly
        Language   Language

$C300   $A0 $7E    LDY #$7E    ; Load Y register with decimal 126
$C302   $A2 $7E    LDX #$7E    ; Load X register with decimal 126
$C304   $CA        DEX         ; Make X register smaller by 1
$C305   $D0 $FD    BNE $C304   ; Branch back if not end of loop
$C307   $88        DEY         ; Make Y register smaller by 1
$C308   $D0 $F8    BNE $C304   ; Branch back if not end of loop
$C310   $00        BRK         ; QUIT!!!!
```

As can be seen, there is no change in the actual machine code between the Apple and C-64.

Use the clear (CL) command to set all the safe area to $00 and then load the program using the L command. It should look exactly like Fig. 9-3, except that your safe area will be listed rather than

```
                          ! IR $00  PC $00
                          ! DR $00  AR $00
C I N V Z                 !         SC $0000
? ? C ? C                 ! X  $00  Y  $00
                          !-----------------------


MEMORY STARTING AT $0300
0300: A0 7E A2 7E CA D0 FD 88
0308: D0 F8 00 00 00 00 00 00
0310: 00 00 00 00 00 00 00 00
0318: 00 00 00 00 00 00 00 00
0320: 00 00 00 00 00 00 00 00
0328: 00 00 00 00 00 00 00 00
0330: 00 00 00 00 00 00 00 00
0338: 00 00 00 00 00 00 00 00



TYPE 'HELP' FOR COMMANDS
YOUR WISH, MASTER?
```

Fig. 9-3. Screen display showing the double-loop machine language program loaded.

mine. That is one of the advantages of using branch instructions rather than jump instructions. With jump instructions you have to say *exactly* where to go. Branch instructions automatically calculate what to do. If you have the disassembler working, use it to check that things are loaded correctly. Figure 9-3 shows what the double loop program looks like when stored in the memory.

Before you use the W instruction to see if it works, do some thinking. We are going to make X get smaller 126 times. We are also going to make X get smaller the 126 times that Y gets smaller by 1. That means that we are going to be doing about 126 × 126 instructions—which, I know without doing any calculation, is going to take a very long time. We just want to check our program to see if it works. We don't need to see it work all the way. If it works for X and Y counting down from 2 then it will work counting down from 126.

Using the CH change instruction, change both the $7E to equal $02. Now use the W instruction.

In order to make the machine language code easy to program, we had to change the form of the two-loop BASIC program to this:

```
1 Y = 126
2 X = 126
3 X = X - 1
4 IF X > 0 THEN 3
5 Y = Y - 1
6 IF Y > 0 THEN 2
7 STOP
```

If you look at the BASIC program as the simulation works, you will see what is happening. In machine languageit is often easier to count down, rather than count up as happens in FOR . . . NEXT loops. As long as everything gets done, it does not really matter which way we go.

Using the CH instruction, change both the $02 back to $7E, so that we count the full 126 times. Use the GO instruction and your watch. This is a real test of how fast machine language programs work. We are going to do more than 126 × 126 = 15,876 instructions. When you try it, I'll bet that the computer is still faster than you can time. This means that the machine does more than 15,876 instructions every second. We will have to wait for some other instructions before we can do things that take long enough that we can properly time things.

**GETTING AND STORING**

In the last part we introduced the immediate instructions that load the X and Y Registers with a fixed number. Suppose we want to load X and Y with a different number each time we use the program, something like this BASIC program:

```
1 FOR Y = 1 to J : REM allow the loop size to be changeable
2 X = X + 3
3 NEXT Y
4 K = X : REM store X some-where
```

Let's turn this into the form that can be used for machine language and put beside it what we know how to do using assembly language:

```
1 Y = J                  $300:  ??
2 X = X + 3              $303:  INX
                         $304:  INX
                         $305:  INX
3 Y = Y - 1              $306:  DEY
4 IF Y <> 0 THEN 2       $307:  BNE $303
5 K = X                  $309:  ??
6 STOP                   $30D:  00
```

You can see that there are two things we can't do at the moment. The variable J is somewhere in memory. We need to get it and load it into the Y Register. That is the problem in line 1. In line 5, we need to store the X Register somewhere in memory so we can look at it later.

For Problem 1 we need X and Y Register instructions which load the X and Y Registers with things stored in memory. The other problem needs instructions that STORE the X and Y Registers into memory locations.

Let's get the STORE animation working first. This is what the EXECUTE logic must do.

1) Using the Program Counter, get another value from memory and put into the Scratch Register. (That is just like the LOAD IMMEDIATE instruction.)
2) Using the Program Counter again, get another value from memory, multiply this new value by 256 and add it to the value already stored in the Scratch Register. Place the

answer back into the Scratch Register. (This is rather like what the JMP instruction did.)

3) Now, using the Scratch Register, pick out the memory location where the value in the X Register must be stored.
4) Since the computer has just handled a number, we must set the N and Z flags.

Notice how we mentioned before that the branch and the LDX immediate instructions were very similar. In this case the store instruction is very similar to the jump instruction. This similarity means that the EXECUTE logic can have bits that are used by *both* instructions. That makes for easier microprocessor building.

```
30160 IF IR = 142 THEN 32300 : REM <<stx-memory>>
30170 IF IR = 140 THEN 32400 : REM <<sty-memory>>

32300 GOSUB 51000 : REM <<fetch-another>>
32310 GOSUB 51500 : REM <<use-PC-yet again>>
32320 POKE(SC) , XREG : REM store the X-register
32330 RETURN : REM <<end stx-memory>>

32400 You provide the
32410 code for the
32420 sty memory
32430 machine language instruction

51500 SC = SC + 256 * PEEK(PC)
      : REM get the new value from memory
51510 PC = PC + 1 : REM adjust the PROGRAMME COUNTER
51520 RETURN : REM <<end use-pc-yet-again>>

60720 MN$(142) = "STX" : TYPE%(142) = 2
60730 MN$(140) = "STY" : TYPE%(140) = 2
```

Now we can try out the simulation. Let us do the machine language program that is the same as this BASIC program.

```
1 X = 6       $300:  $A2 $06              LDX #$6
2 X = X + 3   $302:  $E8                  INX
              $303:  $E8                  INX
              $304:  $E8                  INX
3 K = X       $305:  $8E $08 $03          STX $308
              $308:  $00             K    DS  $1
```

There is something strange in the assembly language program. There is a new instruction called DS, but there was no BASIC code for it. The reason for this is that DS stands for *define space* or, in English, "Leave room for." When we say

K = X

that helpful little monitor program nips around memory and automatically finds room for K. When we are doing machine language programming, *we* have to nip around memory trying to find some space. Since $308 was not in use at the moment, that's the place we decided to put K. For the Commodore 64, change line 5 to read

```
$C305:  $8E $08 $C3              STX $C308
```

Notice the K before the DS. That is a special comment called a *label*. It does not do the computer any good, but it is a simple way of putting a marker on location $308 to remind us that K is going to be placed there. Imagine what would happen if we had to make space for the variables J, K, L, M, N, O, . . . Z. We would quickly lose our place. Just like on a book, we put a title or label on the "outside" of the memory location. Later on we shall discuss a special software tool that you can buy called an *assembler*. Commercial versions of this special tool allow us to turn assembly language programs into machine code almost as quickly as you can write BASIC. These assemblers find that labels are very useful and cut down the time needed to do programming.

When the program is loaded, it should look like Fig. 9-4. Use the W instruction to make the animation work. Save the BASIC program as CHAP.9B.

## A PROBLEM

How come bells started to ring and the program did not stop until after instruction $308 was done? Instruction $308 was not *meant* to be an instruction; it was meant to be data, or the place to store K. We have come across a very important problem in machine language programming. We did not make sure that our program and data places were different. In BASIC this problem never occurred, because that monitor program was making sure it never happened. When we checked the program we saw that location $308 was $00 or a BRK instruction. Look at it now. It has become $06. This is the number that the STX instruction put into location $308. The $06 we

```
                            ! IR $00 PC $00
                            ! DR $00 AR $00
C I N V Z                   !        SC $0000
? ? C ? C                   ! X  $00 Y  $00
                            !-----------------------


MEMORY STARTING AT $0300
0300: A2 06 E8 E8 E8 8E 08 03
0308: 00 00 00 00 00 00 00 00
0310: 00 00 00 00 00 00 00 00
0318: 00 00 00 00 00 00 00 00
0320: 00 00 00 00 00 00 00 00
0328: 00 00 00 00 00 00 00 00
0330: 00 00 00 00 00 00 00 00
0338: 00 00 00 00 00 00 00 00



TYPE 'HELP' FOR COMMANDS
YOUR WISH, MASTER?
```

Fig. 9-4. A machine language program that adds 3 to the X Register.

put there is an instruction our animation does not know. It therefore rang a bell. We thought that location $308 was *not* in use. Well, it was. It was being used as the BRK instruction. To get the program to work properly, we must change a few things.

Using the CH (change) instruction, make the following *patches*:

```
$306 -> $20
$308 -> $00
```

Our program will now be the same as this:

```
1 X = 6             $300: $A2 $06          LDX #$6
2 X = X + 3         $302: $E8              INX
                    $303: $E8              INX
                    $304: $E8              INX
3 K = X             $305: $8E $20 $03      STX $320
                              (C64 use     STX $C320)
```

```
$308:  $00          BRK

$320:  $00          K   DS  $1
```

We have really separated the data and the program. Use the W instruction now and things should happen properly.

Now use the CH instruction to change instruction $320 *back* to $00. We can now try the program using the GO instruction. You should find that the real microprocessor can do the job just as well as our simulation. You will be able to see what is in memory, provided you don't power off. Hit RESET (or, on a Commodore computer, type X then return) after the crash, and then run the BASIC animation program and things will be great. In the chapter on machine language subroutines we will solve the crashing problem. Actually an early chapter has already suggested a method for stopping the crashing. What was it?

*Question: Why did we have to change location $320 back to $000 before running with the GO instruction?*

We are nearly in the position to do that FOR . . . NEXT loop. We can store X into memory. How can we fetch J out of memory and put it into Y? We need to use the LDY instruction. This is like the STX instruction except for two small parts.

1) Using the Program Counter, get another value from memory and put into the Scratch Register. (That is just like the LOAD IMMEDIATE instruction.)
2) Using the Program Counter again, get another value from memory, multiply this new value by 256, and add it to the value already stored in the Scratch Register. Place the answer back into the Scratch Register. (This is rather like what the jump instruction did.)

This is no different than the STX and STY instructions, is it?

3) Now, using the Scratch Register, *fetch* the value from memory and put it into the Y Register.
4) Since the computer has just handled a number, we must set the N and Z flags.

Notice that this time, instead of using the Program Counter to do the fetching, we used the Scratch Register. That is why there must be a wire that connected the Scratch Register and the Address Register in the microprocessor. Figure 9-5 shows the interior

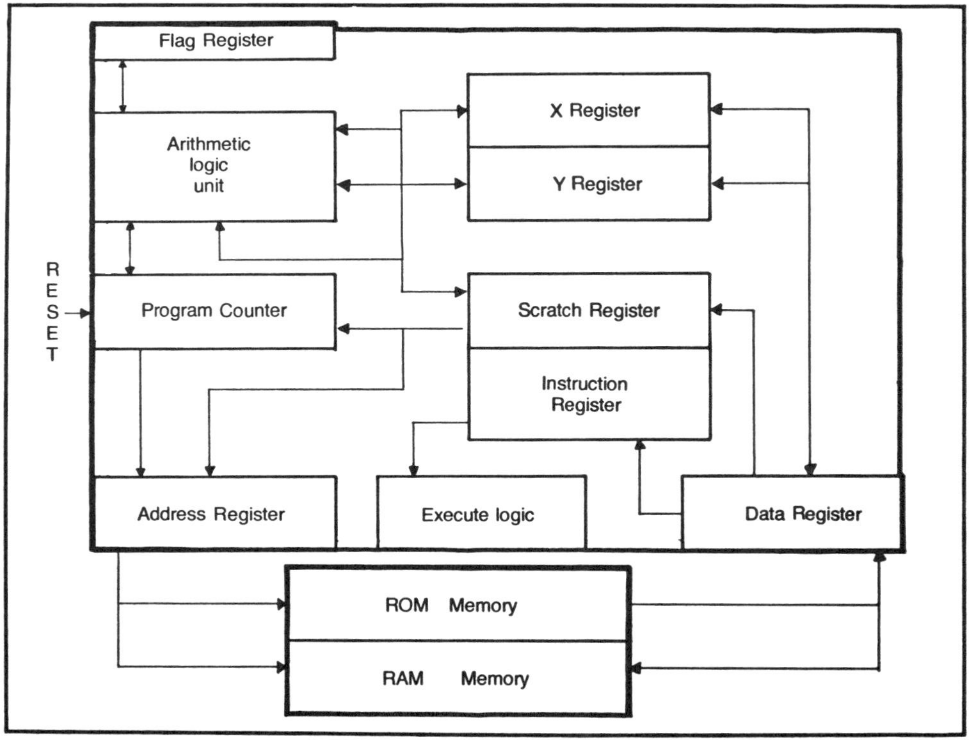


Fig. 9-5. The data path that allows using the Scratch Register to locate things in memory.

connections (*architecture*) of the microprocessor with this new logic.

Let's add the LDX and LDY memory instructions to the animation:

```
30180 IF IR = 174 THEN 32500 : REM <<ldx-memory>>
30190 IF IR = 172 THEN 32600 : REM <<ldy-memory>>

32500 GOSUB 51000 : REM <<fetch-next-memory>>
32510 GOSUB 51500 : REM <<use-PC-again>>
32520 SC = PEEK(SC) : REM use the SCRATCH REGISTER to FETCH
32530 ADJUST = SC : GOSUB 52000 : REM <<set-N-and-Z-flags>>
32540 XREG = ADJUST :REM load the X-register
32550 RETURN : REM <<end ldx-memory>>

32600 GOSUB 51000 : REM <<fetch-next-memory>>
32610 GOSUB 51500 : REM <<use-PC-again>>
32620 SC = PEEK(SC) : REM use the SCRATCH REGISTER to FETCH
32630 ADJUST = SC: GOSUB 52000 : REM <<set-N-and-Z-flags>>
32640 YREG = ADJUST : REM load the Y-register
32650 RETURN : REM <<end ldy-memory>>

60740 MN$(174) = "LDX" : TYPE%(174) = 2
60750 MN$(172) = "LDY" : TYPE%(172) = 2
```

Now we can complete that machine language program.

```
1 Y = J              $300:  $AC $20 $03      LDY $320 ; Get J
2 X = X + 3          $303:  $E8              INX
                     $304:  $E8              INX
                     $305:  $E8              INX      ; X + 3
3 Y = Y - 1          $306:  $88              DEY      ; Y - 1
4 IF Y <> 0 THEN 2   $307:  $D0 $FA          BNE $303 ; Loop!
5 K = X              $309:  $8E $21 $03      STX $321 ; Store K
6 STOP               $30C:  00
                     $320:  00             J DS 1   ; Leave room
                     $321:  00             K DS 1   ; Leave room
```

For the Commodore 64:

```
1 Y = J     $C300:  $AC $20 $C3     LDY $C320 ; Get J
5 K = X     $C309:  $8E $21 $C3     STX $C321 ; Store K
```

That must be the longest machine language program so far. It is a good thing that the LOAD (L) instruction is automated. Can you imagine how long it would take to load it using the methods we first used in Chapter 3!

```
                    ! IR $00 PC $00
C I N V Z           ! DR $00 AR $00
? ? C ? C           !           SC $0000
                    ! X  $00 Y  $00
                    !------------------

MEMORY STARTING AT $0300
0300: AC 20 03 E8 E8 E8 88 D0
0308: FA 8E 21 03 00 00 00 00
0310: 00 00 00 00 00 00 00 00
0318: 00 00 00 00 00 00 00 00
0320: 01 00 00 00 00 00 00 00
0328: 00 00 00 00 00 00 00 00
0330: 00 00 00 00 00 00 00 00
0338: 00 00 00 00 00 00 00 00


TYPE 'HELP' FOR COMMANDS
YOUR WISH, MASTER?
```

Fig. 9-6. A machine language routine that multiplies by 3.

Once you have loaded the program, use the CH instruction to put a $1 in location $320. Your screen should look like Fig. 9-6. Use the W (work) instruction. If things go right then you should end up with a $03 in location $321 (location $C321 for the C-64).

Now try using the GO instruction and get the microprocessor to do the work. Notice that our program does not work any more. How come? Well, in our animation the X Register started at $00. That means that after three INX instructions it becomes 3. However, when the real microprocessor starts using our program, it has just come from doing BASIC. That means there could be just about any number in the X Register. After three INX instructions, who knows what number might end up in location $321 (K). What we need to do is to *clear* the X Register to 0 before using it. When we run a BASIC program, that friendly monitor program makes sure that all variables start off as 0. When we use machine code, then *we* have to make sure that things start up correctly.

Rather than rewriting the machine language program to put the new instructions at the start of our program, we add the instructions to the end. This is a *temporary* patch or fix. Fixes are used to test out things you think might be wrong. There is no good point in making large changes to a program when the changes might not be useful. Test the patches first and then make the changes permanent later.

Use the LOAD instruction and add

```
$310:     $A2 $00         LDX #$0         ; Clear the X-reg
$312:     $4C $00 $03     JMP $300        ; Jump to old program
```

Commodore 64 users should substitute:

```
$C310:    $A2 $00         LDX #$0         ; Clear the X-reg
$C312:    $4C $00 $C3     JMP $C300       ; Jump to old program
```

Now use the GO instruction. It was just as bad, wasn't it?

When you used the GO command, did you tell the program to start at $300 or $310? With this patch, the program now starts at $310, does something, then jumps back to $300 and finishes off. Rather confusing! That's why we must fix the program later to make it easier to understand. Try the GO instruction again and use $310 as the start instruction.

Since things are working correctly, we need to make the changes more understandable. Unlike BASIC, where we just use another line number, we have to move all the machine language instructions up in memory. Really, in BASIC, everything also gets moved up in memory. Sometimes, when you have inserted an extra line in a long program, you may have noticed that a short wait happened. While you were waiting for BASIC to "come back," that friendly monitor program was busy moving the BASIC program up in memory. Move the program so:

```
0 X = 0              $300:  $A2 $00          LDX #$0   ; Clear X
1 Y = J              $302:  $AC $20 $03      LDY $320  ; Get J
2 X = X + 3          $305:  $E8              INX
                     $306:  $E8              INX
                     $307:  $E8              INX       ; X + 3
3 Y = Y - 1          $308:  $88              DEY       ; Y - 1
4 IF Y <> 0 THEN 2   $309:  $D0 $FA          BNE $305  ; Loop!
5 K = X              $30B:  $8E $21 $03      STX $321  ; Store K
6 STOP               $30E:  00
                     $320:  00             J DS 1      ; Leave room
                     $321:  00             K DS 1      ; Leave room
```

Or for the Commodore 64:

```
$C302:  $AC $20 $C3        LDY $C320
$C30B:  $8E $21 $C3        STX $C321
```

The final program as stored in memory looks like Fig. 9-7.

Notice something interesting. Although we moved up the branch instruction, we did not have to change how far it branched! This is because branch instructions are *relative*. They jump a fixed distance. It does not matter where they are located. They always jump by the same amount. If we were using a proper JMP instruction, then this would not be true.

Now use the CH command and put a $02 into location $320 before typing GO. You should get $06 in location $321. If you put $03 into location $320, then you will get $09. We have taught the computer to do the 3-times multiplication table.

*Question: How do you get the computer to do the 16-times table?*

```
                        ! IR $00 PC $00
                        ! DR $00 AR $00
C I N V Z               !        SC $0000
? ? C ? C               ! X  $00 Y  $00
                        !--------------------

MEMORY STARTING AT $0300
0300: A2 00 AC 20 03 E8 E8 E8
0308: 88 D0 FA 8E 21 03 00 00
0310: 00 00 00 00 00 00 00 00
0318: 00 00 00 00 00 00 00 00
0320: 01 00 00 00 00 00 00 00
0328: 00 00 00 00 00 00 00 00
0330: 00 00 00 00 00 00 00 00
0338: 00 00 00 00 00 00 00 00

TYPE 'HELP' FOR COMMANDS
YOUR WISH, MASTER?
```

Fig. 9-7. A version of the program in Fig. 9-6 that can be used directly from BASIC.

Try to get the computer to do the decimal 16-times table ($10). Notice that strange things seem to get stored in K if you do the $10 (16) table—especially if you ask the computer to do $10 × $10. Why?

Store this program as CHAP.9.

## IMPROVING THE DISPLAY

In this chapter we have been using instructions that store things both in registers and the memory. Although the values in the registers have been changing with the display, the memory values have not. The following BASIC statements allow the updating of the memory without having to rewrite all the memory part of the screen. If we had to update the whole screen, the animation would become very slow.

The secret behind updating only that part of the memory display that changes is the number stored in the Scratch Register. This always contains the address of the last memory location changed. We can use its value to check if the screen needs updating. If it does, then we can change only that screen value.

```
54820 IF (SC > NSAFE) OR (SC < SAFE) THEN 54900
54825 REM nothing on the screen needs changing
54830 TSC = SC - SAFE : REM where in the SAFE area?
54840 DOWN = 9 + INT(TSC / 8) : GOSUB 61200
54850 OVER = 7 + 3 * (TSC - 8 * INT(TSC / 8)) : GOSUB 61500
54870 PRINT HEX$(PEEK(SC));
```

I would like to thank Doug Maynard of Calgary for pointing out this simple and elegant way of quickly updating the screen.

# Chapter 10
# Doing Mathematics

In Chapter 8 we had the computer doing some multiplication. Our machine language program was able to do 3 multiplied by anything. It needed three INX instruction for it to work. If you tried the $10 multiplication table, then you would have found that it needed $10 (decimal 16) INXs. This uses a lot of memory and, in machine language terms, it rather slow and inefficient. Why can't we just add 16 to the X Register, instead of increasing it by 1 sixteen times? The answer is simple: the 6502 microprocessor just does not work that way. If you can't do proper arithmetic with the X and Y Registers, then how *can* you do it?

## THE ACCUMULATOR

Since all computers need to be able to add and subtract, the microprocessor manufacturers added a special register called the *Accumulator* or *A Register*. This special register is able to do all the things the X and Y Registers can do and, in addition, a few other things. The obvious question that you should ask is, "Why a special register? Why not have the X and the Y as well as the A Register be able to do arithmetic?" When the 6502 was first made, perhaps the manufacturer thought that it was unnecessary, or too expensive, or there was not enough room on the chip, or because nobody else was doing it. I don't really know why. Even some of the newer chips work the same way, while others allow you to do arithmetic with all memory locations and registers. It does not really matter. With just one special register, you can do everything you need. If you have two special registers, then a few things might be able to be done faster.

Just like the X and Y Registers, you can load a number into the A Register (LDA immediate). You can also load and store from memory (LDA memory and STA memory). However, when we start using the A Register for addition and subtraction, some strange things happen unless the C and V flags are used correctly. More will be said about these two new flags in the next chapter. In this chapter, we are going to use programs that make sure the problems don't occur. However, we are going to leave room for the changes to the simulator we will have to make. Watch the line numbers so you don't make any programming errors. With the new A Register, the internal arichitecture of the microprocessor looks like Fig. 10-1.

We are going to add six new machine language animated instructions. They are:

| ASSEMBLY LANGUAGE MNEMONIC | MACHINE LANGUAGE CODE | WHAT THE INSTRUCTION DOES |
|---|---|---|
| CLC | $18 | Clear the C flag. |
| CLV | $B8 | Clear the V flag. |
| SEC | $38 | Set the C flag. |
| LDA # | $A9 | Load the A register with a number. |
| LDA (memory) | $AD | Load the A register using the value stored in memory. |
| STA (memory) | $8D | Store the A register into a memory location. |

The *flag* instructions are very obvious, and the A Register instructions are exactly the same as the X and Y Register instructions. We can jump straight into the BASIC program for the animation with no major explanation outside of the REMs.

The decision logic:

```
30200 IF IR = 24 THEN 32700 : REM <<clc>>
30210 IF IR = 184 THEN 32800 : REM <<clv>>
30220 IF IR = 56 THEN 32900 : REM <<sec>>
30230 IF IR = 169 THEN 33000 : REM <<lda #>>
30240 IF IR = 173 THEN 33100 : REM <<lda-memory>>
30250 IF IR = 141 THEN 33200 : REM <<sta-memory>>
```

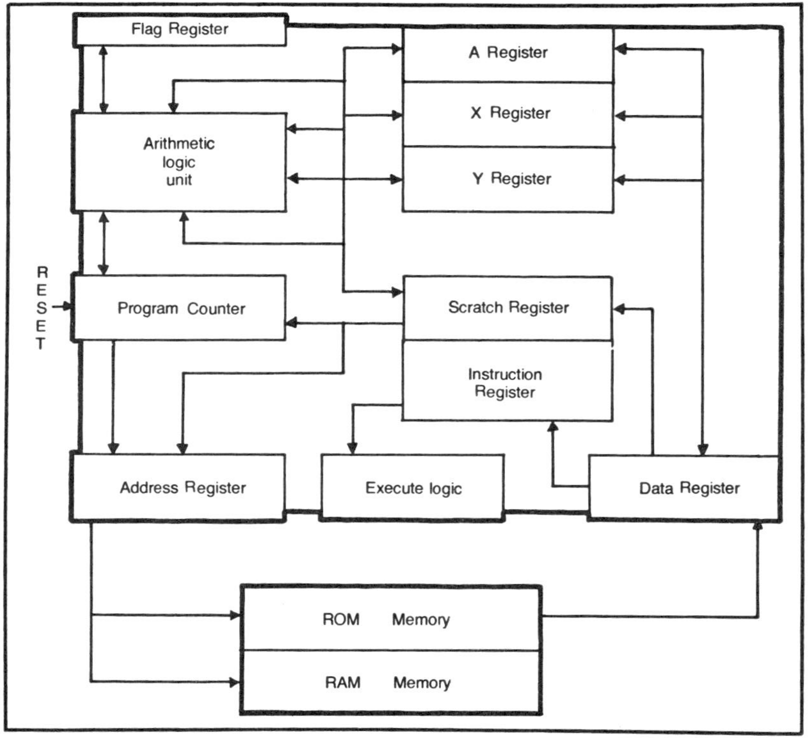


Fig. 10-1. Data paths to the A Register.

The execution logic:

```
32700 C$ = "C"
32710 RETURN : REM <<end clc>>
32800 V$ = "C"
32810 RETURN : REM <<end clv>>
32900 C$ = "S"
32910 RETURN : REM <<end sec>>
33000 GOSUB 51000: REM <<fetch-another>>
33010 ADJUST = SC : GOSUB 52000 : REM <<set-N-and-Z-flags>>
33020 AREG = ADJUST : REM load the A-register
33030 RETURN : REM <<end lda #>>
33100 GOSUB 51000 : REM <<fetch-next-memory>>
33110 GOSUB 51500 : REM <<use-pc-yet-again>>
33120 SC = PEEK(SC) : REM use SCRATCH REGISTER to FETCH
33130 ADJUST = SC: GOSUB 52000 : REM <<set-N-and-Z-flags>>
33140 AREG = ADJUST : REM load the A register
33150 RETURN : REM <<end lda memory>>
33200 GOSUB 51000 : REM <<fetch-another>>
33210 GOSUB 51500 : REM <<use-PC-yet-again>>
33220 POKE (SC) , AREG : REM store A register
33230 RETURN : REM <<end sta-memory>>
```

Additions to the register display:

```
54400 GOSUB 61500 : REM <<move-over>>
54410 PRINT "! A  $";
54420 HEX = AREG : GOSUB 58000 : REM <<print-hex>>
54430 PRINT
```

Additional explanation codes:

```
60760 MN$(24) = "CLC" : TYPE%(24) = 5
60770 MN$(184) = "CLV" : TYPE%(184) = 5
60780 MN$(56) = "SEC" : TYPE%(56) = 5
60790 MN$(169) = "LDA" : TYPE%(169) = 1
60800 MN$(173) = "LDA" : TYPE%(173) = 2
60810 MN$(141) = "STA" : TYPE%(141) = 2
```

Save the program as CHAP.10A. We can test the new animation with a simple program:

```
$300:   $18            CLC          ; Clear the C-flag
$301:   $B8            CLV          ; Clear the V-flag
$302:   $38            SEC          ; Set the C-flag
$303:   $A9 $01        LDA #$01     ; Load A-reg with 1
$305:   $8D $20 $03    STA $320     ; Store A at $320
                                      (C64 use $C320)
$308:   $AD $00 $03    LDA $300     ; Load A from $300
                                      (C64 use $C300)
$30B:   $00            BRK          ; QUIT!!!
```

**ADD WITH CARRY INSTRUCTIONS**

The 6502 microprocessor can add numbers into the A Register. For example, the instruction

ADC #$5

will add $5 to whatever is already in the A Register. On the other hand, the instruction

ADC #$FF

will add $FF or −1 to whatever is already in the A Register. There is a problem, however. Notice the instruction is not *ADD* but *ADC*. There is a difference. If you used a true add instruction:

ADD #$5

when there is $1 already in the A Register, then you will get $6 just as you would expect. However if you use

ADC #$5

when there is $1 already in the A Register, then you will get one of two answers. If the C flag is clear or 0, then you get $1+$5+$0=$6. If the C flag is set or 1, then you get $1+$5+$1—which is $7. The instruction *ADC* means add *with carry*. If the C flag is zero, then you add 0. If the C flag is 1 (set) then you must add an additional $1. Rather confusing.

This seems rather strange. In a later chapter, after the C flag has been explained, you will see that this is very useful. It enables the microprocessor to handle numbers bigger than 255. At the moment, we must make sure that when we use the ADC instruction we always use the CLC or *clear C flag* instruction first. In this way, the ADC instruction will always act as though it were an add instruction. The ADC instruction also causes changes in the state of the C and V flags. In this chapter, you will see the reason for these flags, although how they solve problems will be explained in the next chapter.

| ASSEMBLY LANGUAGE | HEX CODE | WHAT THE INSTRUCTION DOES |
|---|---|---|
| ADC #$%% | $69 | Add the number $%% to A-register plus the Carry |
| ADC $%%%% | $6D | Add the number stored at $%%%% to A plus Carry |

There are two ADC instructions. One is an immediate instruction which adds a number to the A Register (and the carry flag). The other is a memory instruction. This one gets the value stored in a memory location and then adds that value to the A Register, with the carry. This is very much like what the LDA instructions did. The BASIC code for the animation is very similiar, except that we must leave room for adjusting the C and V flags. The decision logic:

```
30260 IF IR = 105 THEN 33300 : REM <<adc #>>
30270 IF IR = 109 THEN 33400 : REM <<adc-memory>>
```

The execute logic:

```
33300 GOSUB 51000: REM <<fetch-another>>
33310 AREG = AREG + SC : IF C$ = "S" THEN AREG = AREG + 1
            : REM add
33320 ADJUST = AREG : GOSUB 52500
            : REM set the N, Z, V and C flags
33330 AREG = ADJUST : REM  the extra 1 MIGHT change things
33340 RETURN : REM <<end adc #>>
33400 GOSUB 51000 : REM <<fetch-next-memory>>
33410 GOSUB 51500 : REM <<use-pc-yet-again>>
33420 SC = PEEK(SC) : REM use SCRATCH REGISTER to FETCH
33430 AREG = AREG + SC : IF C$ = "S" THEN AREG = AREG + 1
            : REM add
33440 ADJUST = AREG : GOSUB 52500
            : REM set the N, Z, V and C flags
33450 AREG = ADJUST : REM the extra 1
33460 RETURN : REM <<end adc memory>>
```

```
52490 REM <<adjust V and C flags>>
52500 GOTO 52000
      : REM  worry about the V and C flags in next chapter
```

Additional explanation codes:

```
60820 MN$(105) = "ADC" : TYPE%(105) = 1
60830 MN$(109) = "ADC" : TYPE%(109) = 2
60840 MN$(96) = "RTS" : TYPE%(96) = 5
```

Save this as program CHAP.10B. We have also put in the mnemonics for the RTS instruction we used in Chapter 4 for testing out the GO instruction.

To test out these new instructions we will use a very large loop. Our last timing loop used the X and the Y Registers; that gave us 126 × 126 = 15,876 machine instructions, which the machine program did so quickly that we could not time it. Now we are going to use three loops to give us 126 × 126 × 126 = 2,000,376—over 2 million instructions. We *should* be able to time that with some accuracy!

The equivalent BASIC program will be:

```
1   FOR A = 1 TO 126
2   FOR Y = 1 TO 126
3   FOR X = 1 TO 126
4   NEXT X
5   NEXT Y
6   NEXT A
7   STOP
```

To make this easier to convert this to a machine language program, we need to count things backwards. Our program becomes:

PROGRAM 1

```
1  A = 126
2  Y = 126
3  X = 126
4  X =  X - 1 : IF X <> 0 THEN 4
5  Y =  Y - 1 : IF Y <> 0 THEN 3
6  A =  A - 1 : IF A <> 0 THEN 2
7  STOP
```

```
                                 ! IR $00 PC $00
                                 ! DR $00 AR $00
C I N V Z                        !        SC $0000
? ? C ? C                        ! X  $00 Y  $00
                                 ! A  $00
                                 !--------------------

MEMORY STARTING AT $0300
0300: A9 7E A0 7E A2 7E CA D0
0308: FD 88 D0 F8 18 69 FF D0
0310: F1 60 00 00 00 00 00 00
0318: 00 00 00 00 00 00 00 00
0320: 00 00 00 00 00 00 00 00
0328: 00 00 00 00 00 00 00 00
0330: 00 00 00 00 00 00 00 00
0338: 00 00 00 00 00 00 00 00


TYPE 'HELP' FOR COMMANDS
YOUR WISH, MASTER?
```

Fig. 10-2. A triple machine language loop.

Use the space at the beginning of memory and enter BASIC Program 1 and time it. (It took my computer 130 seconds.)

Now clear the extra BASIC lines and run the animation. Use the CL and load menu commands to enter the following program:

```
$300:  $A9 $7E      LDA #$7E     ; A = 126
$302:  $A0 $7E      LDY #$7E     ; Y = 126
$304:  $A2 $7E      LDX #$7E     ; X = 126
$306:  $CA          DEX          ; X = X - 1
$307:  $D0 $FD      BNE $306     ; IF X <> 0
$309:  $88          DEY          ; Y = Y - 1
$30A:  $D0 $F8      BNE $304     ; IF Y <> 0
$30C:  $18          CLC          ; Cleared C flag makes ADC
                                   like ADD
$30D:  $69 $FF      ADC #$FF     ; A = A + -1
$30F:  $D0 $F1      BNE $302     ; IF A <> 0
$311:  $60          RTS          ; special return to BASIC
$312:  $00          BRK
```

Your screen should look like Fig. 10-2 or Fig. 10-3.

We have added a new assembly language instruction RTS. Our animation does not know how to do this, so it rings the bell when we use the W instruction. However, the real microprocessor *will* use it when we do a GO command as an instruction to return to BASIC. That will stop those crazy crashes.

"Why did you not tell me how to stop those crashes before?" I hear you cry. The answer is simple. After you have finished this book, I hope you will go onto more complicated books and magazine articles. Since you are working on your own, expect system crashes about one in every five programs. I think I'm good, because I only crash one in six! You are now so used to crashes that you realize it is *no big deal.*

In addition, you have not been paying attention if your computer has been crashing. In Chapter 4 we had to test the GO menu instruction. Look back there. What instruction did I tell you to add to stop the BASIC programs from crashing? Right, $60 or RTS. You

```
                          ! IR  $00 PC  $00
                          ! DR  $00 AR  $00
C I N V Z                 !         SC  $0000
? ? C ? C                 ! X   $00 Y   $00
                          ! A   $00
                          !--------------------

MEMORY STARTING AT $C300
C300: A9 7E A0 7E A2 7E CA D0
C308: FD 88 D0 F8 18 69 FF D0
C310: F1 60 00 00 00 00 00 00
C318: 00 00 00 00 00 00 00 00
C320: 00 00 00 00 00 00 00 00
C328: 00 00 00 00 00 00 00 00
C330: 00 00 00 00 00 00 00 00
C338: 00 00 00 00 00 00 00 00



TYPE 'HELP' FOR COMMANDS
YOUR WISH, MASTER?
```

Fig. 10-3. The triple loop on the Commodore 64.

could have added it and improved my machine language programs any time you wanted. That is something you have to look out for with machine language programming. A program may do what it was supposed to do but there may be a better and simpler way of doing things. Many magazine authors come to think that they have found such a wonderful way of doing something that they can't see that there's an easier way.

Back to the three-loop machine language program. If you have the disassembler command working, check that you have loaded the machine code correctly. Since we are going to check the working of the machine language program using the simulation and there will be more than 2 million instructions executed, then we shall be here until next winter. Before testing, change all $7E into $02 and then use the W command; time how long the animation takes to do 2 × 2 × 2 instructions.

Now use the GO instruction and time the real execution. Don't forget to use the CH instruction to turn the $02 back into $7E before doing that.

My microprocesor took 11 seconds. My BASIC simulation (three loops) took 130 seconds. If we had left *all* the loops in the simulation, then each time round the loop would have taken 63 times longer. That makes 130 × 63 × 63 × 63 = 32,506,110 seconds. Since 1 million seconds is 10 days, then we would have been waiting 320 days.

The machine language programming speed is:

$$\frac{\text{time BASIC took in seconds}}{\text{time machine language took}} \times 100\% \text{ faster than the animation}$$

$$\frac{32506110}{11} \times 100\% = 29{,}000{,}000\% \text{ faster}$$

It is obvious that machine language programs are quite a bit faster than the animation doing the same thing using BASIC.

## SUBTRACTING

Just as there is an add instruction for the A Register, there is also a SUB or subtract instruction. Like the add instruction, which is really ADC (add with carry), the subtract instruction also involves the C flag and is called SBC. Just like the ADC instruction, there are two forms of the SBC instruction, a "subtract a number with carry" and a "subtract using memory with carry." The EXECUTE logic for both ADC and SUB are very similiar.

| ASSEMBLER LANGUAGE MNEMONIC | HEX CODE | WHAT THE INSTRUCTION DOES |
|---|---|---|
| SBC #$ZZ | $E9 | Subtract number $ZZ from A register with Carry |
| SBC $ZZZZ | $ED | Subtract location $ZZZZ contents from A with Carry |

The only big difference is the way the C flag is used. Suppose that the A Register contains an $8. If we did a

SUB #$5

instruction (which does not exist) then we get a normal subtraction 8 − 5 = 3. Suppose instead we do a

SBC #$5

instruction. Then we get the answer 8 − 5 − 1 + carry. This means that if the C flag is set, then we get a normal subraction of 8 − 5 − 1 + 1 = 3. However, if the C flag is clear, then we get 8 − 5 − 1 + 0 = 2, which is smaller than expected. Again, this trick is very useful when we want to handle numbers bigger than 256. For the moment, we must remember to use the SEC (set the C flag) instruction, so that the SBC instruction acts like a SUB.

The decision logic is as follows:

```
30280 IF IR = 233 THEN 33500 : REM <<sbc #>>
30290 IF IR = 237 THEN 33600 : REM <<sbc-memory>>
```

The execute logic:

```
33500 GOSUB 51000: REM <<fetch-another>>
33510 AREG = AREG - SC - 1 : IF C$ = "S" THEN AREG = AREG + 1
33520 ADJUST = AREG : GOSUB 52500
              : REM set the N, Z, V and C flags
33530 AREG = ADJUST : REM  the extra 1 MIGHT change things
33540 RETURN : REM <<end sbc #>>
33600 GOSUB 51000 : REM <<fetch-next-memory>>
33610 GOSUB 51500 : REM <<use-pc-get-again>>
33620 SC = PEEK(SC) : REM use SCRATCH REGISTER to FETCH
33630 AREG = AREG - SC - 1 : IF C$ = "S" THEN AREG = AREG + 1
```

```
33640 ADJUST = AREG : GOSUB 52500
              : REM set the N, Z, V and C flags
33650 AREG = ADJUST : REM the extra 1
33660 RETURN : REM <<end sbc memory>>
```

Some additional explanation:

```
60850 MN$(233) = "SBC" : TYPE%(233) = 1
60860 MN$(237) = "SBC" : TYPE%(233) = 2
```

Save the program as CHAP.10. We can test the animation by doing that long loop again. This time, instead of having to use "add −1," we can instead use the better "subtract 1," which is more like normal mathematics. Rather than retyping the whole of the program, just use the CH command. Remember, we have to use the SEC instruction first so that the SBC acts like a SUB instruction.

```
$300:  $A9 $7E        LDA #$7E     ; A = 126
$302:  $A0 $7E        LDY #$7E     ; Y = 126
$304:  $A2 $7E        LDX #$7E     ; X = 126
$306:  $CA            DEX          ; X = X - 1
$307:  $D0 $FD        BNE $306     ; IF X <> 0
$309:  $88            DEY          ; Y = Y - 1
$30A:  $D0 $F8        BNE $304     ; IF Y <> 0
$30C:  $38            SEC          ; Setting C flag makes
                                     SBC like SUB
$30D:  $E9 $01        SUB $01      ; A = A - 1
$30F:  $D0 $F1        BNE $302     ; IF A <> 0
$311:  $60            RTS          ; special return to BASIC
$312:  $00            BRK
```

Notice that the changes are needed in bytes $30C and $30D only.

## USING *ADC* AND *SBC* INSTRUCTIONS

In this section we shall be using the ADC and SBC instructions and we'll see what problems can occur. This will help explain why the designers of microprocessor chips found it necessary to put in those extra flags C and V.

First of all, we are going to add $20 (decimal 32) to itself nine times. This program will only show what goes wrong if you use the work instruction. The GO instruction uses the real microprocessor and does not have this problem.

```
                                 !  IR  $00  PC  $00
                                 !  DR  $00  AR  $00
C  I  N  V  Z                    !           SC  $0000
?  ?  C  ?  C                    !  X   $00  Y   $00
                                 !  A   $00
                                 !-------------------------

MEMORY STARTING AT $0300
0300:  18  A9  00  69  20  69  20  69
0308:  20  69  20  69  20  69  20  69
0310:  20  69  20  60  00  00  00  00
0318:  00  00  00  00  00  00  00  00
0320:  01  03  00  00  00  00  00  00
0328:  00  00  00  00  00  00  00  00
0330:  00  00  00  00  00  00  00  00
0338:  00  00  00  00  00  00  00  00



TYPE 'HELP' FOR COMMANDS
YOUR WISH, MASTER?
```

Fig. 10-4. A program demonstrating problems with the N and Z flags.

Our program is quite simple. Add $20 to itself 9 times:

```
$300:  $18              CLC          ; CLear that C flag
$301:  $A9 $00          LDA #$0      ; A = 0
$303:  $69 $20          ADC #$20     ; A =  A + 20
$305:  $69 $20          ADC #$20
$307:  $69 $20          ADC #$20
$309:  $69 $20          ADC #$20
$30B:  $69 $20          ADC #$20
$30D:  $69 $20          ADC #$20
$30F:  $69 $20          ADC #$20
$311:  $69 $20          ADC #$20
$313:  $60              RTS          ; Special BASIC return
$314:  $00              BRK          ; QUIT!
```

Your screen should look like Fig. 10-4 or Fig. 10-5.

Run the program using the W instruction. Watch what happens to the N flag and what is stored in the A Register. If things go too

```
                                ! IR $00 PC $00
                                ! DR $00 AR $00
C I N V Z                       !        SC $0000
? ? C ? C                       ! X  $00 Y  $00
                                ! A  $00
                                !-----------------

MEMORY STARTING AT $C300
C300: 18 A9 00 69 20 69 20 69
C308: 20 69 20 69 20 69 20 69
C310: 20 69 20 60 00 00 00 00
C318: 00 00 00 00 00 00 00 00
C320: 01 03 00 00 00 00 00 00
C328: 00 00 00 00 00 00 00 00
C330: 00 00 00 00 00 00 00 00
C338: 00 00 00 00 00 00 00 00



TYPE 'HELP' FOR COMMANDS
YOUR WISH, MASTER?
```

Fig. 10-5. Commodore 64 display demonstrating problems with the N and Z flags.

fast, then use CTRL-S (on the Apple) to stop the screen scroll and any other key (space bar is good) to restart it again. What you should see is this:

| Step | A-register | N-flag | Z-flag |
|---|---|---|---|
| 1 | $00 | C | S |
| 2 | $20 | C | C |
| 3 | $40 | C | C |
| 4 | $60 | C | C |
| 5 | $80 | S | C |
| 6 | $A0 | S | C |
| 7 | $C0 | S | C |
| 8 | $E0 | S | C |
| 9 | $00 | C | S |

Steps 1 through 4 look exactly as you would expect. Steps 5 through 8 look right. The number in the A Register is still going up in increments of $20, but notice that the N flag has become set. This means that although we are adding a positive number to the A Register, we have ended up with a negative number. Step 9 is a little better; at least it is not negative. The only trouble is that instead of being $100, we have instead $00. If we were using this computer for doing mathematics then we would be in real trouble. Five mistakes and all we did was add $20 to itself nine times!

The problem is with the way numbers are stored in the computer. Remember, you can't use POKE to put a −1 into memory. Instead we had to add 256 ($100) to it and store it as $FF. This means that the computer is only able to store the negative numbers from −1 down to −128 ($FF down to $80). If the numbers $80 to $FF are used for negative numbers, then the computer can only use the numbers $00 to $7F to store positive numbers. That means the computer can only store 0 to 127. This means that if we add $20 to $60, and negative numbers start at $80, then doing the addition will give $80, a negative number and an error. This is called an *overflow error*. When this sort of error happens, the computer programmer needs to know, so that the necessary programming can be done to correct the error. For this we need another flag, called the *overflow flag* or V flag.

Notice we said, "If we store negative numbers from $80 to $FF." We don't have to, you know. If our program (like the one just used) only uses positive numbers, then we can use the computer to store the numbers 0 to 255, rather than −128 to 127. If that suits us (and it does sometimes), then we do it. In this case, the fact that when we get to $80 the N flag gets set, we say "So what." Since we are storing the numbers 0 to 255, negative numbers don't exist and the N flag can be ignored. This makes the behavior of the flags on steps 5 through 8 correct.

In our machine language program we have decided that we are not going to worry about negative numbers. That means that only step 9 is still wrong. Well, not really. Look at the following two additions using decimal mathematics:

```
10+    80+
30     30
--     --


--     --
```

The first one is easy, and the answer is 40. The second one is more difficult. The answer is 10, with a *carry* of 1 into the hundreds column. That makes the answer 110.

Notice the word *carry*. When $20 is added to $E0 the answer is $00 with a carry of $1 into the $100s. That makes the answer $100. The only trouble is, $100 is 256 and we can't store that. Instead we store $00 and put the carry into the carry flag. In the next chapter we shall go into these complicated flags in more detail. For the moment, look at what the results from the last program would have been if we had the C and V flags working properly.

| Step | A-register | N-flag | Z-flag | V-flag | C-flag |
|---|---|---|---|---|---|
| 1 | $00 | C | S | C | C |
| 2 | $20 | C | C | C | C |
| 3 | $40 | C | C | C | C |
| 4 | $60 | C | C | C | C |
| 5 | $80 | S | C | S | C |
| 6 | $A0 | S | C | C | C |
| 7 | $C0 | S | C | C | C |
| 8 | $E0 | S | C | C | C |
| 9 | $00 | C | S | C | S |

Notice that the V flag and the C flag only get set when the error occurs. After line 5, as far as the computer knows you are adding a positive number to a negative number and getting an answer that is negative. That is quite all right as far as it is concerned. That's no error, so there are no further error messages.

Now you can see that machine language programming is just a little bit trickier than BASIC. See if you can work out the correct ways of animating the C and V flags before reading the next chapter. You will probably have to read another machine language book to get it right!

*Question: What should all the flags be doing if you started with $00 and subtracted $20 nine times?*

# Chapter 11

# Would Those Contradictions Please Stop Waving Flags?

The last chapter seemed to be full of contradictions. First I said that it was only possible to store numbers between 0 and 255. To show that this is the case try the following program:

```
10  POKE 0, 255
20  POKE 0, 256
```

If you try it then you will find that the computer responds:

```
ILLEGAL QUANTITY IN 20
```

This shows that the number 255 can be stored, but not the number 256.

Then I confused the issue by saying that really it was only the numbers between −128 and +127 that could be stored. Then I really went too far; I started to use numbers like 60100 for line numbers in the animation program. Now the 60100 is stored in the computer and it is not between either 0 to 255 or −128 to +127. If only those ranges of numbers can be stored, how can BASIC use large line numbers? Anyway, the following program shows that *both* decimal numbers and letters can also be stored inside a computer as well.

```
10 A$ = "THE ANSWER IS "
20 B = 2.456
```

```
30 C = B + 1
40 PRINT A$, C
50 STOP
```

Finally, what's this guff about positive numbers being negative (or was it negative numbers being positive) and what are these C and V flags waving around? It does not seem to make sense.

Let's take the problems one at a time. Save the last program (CHAP.10) if you have not already done so and clear the memory with a NEW. Let's try to put things into memory. We can then pull them out of memory and check if they went in correctly.

```
PROGRAM 1
10 POKE 0, 4: REM Check that location is not ROM
20 PRINT PEEK(0)

PROGRAM 2
10 POKE 0, 2.34 : REM check on decimals
20 PRINT PEEK(0)

PROGRAM 3
10 POKE 0, 456 : REM check on large numbers
20 PRINT PEEK(0)

PROGRAM 4
10 POKE 0, "H" : REM check on letters
20 PRINT PEEK(0)
```

Try them out and see what you get. Make a note of what happens in each program.

On my computer, this is what I get and what it means

- Program 1 works. This means that the computer can store numbers between 0 and 255.
- Program 2 works a bit; 2.34 goes in but 2 comes out. This means the computer can't store decimal numbers, only whole numbers.
- Program 3 gives ILLEGAL QUANTITY IN 20. This means that the computer can't store large whole numbers.
- Program 4 gives TYPE MISMATCH IN 20. This means the computer can't store letters.

These four programs say that the computer can't do things that we know that it can do. Why?

There is one big difference between BASIC doing something to memory and us using PEEKs and POKEs to do things to memory. The difference is that very hardworking monitor that the computer manufacture has built into our computer. That monitor is somehow performing magic.

In actual fact, the monitor is acting more like a spy than a magician. What it is doing is what a spy does to make sure his/her message is not intercepted by the enemy. The monitor is *encoding* the information somehow. When you receive a message from a spy, you might find something like this

erty/Y612/sdfg/8956/aswe/qwer

which in English means

My chicken lays purple eggs

or something of equal importance. Notice that the spy breaks the message up into chunks of certain sizes. This makes it more difficult for the spymasters to break the code. The monitor has to take our message in a PRINT statement

10 PRINT "MY CHICKEN LAYS PURPLE EGGS"

and break it up into certain sized pieces, a memory location for each letter. Then, using a special code called *ASCII*, the monitor takes each letter and turns it into a number between 0 and 255 and stores it in the memory. The BASIC command ASC can show us how the letters are stored. Enter the following program and get it to run.

```
10 GET A$ : IF A$ = "" THEN 10
20 PRINT "LETTER "; A$; " ASCII CODE "; ASC(A$)
30 GOTO 10
```

Try typing in "MY CHICKEN LAYS PURPLE EGGS" and see the ASCII code.

**THE D FLAG**

Large numbers are also encoded. We have actually already been using this encoding in a number of the instructions, the JMP and the LDA instructions, for example. What has to be done is split up the number into two sections called the high byte and the low byte, using the following formula:

$$\text{HIGH BYTE} = \frac{\text{NUMBER}}{256} \text{ and ignore any remainder}$$

$$\text{LOW BYTE} = \text{NUMBER} - 256 * \text{HIGH BYTE.}$$

For example, the decimal number 259 becomes

$$\text{HIGH BYTE} = \frac{259}{256} = 1$$

$$\text{LOW BYTE} = 259 - 1 \times 256 = 3$$

In hexadecimal notation, it is very easy to split a number into its high and low bytes. In hexadecimal notation 259 is $103. That means its high byte is $01 and its low byte is $03.

The method mentioned above is only one way of storing large numbers. It is probably one of the most common. The 6502 microprocessor has also been designed to handle numbers in another way. Remember from Chapter 1 that each memory location had 8 bits or rooms. If those rooms are grouped in fours, then it is possible to store two decimal numbers in each memory location. For example the number 1,934 could be stored as

| | | | | |
|---|---|---|---|---|
| word 1 | | word 2 | | |
| 1 | 9 | 3 | 4 | |
| 0001 | 1001 | 0011 | 0100 | |
| $19 | | $34 | | (as stored in memory) |
| 25 | | 52 | | (if thought of in decimal) |

The question you will be asking yourself is, "If the numbers $00 to $FF (or 0 to 255) mean so many things, how can the computer sort things out?" The answer is "carefully." The monitor uses a lot of memory aids. For example, that specialized way of storing numbers is remembered using a flag called the *D* or *decimal flag.* When this D flag gets set, the computer goes into a mode where many of the instructions do things slightly differently. The computer can add together 12 and 34 stored in this strange fashion and still automatically get the correct answer. By "correct answer" I mean that the answer is also coded in this special form. There is a special machine language instruction called *CLD* or *clear decimal flag* ($D8) that can be used to make sure that the computer does not accidentally get into this strange mode. It might be a good idea to put this instruction at the beginning of all your machine language programs to make sure.

To see the effect of the D flag, lets us add 8 and 9 together with the D flag both on and off. Let's do the "off" condition first:

```
$300:  $D8           CLD        ; Clear D-flag
$301:  $18           CLC        ; Clear C-flag
$302:  $A9 $08       LDA #$8    ; A = 8
$304:  $69 $09       ADC #$9    ; + 9
$306:  $8F $20 $03   STA $320   ; Store at $320
$309:  $60           RTS        ; BASIC return
$30A:  $00           BRK        ; QUIT!
```

If you use the GO instruction, then $320 will have $11 in it, which is 17 decimal. Now change location $300 to $F8, which is the SED instruction; this causes the mathematics to work differently. Use the GO instruction and I'll bet you get an error you did not expect!

The system crashed. Type RUN to get the animation to restart and then look at location $320. It has $17 in it. That's the encoded form of 8 + 9. Why did it work correctly, but crash the system? It is that monitor again. The monitor is expecting to work with the D flag off. When we turned it on, the monitor started to do its pointer arithmetic incorrectly. Hence the SYNTAX ERROR message. We must therefore remember that if we turn the D flag on in a machine language instruction, we must turn it *off* before returning to BASIC.

Although with the D flag on, the answers to the mathematics are in decimal, there is a disadvantage to doing machine language programs this way. With the D flag on, the largest number that can be stored in memory is only 99, instead of 256.

The methods of storing and encoding letters and large numbers are different. The monitor uses certain locations of memory as *pointers* to remind it which bit of memory it is using as "storage for letters," other pointers are used for "storage of large numbers," and "storage of program." That's how crashes happen. The monitor gets confused and the pointers get messed up. The monitor starts using "storage for letters" instead of "storage for program."

These different ways of storing things are called *representations*. Figure 11-1 shows a number of different ways that the numbers $00 to $FF are used to represent numbers, letters, and BASIC commands. Not all the information is there. If you want greater detail, you'll have to read your user's manual.

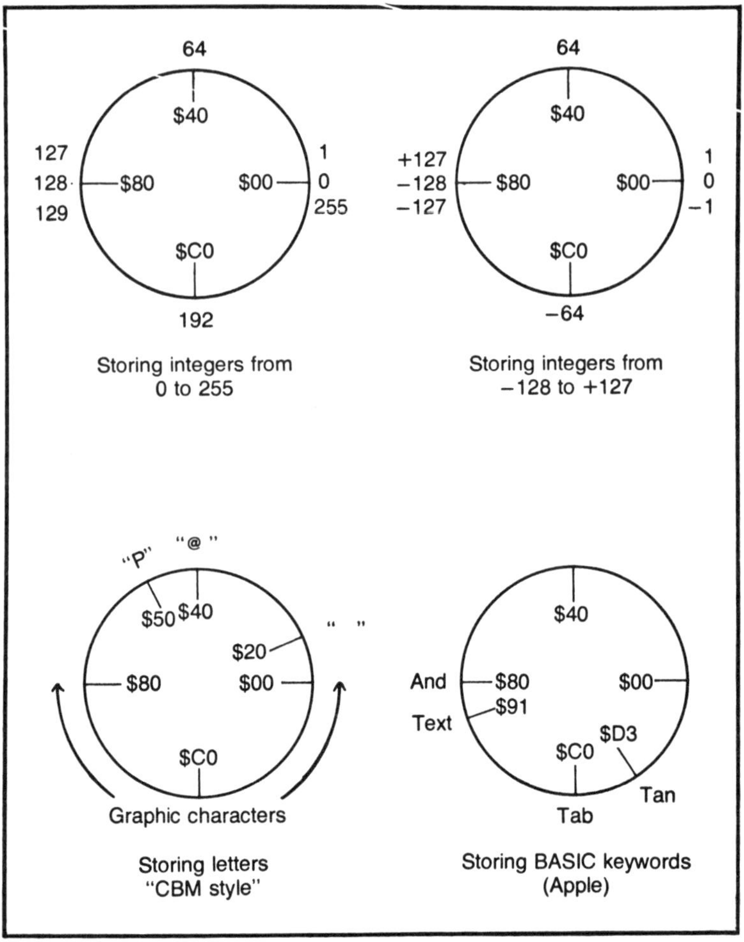


Fig. 11-1. Different representations of memory storage.

We can write a very simple program to show how the things are stored. We can do this by printing out the same locations from memory in three different ways.

```
10 PRINT "AS NUMBERS "
20 FOR J = 1 TO 10
30 PRINT "LOCATION "; J; PEEK (J)
40 NEXT J
50 PRINT "AS LARGE NUMBERS "
60 FOR J = 1 TO 20 STEP 2
70 PRINT "LOCATION "; J; PEEK(J) + 256 * PEEK(J + 1)
```

```
80 NEXT J
90  PRINT "AS LETTERS"
100 FOR J = 1 TO 300
110 PRINT "LOCATION "; J; CHR$(PEEK(J))
120 NEXT J
130 STOP
```

When you run the program, statements 90-120 can print some funny things. The code ASCII is not only used to store letters "A" through "Z" and "a" through "z", it can also be used to store things like "clear screen," "move cursor up," or "ring a bell." The last one can be done by typing

PRINT CHR$(7)

since ASCII code 7 means "bell."

## THE C FLAG

We mentioned that the D flag was used when we want to store numbers, in two's. The flag helped the programmer handle this special representation. The other flags also help. The *C flag* is helpful when we are trying to use the representation or encoding that puts large numbers into two memory locations. Let us do a simple program that counts up from 0 to 65,536 and then stops. We need two locations in memory to store how far we have counted, because any number bigger than 256 needs two locations for its representation. The method is this:

1) Add one into the low byte of the number.
2) Keep adding 1 until we have 255 stored.
3) Add one more and cause the C flag to be set.
4) Add one to the high byte and go back to step 1.
5) Keep on doing this until the high byte has 255 in it.
6) When we add just one more into the high byte, the C flag will become set and we can stop.

Before entering this program, call back program CHAP.10 from your disk or tape. We need a new instruction called BCC or "branch if carry clear" ($90). We want the computer to add up to 255 automatically without us having to worry.

```
$300: $A9 $00        LDA #$0     ; A = 0
$302: $8D $30 $03    STA $330    ; Make LO-BYTE = 0 (C64 $C330)
```

```
$305: $8D $31 $03      STA $331     ; Make HI-BYTE = 0 (C64 $C331)
$308: $D8              CLD          ; Clear Decimal flag
$309: $EA              NOP          ; spacer before loop
$30A: $AD $30 $03      LDA $330     ; Fetch LO-BYTE (C64   $C330)
$30D: $18              CLC          ; Clear Carry
$30E: $69 $01          ADC #$1      ; A = A + 1. This MAY set C
                                      flag
$310: $8D $30 $03      STA $330     ; Put back LO-BYTE (C64 $C330)
$313: $90 $F4          BCC $30A     ; Branch back if Carry clear
$315: $EA              NOP
$316: $18              CLC          ; Clear Carry so we can use ADC
$317: $AD $31 $03      LDA $331     ; Fetch HI-BYTE (C64   $C331)
$31A: $69 $01          ADC #$1      ; A = A + 1. This MAY set C
                                     flag
$31C: $8D $31 $03      STA $331     ; Put back HI-BYTE (C64 $C331)
$31F: $90 $E9          BCC $30A     ; Keep going if Carry clear.
$321: $60              RTS          ; Special BASIC return
$322: $00 $00 $00      BRK          ; QUIT!!!!

$330: $XX          LO: DS $1        ; Make room
$331: $XX          HI: DS $1
```

After you have loaded up your program, it should look like Fig. 11-2, (Fig. 11-3 for the C-64) except that it will be in your safe area. Notice the $XX at locations $330 to $331 in the listing above. This means "don't care" values. It does not matter what is in these values, because the first thing that our program does is to put a $00 in the A Register and store the zero in locations $330 and $331. This means that after the third instruction those places become zero. We don't care what is there before, because it will become 0 just as soon as the program starts. We have cleared those locations or *initialized* them.

Since our animation can't do the instruction BCC yet, we can't test it using the W instruction; we'll have to use the GO instruction. The program will not do anything very exciting. It will quietly go away, count, and then come back—provided you typed things in correctly. Memory locations $330 and $331 will have been made 0 and then 1 and then 2, all the way up to $FF; then, when they become 0 again, that C flag gets set. For us to see what is happening, we shall have to get the animation working properly. For that we need the following new instructions.

```
                          ! IR $00 PC $00
                          ! DR $00 AR $00
C D I N V Z               !        SC $0000
? ? ? ? ? ?               ! X  $00 Y  $00
                          ! A  $00
                          !-----------------

MEMORY STARTING AT $0300
0300: A9 00 8D 30 03 8D 31 03
0308: D8 EA AD 30 03 18 69 01
0310: 8D 30 03 90 F4 EA 18 AD
0318: 31 03 69 01 8D 31 03 90
0320: E9 60 00 00 00 00 00 00
0328: 00 00 00 00 00 00 00 00
0330: 00 00 00 00 00 00 00 00
0338: 00 00 00 00 00 00 00 00



TYPE 'HELP' FOR COMMANDS
YOUR WISH, MASTER?
```

Fig. 11-2. A machine language program that can count to 65,536 with the help of the C flag.

| ASSEMBLY LANGUAGE MNEMONIC | MACHINE LANGUAGE | WHAT THE INSTRUCTION DOES |
|---|---|---|
| CLD | $D8 | Clears the D flag |
| SED | $F8 | Sets the D flag |
| BCC | $90 | Branch on Carry Clear |
| BCS | $B0 | Branch on Carry Set |

We also need to make sure that the C flag is used correctly. Only two of our instructions use the C or carry flag. They are ADC (both forms) and SBC (both forms). So there is not much to change.

The BASIC animation subroutines needed for the two branch instructions are very similar to the branch subroutines that use the N and Z flags. For the D flag instruction, we must make a small change to the register display. The decision logic:

```
30300 IF IR = 216 THEN 33700 : REM <<cld>>
30310 IF IR = 248 THEN 33800 : REM <<sed>>
30320 IF IR = 144 THEN 33900 : REM <<bcc>>
30330 IF IR = 176 THEN 34000 : REM <<bcs>>
```

The execution logic:

```
33700 D$ = "C"
33710 RETURN : REM <<cld>>
33800 D$ = "S"
33810 RETURN : REM <<sed>>
33900 GOSUB 51000 : REM <<fetch-the-next-memory-location>>
33910 IF C$ <> "C" THEN RETURN
33920 GOSUB 50000 : REM <<change-the-program-counter>>
33930 RETURN : REM <<end bcc>>
34000 GOSUB 51000 : REM <<fetch-the-next-memory-location>>
34010 IF C$ <> "S" THEN RETURN
34020 GOSUB 50000 : REM <<change-the-program-counter>>
34030 RETURN : REM <<end bcs>>
```

Changes to the register display:

```
54920 PRINT "C D I N V Z" : REM  add the extra flag
54930 PRINT C$; " "; D$; " "; I$; " "; N$; " "; V$; " "; Z$
60600 D$ = "?" : N$ ="?" : Z$ = "?" : REM make room
```

Additional explanation:

```
60870 MN$(216) = "CLD" : TYPE%(216) = 5
60880 MN$(248) = "SED" : TYPE%(248) = 5
60890 MN$(144) = "BCC" : TYPE%(144) = 11 : REM signal BRANCH
60900 MN$(176) = "BCS" : TYPE%(176) = 11 : REM signal BRANCH
```

Save this program as CHAP.11A

If anybody was in a hurry to find out if the new instructions worked, you'll have noticed that they did not. The reason why they didn't work using the W instruction is that the C flag remained cleared (or C) the whole time. We need to change the subroutine at 52500 to set this flag. If we were using the GO instruction, the EXECUTE logic would have taken care of setting the C flag for us.

```
                         ! IR $00 PC $00
                         ! DR $00 AR $00
C D I N V Z              !           SC $0000
? ? ? ? ? ?              ! X  $00 Y  $00
                         ! A  $00
                         !------------------

MEMORY STARTING AT $C300
C300: A9 00 8D 30 C3 8D 31 C3
C308: D8 EA AD 30 C3 18 69 01
C310: 8D 30 C3 90 F4 EA 18 AD
C318: 31 C3 69 01 8D 31 C3 90
C320: E9 60 00 00 00 00 00 00
C328: 00 00 00 00 00 00 00 00
C330: 00 00 00 00 00 00 00 00
C338: 00 00 00 00 00 00 00 00



TYPE 'HELP' FOR COMMANDS
YOUR WISH, MASTER?
```

Fig. 11-3. Commodore 64 version of the to count to 65,536.

The subroutine at 52500 must act as our EXECUTE logic. We have to write a subroutine to decide whether or not the C flag needs to be changed.

Remember, the C flag is used to help the machine language programmer handle numbers that get too large or too small to store normally as numbers $00 to $FF in memory. Here are six examples of additions and subtractions. Figure 11-3 shows how to determine if the C flag gets set or not.

| DECIMAL | HEXADECIMAL | ANSWER | C-FLAG |
|---|---|---|---|
| 8 + 10 | $8 + $A | 18 ($12) | Clear |
| 4 + 254 | $4 + $FE | 258 ($02) | Set |
| 4 + 250 | $4 + $FA | 254 ($FE) | Clear |
| | | | |
| 10 − 8 | $A − $8 | 2 ($02) | Set |
| 4 − 254 | $4 − $FE | −250 ($FA) | Clear |
| 254 − 4 | $FE − $4 | 250 ($FA) | Set |

The rules for the C flag are

1) If you go past the $00 mark when doing an addition, you must SET the C flag, otherwise CLEAR it.
2) If you go past the $00 mark when doing a subtraction, you must CLEAR the C flag, otherwise SET it.

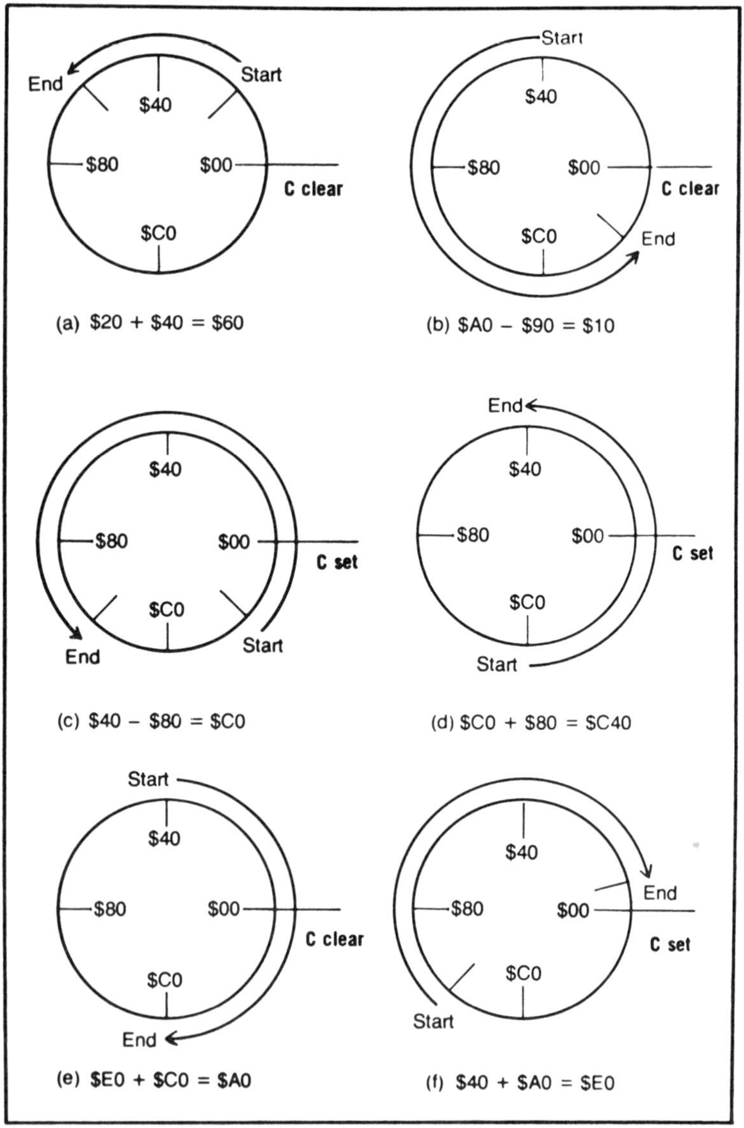


Fig. 11-4. How to determine if the C flag will be set.

That is easy to program in BASIC because when the program calls subroutine 52500, it passes the parameter ADJUST. We just have to check that ADJUST is neither too big nor too small.

```
52500 C$ = "C" : REM clear the C flag
52510 IF (ADJUST > 255) AND ((IR = 105) OR
      (IR = 109)) THEN C$ = "S"
52520 IF (ADJUST > 0) AND ((IR = 233) OR
      (IR = 237)) THEN C$= "S"
52530 REM  worry about the V flag later
52540 GOTO 52000 : REM <<go-adjust-the-N-and-Z-flags>>
```

Save this program as CHAP.11B.

Before using the work (W) instruction, we want to make things such that the program does not go for too long. First, using the CH instruction, make $330 = $FE and $331 = $FF. This means that the program will do the first loop twice, since as we have started the double loop right near its end. Since this will use the BCC instruction, it will be sufficient to check that the animation works. There is still one problem. If we start the program at the same start address as when we used the GO instruction, what is the first thing that is going to happen? Right, those carefully changed locations will be changed back to 0 and the program will do 65,535 loops—which will take forever. To avoid this, make sure that you start your program at the first NOP. If you look at the picture in Fig. 11-4, you can see that this is $30A for me. (The C64 uses $C30A). When the program has finished, you should notice that locations $330 and $331 have been changed back to 0. As the animation works, notice what changes occur with the C flag.

## THE V FLAG

We have said that the microprocessor has to encode things to fit into the available word size of $00 to $FF (0 to 255). We showed that the D flag was useful when we encoded two decimal numbers side-by-side into one word. The C flag was useful when we were trying to work with large numbers. The last flag we shall consider in this book is the *V* or *overflow flag*. This flag is used when the microprocessor is used to encode numbers in the range −128 to +128 to fit inside the word size of $00 to $FF (0 to 255). Just to remind you, here are some numbers and the way that they are encoded:

| DECIMAL NUMBER | ENCODED NUMBER |
|---|---|
| 0 | $00 (0) |
| 1 | $01 (1) |

| DECIMAL NUMBER | ENCODED NUMBER |
|---|---|
| −1 | $FF (255) |
| 127 | $FF (255) |
| −128 | $80 (128) |
| −127 | $81 (129) |

The N flag had already been used to help us when numbers were stored like this in memory. This flag, the negative flag, was set if the number stored was $80 or larger. If it was $80 or more then it was negative because the high was set. If we never did any additions or subtractions, then this flag would be enough. When we start using additions and subtractions, the encoding comes into trouble. Let us take a look at some examples.

| ENCODED FORM | DECIMAL FORM | DECIMAL ANSWER | ENCODED ANSWER | TROUBLE |
|---|---|---|---|---|
| $01 + $02 | 1 + 2 | 3 | $03 | no |
| $FF + $01 | −1 + 1 | 0 | $00 | no |
| $FF + $FF | −1 + (−1) | −2 | $FE | no |
| $01 + $7F | 1 + 127 | 128 | $80 | YES |
| $80 + $81 | −128 + (−127) | −257 | $01 | YES |

The first three examples are okay. The carry flag may get set but the encoded answer is exactly what we expect.

The fourth answer is wrong? Yes! When the computer adds together 1 and 127, it does not care that we have encoded these numbers. It just does it. The sum of 1 and 127 is 128, and that can be stored as $80, period. The computer is happy but we are not, because $80 is the encoded form of −128 not the encoded form of +128. That means we added together two positive numbers and got a negative number. In a program, that means that our final answer is no longer valid. We could ask the question

Is 1 + 127 bigger than −1?

In the encoded form the question becomes

Is $01 + $7F bigger than $FF?

Since $80 is less than $FF, we would say "no" and be wrong. As programmers, we must be warned when this kind of thing happens.

When we had carry problems, because we added together numbers that got too large, we adjusted our program. The same is true here. When we add together two positive numbers and get a negative number, we have stepped outside our number range. We have overflowed. To help the machine language programmer know this has happened, the microprocessor sets the V flag.

Since we chose the numbers 1 and 127, we knew that something had happened. In a program, however, the programmer does not know what numbers to expect. This flag then becomes very useful when you do serious programming. It is however, one of the least-used flags. Other than making sure that it gets set and cleared correctly, we shall not be using it.

*Question: Why would the V flag set in example 5? In what way has an overflow occurred?*

The V flag is only set when something is added or subtracted from one of the registers. For us at the moment, that means only the ADC and the SBC instructions will change the V flag (or the C flag, for that matter). Let's look at some of the subtraction problems:

| ENCODED FORM | DECIMAL FORM | DECIMAL ANSWER | ENCODED ANSWER | TROUBLE |
|---|---|---|---|---|
| \$03 – \$02 | 3 – 2 | 1 | \$01 | no |
| \$01 – \$FE | 1 – –2 | 3 | \$03 | no |
| \$FF – \$FE | –1 – –2 | 1 | \$01 | no |
| \$06 – \$07 | 6 – 7 | –1 | \$FF | no |
| \$FE – \$7F | –2 – 127 | –129 | \$7F | YES |
| \$7F – \$80 | 127 – –128 | 255 | \$FF | YES |

The trouble occurs once again when the decimal result, which we and BASIC understand, gets outside the range of numbers (–128 to +127) that we have decided to store in memory. The rules for the V flag are shown in Fig. 11-5. The flag should be set if, after a mathematical operation.

positive + positive gives negative
negative + negative gives positive

positive – negative gives negative
negative – positive gives positive

If you think about normal mathematics, then these four things are impossible. They only happen in the computer because of the way

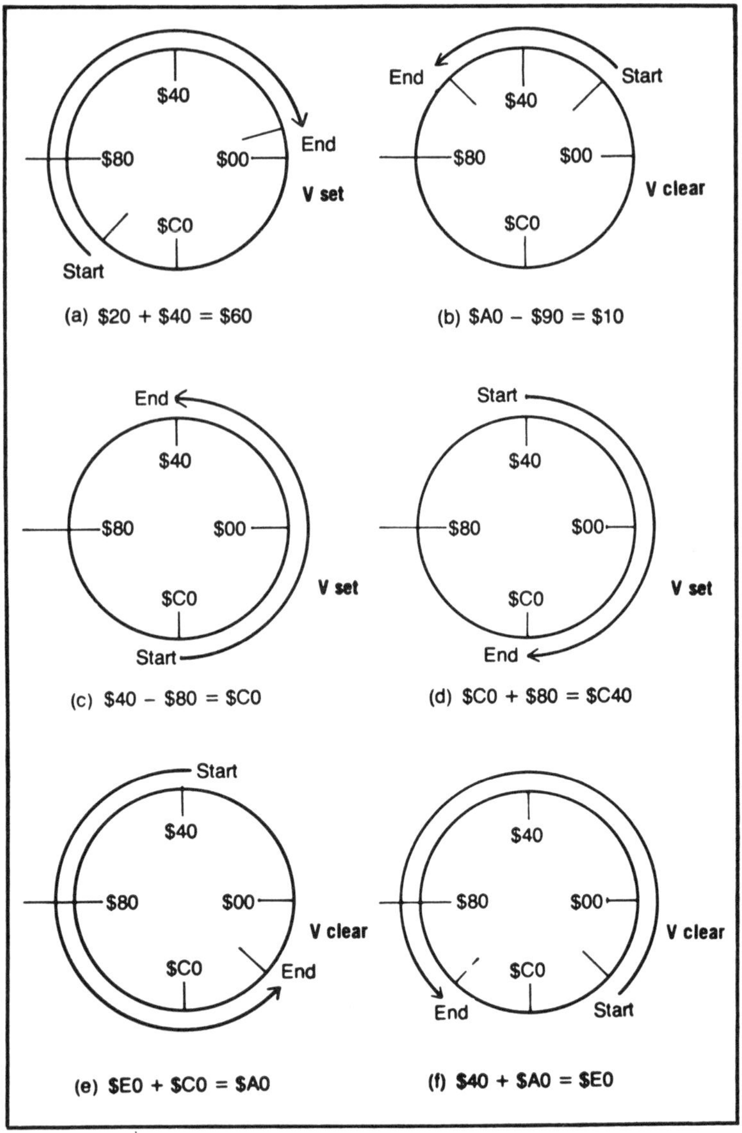


Fig. 11-5. Determining whether the V flag will be set.

we have to store numbers.

In order to check whether or not the V flag needs to be set, then we must use two more parameters in our subroutine. We need to know the two things we are using to start with, plus the answer ADJUST. We have to modify both the ADC and the SBC instructions. We make these changes to encode logic:

```
33305 P1 = AREG : P2 = SC : REM <<adjust adc #>>
33425 P1 = AREG : P2 = SC : REM <<adjust adc memory>>
33505 P1 = AREG : P2 = SC : REM <<adjust sbc #>>
33625 P1 = AREG : P2 = SC : REM <<adjust sbc memory>>
```

Changes to <<set–C–N–Z–V–flags>> :

```
52540 IF (ADJUST > 255) THEN ADJUST = ADJUST - 256
52550 IF (ADJUST < 0) THEN ADJUST = ADJUST + 256
52560 IF (IR = 105) OR (IR = 109) THEN V$ = "C" : GOSUB 52700
52565 REM add instructions
52570 IF (IR = 233) OR (IR = 237) THEN V$ = "C" : GOSUB 52800
52575 REM  sub instructions
52580 GOTO 52000 : REM <<go-adjust-the-N-and-Z-flags>>
```

We must leave room in case we want to animate some other instructions that cause changes in the C flag.

```
52600 GOTO 52000 : REM adjust N and Z ***note line number***
```

The four cases for the V flag to be checked:

```
52700 IF (ADJUST >= 128) OR (ADJUST < 0) THEN 52750
      : REM adjust negative
52710 IF (P1 >= 128) AND (P2 >= 128) THEN V$ = "S"
52720 RETURN : REM made sure that neg + neg <> pos

52750 IF (P1 <= 127) AND (P2 <= 127) THEN V$ = "S"
52760 RETURN
      : REM made sure that pos + pos <> neg <<end add with V>>

52800 IF (ADJUST >= 128) OR (ADJUST < 0) THEN 52850
      : REM adjust negative
52810 IF (P1 >= 128) AND (P2 <= 127) THEN V$ = "S"
52820 RETURN : REM made sure that neg - pos <> pos

52850 IF (P1 <= 127) AND (P2 >=128) THEN V$ = "S"
52860 RETURN
      : REM made sure that pos - neg <> neg  <<end sub-with-V>>
```

The V flag is quite a bit more complicated to program its EXECUTE logic than the C flag. It is one of the more difficult for us to understand, though the microprocessor does it easily. If you asked me in which bit of this book I have most likely made a mistake, I will honestly answer, “Somewhere between 52700 and 52860.” I think the V flag will always get set correctly; if you can find a special case where it is not correct let me know in care of the publisher. Special cases can be really difficult to program and make sure that mistakes are not made.

Since we now have a new flag, we need some branch instructions to use with it. These are the last two branch instructions that you can use with the 6502 microprocessor.

| ASSEMBLY LANGUAGE MNEMONIC | HEX CODE | WHAT THE INSTRUCTION DOES |
|---|---|---|
| BVC | $50 | Branch on V flag Clear |
| BVS | $70 | Branch on V flag Set |

These instructions are just like the BCC and BCS, except that they work on the V flag rather than the C flag.

The decision logic is as follows:

```
30340 IF IR = 80 THEN 34100 : REM <<bvc>>
30350 IF IR = 112 THEN 34200 : REM <<bvs>>
```

The execution logic is:

```
34100 GOSUB 51000 : REM <<fetch-the-next-memory-location>>
34110 IF V$ <> "C" THEN RETURN
34120 GOSUB 50000 : REM <<change-the-program-counter>>
34130 RETURN : REM <<end bvc>>

34200 GOSUB 51000 : REM <<fetch-the-next-memory-location>>
34210 IF V$ <> "S" THEN RETURN
34220 GOSUB 50000 : REM <<change-the-program-counter>>
34230 RETURN : REM <<end bvs>>
```

Additional explanation:

```
60910 MN$(80) = "BVC" : TYPE%(80) = 11
      : REM signal that is BRANCH
60920 MN$(112) = "BVS" : TYPE%(112) = 11
      : REM signal that is BRANCH
```

Save this as CHAP.11.

Try out the animation for the V flag by adding various numbers together. The following program gives you an idea of what you might do.

```
$A9 $08         LDA #$8         ;Load A with 8
$18             CLC
$69 $09         ADC #$9         ;Add a 9. No change in V flag
$18             CLC
$69 $7F         ADC #$7F        ;Add 127. V flag becomes set
$60             RTS             ;BASIC return
$00             BRK             ;Quit W command.
```

In writing the code for the V flag, room was left for some more code to be added. There are other machine language instructions that use and change the V and C flags. I will be describing these, but I will not be animating any other machine language instructions. All the special subroutines are now there and, if you want, you can add these other instructions. I will be explaining the other instructions, and in a few places I will give rather broad hints on how you could simulate them if you wanted to.

Most of the time we shall be using our menu to allow us to run programs using the GO instruction. The simulation or model has, I hope, served its purpose. By now, you should be able to understand what the flags do, and how the Program Counter helps with choosing the next instruction. You know that more mathematics can be done with the A Register than with the X or Y Register. In Chapter 13, I will show you that the X and Y registers can do some things that the A Register cannot.

# Chapter 12

# Making Machine Language Programming Even Simpler

In the last couple of machine language programs, you may have found a number of problems:

1) The programs were getting rather large and it was difficult to check that things had been put correctly into memory.
2) You kept being called away from the computer. Sometimes the machine language program got lost when the computer was turned off.
3) You would have liked to enter in your own programs, but had difficulty in remembering the hex code for the instructions.

With problems like these, it is rather obvious that we are doing a lot of work the computer should be taking care off. We need some more software tools. Problem 1 can be taken care of using a disassembler. Problem 2 means that our menu needs two new instructions, GET and SAVE, for saving and getting machine language programs onto our disk. If we are doing things on the disk we should also add a CATALOG command so we can see what's on the disk. This command will be useful as a separate command or from either the SAVE or GET commands. Problem 3 can be solved using an assembler.

A *disassembler* is a program that takes the machine language code and turns it into a readable English form of the assembly language mnemonics. If we use it, then we can look at what the computer says we typed in and easily compare it to what we wanted to type in. In Chapter 5, a disassembler command was added for the Apple computers that had a disassembler built in. In this chapter we are going to use those mnemonics we stored in MN$ and the information stored in TYPE% to build a disassembler.

Getting and saving machine language programs is something everybody's computer can do. For saving you need to know where the machine language program starts, how long it is, and the name you want to use to store it on disk. For loading a program back into memory, you need to know the name you already used to store it. The information on these things are given in your user's manual.

An assembler is a program that takes the English-like assembly language mnemonics and turns them into machine language instructions. For example, we would answer the following question

```
START ADDRESS?
```

with the answer

```
$300
```

and then type

```
INX
CLC
BNE  $300
```

and the computer would automatically put the correct things into the memory locations, starting at location $300. Also, it should do all the mathematics to calculate the number to be used with the branch instruction.

We have already been using a program to do this. It was stored in the computer of our brain. It was in use for each one of the programs that we turned from BASIC into assembly language mnemonics, and then into machine language code. If you are going to do a lot of machine language programming, then it is worthwhile buying a good assembler. In this chapter we shall build a small assembler that, although not the best in the world, will do a satisfactory job.

## THE DISASSEMBLE COMMAND

Those of you who have already built the disassembler in

Chapter 5 can skip this section, unless you are interested in seeing what sort of things were going on inside their ROM disassembler routine.

First we need to add the disassembler command to the menu:

```
4240  IF TEMP$ = 'D' THEN GOSUB 46000 : GOTO 4000
      : REM <<disassembler>>

45055 PRINT "D  - DISASSEMBLE A MACHINE PROGRAM"

46000 PRINT "DISASSEMBLE"
46010 GOSUB 55500 : REM <<wait>>
46020 RETURN
```

Check that your syntax is correct, that the H (help) function works, and that the BASIC program can understand the new command D (disassemble). Save the program as CHAP.12A.

The first thing that the disassembler must do is get information from the keyboard on where in memory we want to look at the machine language program. Since we might want to look anywhere in memory, we shouldn't place any checks on the starting address.

```
45995 REM  <<disassembler>>
46000 PRINT : PRINT "STARTING AT WHAT ADDRESS? $";
46010 GOSUB 56000 : BEGIN = HEX : REM <<get-hex-number>>
46020 GOSUB 46100 : REM go do it!
46030 PRINT : PRINT "PRESS RETURN TO STOP "
46040 PRINT "ANYTHING ELSE CONTINUES ";
46050 GET ANS$ : IF ANS$ = "" THEN 46050
46060 IF ANS$ <> CHR$(13)  THEN 46020
46070 RETURN

46100 RETURN : REM dummy disassemble subroutine
```

Check that this part of your program is working correctly and save as CHAP.12B.

How does a disassembler work? The steps are basically simple. The program goes into memory and pulls out an instruction. If it does not understand the instruction, then it prints EH? If it does understand the instruction, the disassembler prints out the assembler language mnemonic stored in MN$. Using the information about the type of instruction stored in TYPE%, the disassembler prints out other information about the instruction. For example, what number or address is needed, how far a branch instruction goes, etc.

How can the disassembler not understand an instruction?

There are three reasons:

1) The instruction does not exist, meaning the microprocessor has been told to do something by mistake. Not all the numbers $00 to $FF are instructions.
2) The disassembler has got hold of some data and not an instruction. In our last machine language program, we used the DS pseudoinstruction, which made space available in memory for our variables. The disassembler has *no* idea that data is stored anywhere and treats everything as though it was an instruction. This means that it can get confused.
3) The disassembler can't recognize the instruction although it is valid. This error will remain an error until we have entered in all the instructions into our animation program.

So far we have used four different types of instructions. The difference is remembered by what is stored inside TYPE%.

| TYPE% VALUE | WHAT TYPE |
|---|---|
| 0 | Not currently recognized as a valid instruction |
| 1 | Immediate |
| 2 | Memory (properly called ABSOLUTE) |
| 5 | Simple (properly called IMPLIED) |
| 9 | NEW (properly called ABSOLUTE indexed using X) |
| 10 | NEW (properly called ABSOLUTE indexed using Y) |
| 11 | Branch (properly called RELATIVE) |

The TYPE% value is taken "out of the air" and does not mean anything. It is actually the number of the columns in a reference table in one of the assembly language programming books mentioned in Appendix C.

Believe it or not, there are other, different types of instructions. Many of these are special instructions for the zero page. Since the zero page is very heavily used by the BASIC in our machines, we shall not be considering these. If we used them, it is very likely that BASIC would crash. In the list above there are two new or unexplained types of instructions. These *absolute indexed* instructions will be introduced in Chapter 13 and are used to do things like the BASIC command A(X) = 6, which handles arrays.

For the other instructions not mentioned in the list you'll need a more advanced textbook than this to explain them in great detail.

Our disassembler program must put things nicely on the screen for ease of understanding. There will be three columns like our listings of machine language. The first is the address, the second is the machine language code, and the third is the mnemonic. We need something that looks just like our listings. The fourth column of comments will not be there, however; the reason is that we have never stored the comments in memory. This is the disassembler subroutine:

```
46100 GOSUB 61100 : REM <<clear the page>>
46110 FOR NUM = 1 TO 18 : REM no more than 18 things on a page
```

Print the instruction start address:

```
46120 PRINT "$"; : HEX = BEGIN : GOSUB 58000
      : REM <<print-start-address>>
46130 PRINT ": ";
46140 M1 = PEEK(BEGIN)
      : REM get values we MIGHT need from memory
46150 M2 = PEEK(BEGIN + 1);
46160 M3 = PEEK(BEGIN + 2);

46170 OVER = 8 : GOSUB 61500 : REM <<move-over>>
46180 HEX = M1 : GOSUB 58000 : REM <<hex-print>>
46190 PRINT " "; : REM that print the instruction
```

Handle one-byte instructions:

```
46200 TYPE = TYPE%(M1) : REM  find out type
46210 BEGIN = BEGIN + 1
      : REM keep track of what memory is used
46220 IF (TYPE = 0) OR (TYPE = 5) THEN 46400
      : REM no more printing
```

Handle two-byte instructions:

```
46230 HEX = M2 : GOSUB 58000 : PRINT " ";
      : REM  need more <<hex-print>>
46240 BEGIN = BEGIN + 1 : REM  keeping track
46250 IF (TYPE = 1) OR (TYPE = 11) THEN 46400
```

Handle three-byte instructions:

```
46260 HEX = M3 : GOSUB 58000 : REM need a third <<hex-print>>
46270 BEGIN = BEGIN + 1
46280 IF (TYPE = 2) OR (TYPE = 8) OR (TYPE = 9) THEN 46400
46290 TYPE = 0 : REM getting this far is a mistake
46300 PRINT EH$; EH$ ; : REM do a warning
```

Print out the assembler language mnemonic found:

```
46400 OVER = 20 : GOSUB 61500 : REM <<move-over>>
46410 IF TYPE = 0 THEN PRINT "EH??"; : GOTO 46900
46420 PRINT MN$(M1); " "; : REM print out instruction
```

Handle one-byte instructions:

```
46430 IF (TYPE = 5) OR (TYPE = 0) THEN 46900
```

Handle *immediate* instruction:

```
46440 IF TYPE <> 1 THEN 46470
46450 PRINT "#$"; : HEX = M2 : GOSUB 58000 : REM immediate
46460 GOTO 46900
```

Handle three-byte instructions:

```
46470 IF (TYPE <> 2) AND (TYPE <> 9) AND (TYPE <> 10) THEN 46550
46480 PRINT "$"; HEX = M3 * 256 + M2 : GOSUB 58000
      : REM <<HEX-PRINT>>
46490 IF TYPE = 2 THEN 46900 : REM absolute
46500 IF TYPE = 9 THEN PRINT ",X"; : GOTO 46900
      : REM absolute,x
46510 IF TYPE = 10 THEN PRINT ",Y"; : GOTO 46900
      : REM absolute,y
```

Handle branch instructions. (We need to calculate the jump address for these.)

```
46550 IF TYPE <> 11 THEN 46600
46560 IF M2 > 127 THEN M2 = M2 - 256
      : REM adjust to decimal for branch
46570 PRINT "$"; : HEX = BEGIN + M2 : GOSUB 58000
```

```
46580 GOTO 46900 : REM have printed branch address
46600 REM leave room for others
46900 PRINT : REM move to new line
46910 NEXT NUM : REM end of loop
46920 RETURN

60150 M1 = 0: M2 = 0: M3 = 0: TYPE = 0: REM make room
```

Try this out and save the program as CHAP.12C.

If you retype the last machine language program from Chapter 11 and then use the D (disassembler) instruction, you should get a screen that looks like Fig. 12-1 for the Apple, or like Fig. 12-2 for the C-64.

Since we have put no limits on where this disassembler can look in memory, use it to look at ROM and RAM all over your memory.

## SAVING MACHINE LANGUAGE PROGRAMS ON DISK

The next three software tools are very useful. They are CA to

```
0300:A9 00          LDA #$00
0302:8D 30 03       STA $0330
0305:8D 31 03       STA $0331
0308:D8             CLD
0309:EA             NOP
030A:AD 30 03       LDA $0330
030D:18             CLC
030E:69 01          ADC #$01
0310:8D 30 03       STA $0330
0313:90 F4          BCC $0309
0315:EA             NOP
0316:18             CLC
0317:AD 31 03       LDA $0331
031A:69 01          ADC #$01
031C:8D 31 03       STA $0331
031F:90 E9          BCC $030A
0321:60             RTS
0322:00             BRK

 PRESS RETURN TO STOP
ANYTHING ELSE CONTINUES
```

Fig. 12-1. The new DISASSEMBLE command in operation.

```
C300:A9 00          LDA #$00
C302:8D 30 C3       STA $C330
C305:8D 31 C3       STA $C331
C308:D8             CLD
C309:EA             NOP
C30A:AD 30 C3       LDA $C330
C30D:18             CLC
C30E:69 01          ADC #$01
C310:8D 30 C3       STA $C330
C313:90 F4          BCC $C309
C315:EA             NOP
C316:18             CLC
C317:AD 31 C3       LDA $C331
C31A:69 01          ADC #$01
C31C:8D 31 C3       STA $C331
C31F:90 E9          BCC $C30A
C321:60             RTS
C322:00             BRK

PRESS RETURN TO STOP
ANYTHING ELSE CONTINUES.
```

Fig. 12-2. DISASSEMBLE on the Commodore 64.

catalog what is on the disk, GE to get a program from the disk, and SA to save a program onto disk. Although very useful things to add to our basic operating system for the animation program, the exact BASIC commands you need to get them to work depend on your machine. I will give you as much help as possible, but you'll have to finish the job using your manual.

Let's add the commands to the menu:

```
4560 IF TEMP$ = "CA" THEN GOSUB 61600 : GOTO 4000
     : REM <<catalog>>
4670 IF TEMP$ = "GE" THEN GOSUB 61700 : GOTO 4000
     : REM <<get>>
4680 IF TEMP$ = "SA" THEN GOSUB 41500 : GOTO 4000
     : REM <<save>>
```

The HELP list was getting confusing because so many things are listed altogether. Adding an additional PRINT (line 45058) breaks things up on the screen for easier reading.

```
45035 PRINT "CA - CATALOG FILES ON DRIVE"
45058 PRINT "GE - GET MACHINE LANGUAGE PROGRAM" : PRINT
45075 PRINT "SA - SAVE MACHINE LANGUAGE PROGRAM"
41490 REM <<save-file>>
41500 PRINT "SAVE"
41510 GOSUB 55500 : REM <<wait>>
41520 RETURN
61590 REM <<catalog-disk>>
61600 PRINT "CATALOG"
61610 GOSUB 55500 : REM <<wait>>
61620 RETURN
61690 REM <<get-file>>
61700 PRINT "GET"
61710 GOSUB 55500 : REM <<wait>>
61720 RETURN
```

Test out the program and save it as CHAP.12D. If you use the *H* (help) command, your screen should look like Fig. 12-3.

**The CATALOG Instruction.** This is an easy instruction to

```
VALID COMMANDS
**************

A  - ASSEMBLER FOR MACHINE CODE
CA - CATALOG FILES ON DRIVE
CH - CHANGE ONE MEMORY LOCATION
CL - CLEAR THE SAFE MEMORY AREA
D  - DISASSEMBLE A MACHINE PROGRAM
GE - GET MACHINE LANGUAGE PROGRAM

GO - GO DO MACHINE PROGRAM
L  - LOAD MACHINE PROGRAM
SA - SAVE MACHINE LANGUAGE PROGRAM
ST - STOP THIS PROGRAM
W  - WORKING MODEL OF MICRO-PROCESSOR




PRESS RETURN TO CONTINUE
```

Fig. 12-3. The new HELP command screen.

add. We will need to clear the screen, do the catalog, and then wait for the person to finish reading.

```
61600 GOSUB 61100 : REM <<clear-screen>>
61610 PRINT CHR$(4); "CATALOG"
      : REM xxxchange for your machinexxx
61620 PRINT : PRINT "PRESS RETURN TO CONTINUE ";
61630 GET ANS$ : IF ANS$ = "" THEN 61630
61640 RETURN : REM <<end catalog>>
```

The Commodore 64 version is

```
61600  PRINT "CATALOG NOT AVAILABLE"
61610  GOSUB 55500 : REM <<do-wait>>
61620  RETURN
```

For other Commodore machines, substitute the following line:

```
61610 CATALOG D0
```

**The SAVE Command.** In this instruction we need to ask for the name of a file and then get it from the disk. To help us remember what files are BASIC and what files are machine language programs, we shall add the suffix .OBJ at the end of the name before storing the file. This is standard practice for computer scientists. Machine language programs are called *object files*. BASIC programs and assembly language programs are called *source files*.

The SAVE command needs a number of options. They are to *save* the machine language program. To *not save* is the second option, and we also need a *catalog* of the disk. The program needs to get a filename, together with starting and finishing addresses for the part of memory that needs to be saved.

```
41500 PRINT
41510 PRINT "SAVING"
41520 PRINT "TYPE 'END' TO QUIT, 'CAT' TO CATALOG" : PRINT
41530 INPUT "SAVE AS WHAT NAME? "; NAME$
41540 IF NAME$ = "CAT" THEN GOSUB 61600 : GOTO 41500
41550 IF NAME$ = "END" THEN RETURN
```

Add an .OBJ to the end of the name if needed:

```
41560 IF LEN(NAME$) < 5 THEN 41580 : REM check on '.OBJ'
41570 IF MID$(NAME$, LEN(NAME$) - 3, 4) = ".OBJ" THEN 41590
41580 NAME$ = NAME$ + ".OBJ"
```

Allow any recognized error to get us to start again:

```
41590 PRINT "TYPE 'ERR' WHEN ERROR HAPPENS"
41600 INPUT "STARTING ADDRESS $"; ANS$
41610 IF ANS$ = "ERR" THEN 41500
41620 GOSUB 56010 : REM jump INTO <<get-hex>>
41630 BEGIN = HEX
41640 INPUT "END ADDRESS $"; ANS$
41650 IF ANS$ = "ERR" THEN 41500
41660 GOSUB 56010 : REM jump INTO <<get-hex>>
41670 LAST = HEX : IF LAST < BEGIN THEN PRINT EH$ : GOTO 41640
41680 PRINT : PRINT "SAVING AS "; NAME$
41690 PRINT "START $"; : HEX = BEGIN : GOSUB 58000
      : REM <<print-hex>>
41700 PRINT " LAST $"; : HEX = LAST : GOSUB 58000
      : REM <<print-hex>>
41710 PRINT : INPUT "OKAY ?"; ANS$
41720 IF MID$(ANS$,1,1) = "N" THEN 41500
41730 IF MID$(ANS$,1,1) <> "Y" THEN PRINT EH$; : GOTO 41680
41740 PRINT CHR$(4); "BSAVE "; NAME$; ",A"; BEGIN; " ,L";
      LAST - BEGIN + 1
41750 REM ***change 41740 for your machine***
41760 PRINT "SAVED "; NAME$
41770 GOSUB 55500 : REM <<wait>>
41780 RETURN : REM <<end save>>
60160 LAST = 0
```

Line 41740 needs changing for your machine. My computer requires that I tell it

| | |
|---|---|
| BSAVE file.name | so it knows what file to save. |
| A start.address | so it knows where to start saving. |
| L length | so it knows how much to save. |

Your machine should do something very similiar. Save this program as CHAP.12E.

These are the changes needed to save a machine language program on the C64.

```
41740 NAME$ = "0:" + NAME$
41742 OPEN 1, 8, 15, "I0" : REM position the heads
41744 OPEN 2, 8, 1, NAME$
41746 HI = INT(BEGIN / 256) : LO = BEGIN - HI * 256
41748 PRINT #", CHR$(LO), CHR$(HI) :  REM save the start address
41750 FOR I = (BEGIN) TO LAST
41752 PRINT #2, CHR$(PEEK(I)) : REM  save location
41754 NEXT I
41756 CLOSE 2: CLOSE 1
```

Thanks to Danny Rudiak of Calgary for this technique.

There is a problem with using the disk commands on other Commodore (CBM) machines. If we use commands like DSAVE, the area we are using for our safe area gets written into. For small machine language programs that don't go past $33A, there is no problem. The following is a technique that gets around this difficulty. We can save files using the dynamic keyboard and avoid problems with changing our safe area. This *dynamic keyboard* makes the computer automatically type things into the keyboard. (A real computer ghost story!) By making the computer switch into the monitor built into the computer, save the program and then switch out and back into BASIC, we can avoid writing into our safe area. The special commands that need typing are

```
SYS 4                                          Jump into the monitor
S "0:FILENAME",08,"HEX-START-ADDRESS,HEX-FINISH-ADDRESS"
X                                              Switch back to BASIC
CONT                                           Continue the animation
```

First we need to cause the animation to stop at the correct time:

```
4680 IF TEMP$ = "SA" THEN GOSUB 41500 : STOP : GOTO 4000
     : REM <<save>>
```

Now write the special commands on the screen at the correct positions. (The correct position is done by educated guesswork or trial and error.)

```
41740 PRINT CHR$(147);CHR$(17);CHR$(17);CHR$(17)
41741 REM that clears the screen and cursors down 3 lines
```

```
41742 PRINT " SYS 4" :                    REM set up first command
41743 PRINT CHR$(17);CHR$(17);CHR$(17);CHR$(17);" S";
41744 PRINT CHR$(34);"0:";NAME$;CHR$(34);",08,";
41745 HEX = BEGIN : GOSUB 58000; PRINT ",";
41746 HEX = LAST + 1 : GOSUB 58000 : PRINT
      : REM print second command
41747 PRINT " X" :  PRINT CHR$(17); "CONT": REM other commands
41748 PRINT CHR$(19) : REM home the cursor
```

This is the "ghost" part:

```
41749 REM FOR J = 623 TO 626 : POKE J, 13 : NEXT J
41750 REM POKE 158, 4
```

Try this out first with REMs in lines 41749 and 41750. The SAVE command will ask you for a filename, then a start address (try $300), and then an end address (try $320). Then it will print the things on the screen and stop. Press the Return key once. You will switch into the computer's monitor. Press Return again. The machine language will be saved. Press again and you will switch back to BASIC. Press again and the animation will restart.

If you remove the REMs from lines 41749 and 41750 and try again, then the computer will automatically type in those carriage returns. Don't forget to use a different filename when you save the .OBJ file. (Why?) Save the REM-free version as CHAP.12E.

**The GET Command.** The GET command should have a number of options. It should allow us to get a file or change our minds and not get a file, and should catalog the disk to find out the names of files stored on the disk. To allow a choice between cataloging, getting a file, or quitting, add these lines.

```
61700 GOSUB 61100 : REM <<clear screen>>
61710 PRINT "TYPE 'END' IF NO FILE WANTED"
61720 PRINT "TYPE 'CAT' FOR CATALOG"
61730 INPUT "WHAT FILE NAME? "; NAME$
61740 IF NAME$ = "END" THEN RETURN : REM here by mistake
61750 IF NAME$ = "CAT" THEN GOSUB 61600 : GOTO 61700
```

Add the .OBJ to the name if needed:

```
61800 IF LEN(NAME$) < 5 THEN 61820
      : REM help in case .OBJ already there
```

```
61810 IF MID$(NAME$, LEN(NAME$) - 3,4) = ".OBJ" THEN 61830
61820 NAME$ = NAME$ + ".OBJ"
61830 PRINT : PRINT "FETCHING "; NAME$
61840 INPUT "THIS OKAY? "; ANS$
61850 IF MID$(ANS$,1,1) = "N" THEN 61700
61860 IF MID$(ANS$,1,1) <> "Y" THEN PRINT EH$ : GOTO 61830
```

These lines fetch the file. (Line 61900 must be changed for your machine.)

```
61900 PRINT CHR$(4); "BLOAD "; NAME$
      : REM xxx change for your machine xxx
61910 PRINT : PRINT "GOT "; NAME$; BELL$
61920 GOSUB 55500 : REM <<wait>>
61930 RETURN : REM <<end get>>
60940 NAME$ = ""; REM make room
```

With the Commodore 64 there is a problem. Each time we load a machine language program from BASIC, the BASIC program restarts without clearing any variables. When the restarted program reaches GOSUB 60000 again, we will get a REDIMENSION error. We can avoid this by adding a few BASIC lines that check to see if the program is restarting. If it is, we jump around the GOSUB 60000 and avoid the error.

```
1 REM  first time around all variables will be 0
2 IF F = 1 THEN 40 : REM  avoid that REDIM error
3 F = 1 : REM  show program has started for the first time
```

The changes to the GET subroutine:

```
61900 NAME$ = "0:" + NAME$
61902 OPEN 1, 8, 15, "I0" : REM position the heads
61904 OPEN 2, 8, 0, NAME$
61906 CLOSE 2
61908 LOAD NAME$, 8, 1
```

Thanks again to Danny Rudiak of Calgary for the hint on how to load programs this way.

On other CBM machines, we can overcome all problems by cheating a little. If we stopped the animation and used the com-

```
SYS 4                  get into the CBM machine code monitor
L "FILENAME",08        get the file
X                      back into BASIC
CONT                   restart the program
```

mands then we can avoid using the disk operating commands. What we have used is the built-in monitor commands from the computer. These don't store anything in our safe area. The following program changes allow us to automatically change in and out of the CBM monitor, and continue our program. It is known as using a dynamic keyboard.

```
4670 IF TEMP$ = "GE" THEN GOSUB 61700 : STOP : GOTO 4000
     : REM <<get>>
61900 PRINT CHR$(147);CHR$(17);CHR$(17);CHR$(17)
61901 REM that clears the screen and cursors down 3 lines
61902 PRINT " SYS 4" : REM set up first command
61903 PRINT CHR$(17);CHR$(17);CHR$(17);CHR$(17);" l";
61904 PRINT CHR$(34);"0:";NAME$;CHR$(34);",08"
      : REM print second command
61905 PRINT CHR$(17); CHR$(17); " X" :REM print third command
61906 PRINT CHR$(17); "CONT" :REN print fourth command
61907 PRINT CHR$(19) : REM home the cursor
61908 REM FOR J = 623 TO 626 : POKE J, 13 : NEXT J
61909 REM POKE 158, 4
```

Try the program out. It will stop at line 4670. Press Return to enter the CBM monitor. Press Return again. You will cause the loading of a machine language program if there is one on the disk. Press Return a third time and you will return to BASIC command mode. Finally, press Return one more time to restart your program.

If you now remove the REMs from lines 61908 and 61909, you will automatically cause the carriage returns to be done by your program. Line 61908 causes four carriage returns to be put into the CBM keyboard buffer. Line 61909 tells the CBM that there are four characters to be processed. This "smart" technique of dropping out of a BASIC program, into machine code, and then back into a BASIC program only works *provided you are NOT in a subroutine.*

Save the program above as CHAP.12F.

Since you can now both SAVE and GET files, try the commands out to see if they work together. After you have used SA (save) to put a file on the disk, use the CA (catalog) command to make sure the name you used was correct. Before using the GE (get) command, use the CL (clear) command to clear the save area. Then you can make sure that things were reloaded correctly. You can also check things with the disassemble (D) command.

## IMPROVING THE *GET* AND *SAVE* COMMANDS

These commands are helpful in that they check to see if the person has already added the .OBJ on the end of the filename. However, there are other things that could cause problems. It is up to you to add these other checks if you want to and if you can find out how.

For instance, what would happen if the file you wanted to get does not exist, or if a drive malfunctions? Make a check and warn the user that there is a problem.

What happens if the program you get does not load into the safe area? This could cause a system crash. Checking to see where a disk file will be loaded, if you don't already know, is really tricky. Getting this check to work will require some fancy programming. Check the magazines to see if somebody has already done it for your machine. If not, *be careful.* (It should not be a great problem for files that we have saved with help of the menu, because they should all come from the safe area.)

What happens if you save a machine language program using a name already in use? Do you want to allow that to happen always, never, or after a warning has been given. You don't want to accidentally destroy something.

## THE *ASSEMBLE* COMMAND

We have built a large number of software tools in this chapter We can always do without them, but they are rather nice to have. The last one, the assembler, is probably the one you will find the most time-saving and error-preventing. This command will allow us to type in things like

```
ADC #$FF
```

and have the computer automatically turn it into

```
$69  $FF
```

stored in the correct place in memory. This will remove a lot of mistakes and brain work. The assembler we will build will not be fancy and it will not be fast. An assembler has to do a lot of looking and a lot of checking. In BASIC this is very slow. The commercial programs work in machine language for speed. If we made this assembler as fancy as the commercial ones it would be *very* slow.

This assembler will expect you to be very careful in typing things in. If it does not understand the instruction it will turn the instruction into three BRK instructions ($00, $00, $00). This will cause both the animation and the real microprocessor to stop at that place. It will give you another chance to type in the correct instructions.

If you start the instruction with a $ symbol, the computer will use what you type as a hex number and load it into memory. This will be useful in putting data into memory or for using instructions that the assembler does not know.

The assembler will not be very "intelligent." Being intelligent means more checking of letters and more time. You must not add any unnecessary blanks. The assembler also will not handle comments or labels. You will have to add them yourself after you have used the printer and the disassembler.

This is how the assembler will work:

1) It will get a starting address (no checks made).
2) It will get the assembly language mnemonics from the keyboard.
3) If the mnemonic is an END it will quit.
4) If the mnemonic is an ERR, then it will go back to step 1. This is useful if you suddenly realize that an error exists and you want to go back and change things you have already typed in.
5) If the mnemonic starts with a $, it will load that value straight into the next memory location.
6) It will try to recognize the mnemonic. It could do this by searching through all of MN$. That might take some time, since looking at letters using BASIC is very inefficient. Instead we will use TYPE% to look for the ***right kind*** of instructions. If we find one of the correct kind, then we look at MN$ to see if this is the one we really want. Looking at numbers is a bit faster way of doing a search.
7) In order to know what type of instruction to look for, the assembler must look for some sort of marker in the mnemonic you have typed in. These are the markers we shall look for:

| MARKER | LOCATION | TYPE | |
|---|---|---|---|
| $ | letter 1 | hex code | - |
| only 3 letters | | implied | 5 |
| # | letter 5 | immediate | 1 |
| ,X | end | absolute, x | 9 |
| ,Y | end | absolute, Y | 10 |
| B | letter 1 | branch | 11 |
| everything else | | absolute | 2 |

8) Once the marker has been found, it will decode the number, type in and do the loading into memory of the 1, 2, or 3 hex codes needed.
9) If the mnemonic is not recognized, then it will turn the instruction into a BRK instruction and leave three empty spaces in memory. This allows us to go back and insert the correct code later.

Let's add the new command to our menu

```
4260 IF TEMP$ = "A" THEN GOSUB 44700 : GOTO 4000
     : REM <<assembler>>

45032 PRINT "A  - ASSEMBLER FOR MACHINE CODE"

46690 rem <<ASSEMBLER>>
47000 PRINT "ASSEMBLER"
47010 GOSUB 55500 : REM <<wait>>
47020 RETURN
```

As usual, test the animation program for syntax errors.

Now let's add the recognition parts of the assembler a bit at a time. At each stage, we should make sure that the stage works before moving onto the next task.

```
47000 PRINT : PRINT "ASSEMBLER STARTING ADDRESS? ";
47010 GOSUB 56000 : REM <<get-hex>>
47020 BEGIN = HEX
47030 PRINT "TYPE 'END' TO QUIT, 'ERR' TO RESTART" : PRINT
47040 GOSUB 62000 : REM <<go-to-page-bottom-less-one>>
47050 PRINT "$"; : HEX = BEGIN : GOSUB 58000
      : REM <<print-hex>>
47060 PRINT ": "; BELL$; : INPUT ANS$ : REM get command
47070 IF ANS$ = "END" THEN RETURN
47080 IF ANS$ = "ERR" THEN 47000
47085 IF ANS$ = "BRK" THEN FOUND = 0: GOTO 47230
```

```
47100 GOTO 47040
61990 REM <<move-to-screen-bottom-less-1>>
62000 DOWN = 23
      : REM xxx change for your machine if needed xxxx
62010 GOSUB 61200 : RETURN
```

Test this out. It should just take in an instruction and ignore it unless it is an END or an ERR. The END instruction stops doing the assembling. The ERR instruction allows you to enter a new starting address in case you spot something you need to change.

We're going to do something sneaky to make this command more useful. After an instruction has been loaded (LDA #$30, for example) at location $306, we are going to use the disassembler and write over the top of what we have written in, to make it look like our machine code listings. The thing we typed in will then change to look like this

```
$306: $A9 $30          LDA #$30
```

That way if you are entering in a machine language program from a magazine, you can check to see if it is going in correctly. You may have to adjust the value of DOWN in line 6200 to ensure that it will write over the top of the old line.

Now let's add the $ and the *implied* or simple instructions:

```
47100 IF LEN(ANS$) < 2 THEN PRINT EH$: GOTO 47850 : REM ERROR
47110 IF MID$(ANS$,1,1) <> "$" THEN 47200
      : REM handle '$' commands
47120 GOSUB 56010 : REM jump into <<get-hex>> for a number
47130 IF HEX > 255 THEN PRINT EH$ : GOTO 47850 : REM error
47140 POKE (BEGIN), HEX : REM store
47150 GOTO 47040 : REM <<end '$' instruction>>
47200 IF LEN (ANS$) <> 3 THEN 47300
      : REM find things with no parameters
47210 TYPE = 5 : GOSUB 47900 : REM <<go-look-for-mnemonic>>
47220 IF FOUND = 0 THEN 47850 : REM error if not found!!!
47230 POKE (START), FOUND : GOTO 47800 : REM <<end implied>>
47300 REM dummy continue statement
```

If the mnemonic was found in the <<go-look>> subroutine, then we must move to the line just above the screen bottom, print an empty line to write over the top of the old line, and jump into the disassembler loop and disassemble one line. We shall change the loop in the disassembler so that instead of doing things 18 times, it does things DNUM times. We shall jump into the loop with DNUM = 1 to get just one line disassembled.

```
46105 DNUM = 18
      : REM  patch so that disassembler still does 18 lines
46110 FOR NUM = 1 TO DNUM : REM changed
47800 GOSUB 62000 : REM <<move-to-bottom-line-less-1>>
47810 PRINT "                               "
47820 GOSUB 62000
47830 DNUM = 1 : GOSUB 46110 : PRINT : GOTO 47040
      : REM do more assembling
```

If we get an error, then we should be allowed to try again:

```
47850 PRINT EH$ : INPUT "ERROR - TRY AGAIN? "; ANS$ : PRINT
47860 IF MID$(ANS$,1,1) = "Y" THEN 47040
47870 IF MID$(AND$,1,1) <> "N" THEN PRINT EH$ : GOTO 47850
47880 FOR NUM = 1 TO 3 : POKE (BEGIN) , 0 : BEGIN = BEGIN + 1
47890 NEXT NUM : PRINT : GOTO 47040
      : REM <<end add-3-BRK-for-error>
```

We need to look for the same type of instruction as the one typed in. This is the <<go-look>> mnemonic subroutine:

```
47900 FOUND = 0 : REM not found yet
47910 LOOK$ = MID$(ANS$,1,3) : REM look at first 3 letters only
47920 FOR NUM = 0 TO 255
47930 IF TYPE <> TYPE%(NUM) THEN 47970 : REM wrong type
47940 IF LOOK$ <> MN$(NUM) THEN 47970 : REM wrong one
47950 FOUND = NUM : REM found the right one
47960 RETURN
47970 NEXT NUM : REM keep looking
47980 RETURN : REM <<end look>>
```

Test this for syntax errors and save as CHAP.12F.

Try to load instructions into the safe area. If you use the instructions NOP, INX, etc., they should load okay, be assembled, and then disassemble correctly. Your screen will look like Fig. 12-4 or 12-5.

You'll notice that things are assembled rather slowly. At the

```
                                   !-----------------------------

MEMORY STARTING AT $0300
0300: 00 00 00 00 00 00 EA 03
0308: D8 EA AD 30 03 18 69 01
0310: 8D 30 03 90 F4 EA 18 AD
0318: 31 03 69 01 8D 31 03 90
0320: E9 60 00 00 00 00 00 00
0328: 00 00 00 00 00 00 00 00
0330: 00 00 00 00 00 00 00 00
0338: 00 00 00 00 00 00 00 00



TYPE 'HELP' FOR COMMANDS
YOUR WISH, MASTER? ASSEMBLE

ASSEMBLER STARTING ADDRESS ?330
TYPE 'END' TO QUIT

$0330:E8               INX
$0331:E8               INX
$0332:CA               DEX
$0333: BRK
```

Fig. 12-4. The new ASSEMBLE command in operation.

end of the chapter we will examine why and fix things so that the program assembles things four times faster

Let's handle the ABSOLUTE,X and the ABSOLUTE,Y mnemonics next, because they are easy to recognize by the embedded comma.

```
47300 TYPE = 0 : REM not recognized yet
47310 IF MID$(ANS$, LEN(ANS$) - 1, 1) <> "," THEN 47410
47320 IF MID$(ANS$,LEN(ANS$),1) = "X" THEN TYPE = 9
47330 IF MID$(ANS$, LEN(ANS$), 1) = "Y" THEN TYPE = 10
47340 ANS$ = MID$(ANS$, 1, LEN(ANS$) - 2)
      : REM remove the ',X' or ',Y'
47350 GOSUB 47900 : IF FOUND = 0 THEN 47850 : REM not found!!
47360 POKE (BEGIN), FOUND : REM load instruction
47370 ANS$ = MID$(ANS$, 5, LEN(ANS$) - 4) : REM just get number
```

```
47380 GOSUB 56010 : POKE (BEGIN + 2), INT (HEX / 256)
      : REM HIBYTE
47390 POKE (BEGIN + 1) , HEX - 256 * (PEEK (BEGIN + 2))
      : REM LOBYTE
47400 GOTO 47800 : REM <<end absolute x and y>>
```

The next to do are the branch mnemonics. We need to calculate how far to branch and make sure that we don't try to go too far.

```
47410 IF MID$(ANS$(1,1) <> "B" THEN 47500
47420 TYPE = 11 : GOSUB 47900 : IF FOUND = 0 THEN 47850
47430 POKE (BEGIN) , FOUND : REM load instruction
47440 ANS$ = MID$(ANS$, 5, LEN(ANS$) -4)
      : REM get the number part
```

```
MEMORY STARTING AT $C300
C300:  00  00  00  00  00  00  EA  03
C308:  D8  EA  AD  30  03  18  69  01
C310:  8D  30  03  90  F4  EA  18  AD
C318:  31  03  69  01  8D  31  03  90
C320:  E9  60  00  00  00  00  00  00
C328:  00  00  00  00  00  00  00  00
C330:  00  00  00  00  00  00  00  00
C338:  00  00  00  00  00  00  00  00



TYPE 'HELP' FOR COMMANDS
YOUR WISH, MASTER? ASSEMBLE

ASSEMBLER STARTING ADDRESS ?C330
TYPE 'END' TO QUIT

$C330: E8              INX
$C331: E8              INX
$C332: CA              DEX
$C333:  BRK
```

Fig. 12-5. ASSEMBLE on the Commodore 64.

```
47450 GOSUB 56010 : HEX = HEX - BEGIN - 2 : REM work out how far
47460 IF (HEX > 127) OR (HEX < -128) THEN PRINT "TOO FAR "
      : GOTO 47850
47470 IF HEX < 0 THEN HEX = HEX + 256 : rem adjust for storage
47480 POKE (BEGIN + 1), HEX : REM load
47490 GOTO 47800 : REM <<end branch>>
```

The difference between the IMMEDIATE and the ABSOLUTE mnemonics is the number or pound sign (#).

```
47500 IF MID$(ANS$,5,1) <> "#" THEN 47600
47510 TYPE = 1 : GOSUB 47900 : IF FOUND = 0 THEN 47850
47520 POKE (BEGIN), FOUND : REM load instruction
47530 ANS$ = MID$(ANS$, 6, LEN(ANS$) - 5)
      : REM just number part
47540 GOSUB 56010 : IF HEX > 255 THEN PRINT "TOO LARGE"
      : GOTO 47850
47560 POKE (BEGIN + 1), HEX : GOTO 47800
      : REM <<end immediate>>
47600 TYPE = 2 : GOTO 47350
      : REM absolute can be done like absolute,x
```

Save this as CHAP.12. It is rather a long program but very useful.

If you test this new command with the following program, you should see the way the screen changes as you enter the mnemonics. Figures 12-6 and 12-7 show what should happen after each step.

```
$300
LDA #4
STA $200
CLC
LDA $200
INX
BNE $300
END
```

This is the last software tool. Our system is now complete and we can get down to really serious machine language programming.

## ADDING ASSEMBLER RACING SPEED

The assembler is rather slow at the moment. In Chapter 17 we shall spend time discussing how to make BASIC and machine code

```
            !--------------------

MEMORY STARTING AT $0300
0300: 00 00 00 00 00 00 EA 03
0308: D8 EA AD 30 03 18 69 01
0310: 8D 30 03 90 F4 EA 18 AD
0318: 31 03 69 01 8D 31 03 90
0320: E9 60 00 00 00 00 00 00
0328: 00 00 00 00 00 00 00 00
0330: E8 E8 CA 00 00 00 00 00
0338: 00 00 00 00 00 00 00 00

TYPE 'HELP' FOR COMMANDS
YOUR WISH, MASTER? ASSEMBLE

ASSEMBLER STARTING ADDRESS ?330
TYPE 'END' TO QUIT

$0330:E8              INX
$0331:E8              INX
$0332:CA              DEX
$0333: BNE $300
```

**Before**

```
MEMORY STARTING AT $0300
0300: E8 E8 CA D0 FB 00 EA 03
0308: D8 EA AD 30 03 18 69 01
0310: 8D 30 03 90 F4 EA 18 AD
0318: 31 03 69 01 8D 31 03 90
0320: E9 60 00 00 00 00 00 00
0328: 00 00 00 00 00 00 00 00
0330: E8 E8 CA D0 00 00 00 00
0338: 00 00 00 00 00 00 00 00
TYPE 'HELP' FOR COMMANDS
YOUR WISH, MASTER? ASSEMBLE

ASSEMBLER STARTING ADDRESS ?330
TYPE 'END' TO QUIT

$0330:E8              INX
$0331:E8              INX
$0332:CA              DEX
$0333:D0 CB           BNE $0300
$0335: STA $300
```

**After**

Fig. 12-6. Before-and-after screen displays showing how the DISASSEMBLE subroutine is used to disassemble each new command as it is entered with the ASSEMBLER.

```
                    !-------------------------
 MEMORY STARTING AT $C300
 C300: 00 00 00 00 00 00 EA 03
 C308: D8 EA AD 30 03 18 69 01
 C310: 8D 30 03 90 F4 EA 18 AD
 C318: 31 03 69 01 8D 31 03 90
 C320: E9 60 00 00 00 00 00 00
 C328: 00 00 00 00 00 00 00 00
 C330: E8 E8 CA 00 00 00 00 00
 C338: 00 00 00 00 00 00 00 00

TYPE 'HELP' FOR COMMANDS
YOUR WISH, MASTER? ASSEMBLE

ASSEMBLER STARTING ADDRESS ?C330
TYPE 'END' TO QUIT

$C330:E8           INX
$C331:E8           INX
$C332:CA           DEX
$C333: BNE $C300



 MEMORY STARTING AT $C300
 C300: E8 E8 CA D0 FB 00 EA 03
 C308: D8 EA AD 30 03 18 69 01
 C310: 8D 30 03 90 F4 EA 18 AD
 C318: 31 03 69 01 8D 31 03 90
 C320: E9 60 00 00 00 00 00 00
 C328: 00 00 00 00 00 00 00 00
 C330: E8 E8 CA D0 00 00 00 00
 C338: 00 00 00 00 00 00 00 00

TYPE 'HELP' FOR COMMANDS
YOUR WISH, MASTER? ASSEMBLE

ASSEMBLER STARTING ADDRESS ?C330
TYPE 'END' TO QUIT

$C330: E8          INX
$C331: E8          INX
$C332: CA          DEX
$C333: D0 CB       BNE $C300
$C335: STA $300
```

Fig. 12-7. Figure 12-6 as displayed by the Commodore 64.

go faster. By trying to find the correct TYPE% rather than looking for the correct mnemonic MN$, we have made the assembler instruction a little faster. However it is not by any means fast. The assembler called BIG.MAC described in the appendix on software tools works at over 2000 lines a minute.

Although we can't aim for that sort of speed, we would like an assembler that at least kept up with our typing. The problem we have here, is quite simple. We have a FOR . . . NEXT loop in the <<look-for-instruction>> subroutine (lines 47900-47990) that is used a large number of times. In the middle of the loop, there are GOTO instructions. GOTO instructions in a loop are very slow if they get done very often. Since with our loop the GOTOs are used 254 times out of 255, the loop will be very slow. We need to rewrite the loop so that the GOTO statements are not needed. The following is rather confusing, and is therefore rather poor code. However, on my machine, because the program becomes four times faster, it is worth it.

```
47925 REM *** watch for NEXT in IF statements next TWO lines
47930 IF TYPE <> TYPE%(NUM) THEN NEXT NUM : RETURN
      : REM wrong type
47940 IF LOOK$ <> MN$(NUM) THEN NEXT NUM  : RETURN
      : REM wrong one
```

Having the NEXT in an IF statement can cause a lot of problems. However, we already had the program working and could identify a definite problem. That does not make the bad code good, but it does justify it. Note we have added a warning to the next person reading the code.

A second way of speeding up things is to "just keep typing."Most computers will remember what has been typed in even while they are doing something else. This way, if you are a slow typer, two things can be going on at once. The computer is working out the last command while you are typing in the test. That way, neither of you is kept waiting by the other. Different computers remember different amounts. The Apple seems able to handle up to 255 input characters and the CBMs about 10. I find that the assembler will keep up to me if I am reading code from a magazine and then typing it in. I am a four-fingered hunt-and-peck typist. I can get ahead of it without too much trouble.

# Chapter 13

# "Avast, Knave! Be Careful How Thou Addresses Me!"

In days of old, you had to look out. If a knight came up to your house and asked the way, you had better say "Yes Sire," and "No Sire." If you were not careful in the way you addressed or said things, the knight would take out his sword and cut you off in the middle of your life.

Things haven't changed much. When you are machine language programming, the knight becomes the microprocessor. If you are not careful in the way you address the microprocessor, it will cut you off in the middle of your program. If you had just spent six hours programming—with no backup copy—and you had to use the POWER OFF switch to regain control, then it will be as painful as the sword.

When we built the disassembler we talked about different kinds or types of instructions. The computer scientist says that the different kinds of instructions have different *addressing modes.* Addresses, as we know, are methods of describing what word in memory we are going to use in an instruction. Instructions like INX or DEY have implied or inherent addresses in them. When we say INX we know we are going to use that address called the X Register. The addressing mode for these kinds of instructions is called an *inherent addressing mode*.

Instructions like BCC and BNE are instructions with a *relative address mode* because they do things relative to the value currently in the Program Counter. The ADC #$14 instruction is an example of an instruction with an *immediate addressing mode.* This instruction uses a number immediately, without requiring any more processing. The instruction ADC $300 has an *absolute addressing mode.* The number $300 refers to a memory location calculated from the start of the memory. The address used is absolute, meaning not relative to something that is continually changing. For the ADC instruction there are six other types of addressing modes. Only two of them are in common use and they will be explained in detail. For information on the others consult the more advanced books given in Appendix C.

To see why these additional types of instructions are needed, look at the following BASIC programs:

```
PROGRAM 1
10 FOR X = 1 TO 2
20 G(X) = X
30 NEXT X
40 STOP
```

```
PROGRAM 2
10 FOR X = 1 TO 32
20 G(X) = X
30 NEXT X
40 STOP
```

These are very simple storage programs. Storing things in arrays is very common in any programming language.

Let's turn program 1 into assembly language mnemonics. When you load the program, make sure that you use the new A or assembler instruction.

```
$300:            LDX #$1     ; X = 1
$302:            STX $320    ; G(1) = 1          (C64 use $C320)
$305:            LDX #$2     ; X = 2
$307:            STX $321    ; G(2) = 2          (C64 use $C321)
$30A:   $60      RTS         ; BASIC stop (Type in $60)
$30B:            BRK         ; QUIT!!
$320:          G DS  2       ; Make room         (Don't type in)
```

When you are using the assembler, remember:

- When there is an instruction the assembler does not know about (RTS), put it in as the hex code $60.
- Don't put in the comments.
- Except for the starting address, don't put in the numbers at the beginning of the line.
- Don't type in the pseudoinstructions such as DS, because our assembler does not know how to handle them.
- Don't use labels such as G.

You would have used the assembler like this:

```
A                       Request assembler
$300                    Load starting address
LDX #$1
STX $320
LDX #$2
STX $321
$60                     Load HEX code for unknown instruction
BRK
END                     Leave assembler for main menu
```

If you use either the W or the GO instructions, then you will see that this program really works like the BASIC program.

Suppose instead that you want to do the next program the same way. This would take two instructions (5 memory locations) for each time we went round the loop. That means to store 32 numbers we need 64 instructions, and the program would take up 150 memory locations. That is very inefficient programming. There must be a better way.

## INDEXED INSTRUCTIONS

The better way is the ABSOLUTE,X and the ABSOLUTE, Y instructions. These are also called *indexed* instructions. Let us look at two ways of using the store instruction with the A Register.

```
STA $320    absolute addressing mode
STA $320,Y  absolute adress indexed with the Y register
```

The first instruction says, "Use the following address as a storage location for the A Register." The second instruction is more interesting. It says, "ADD the value stored in the Y Register to the following address. Use the answer as the storage location address

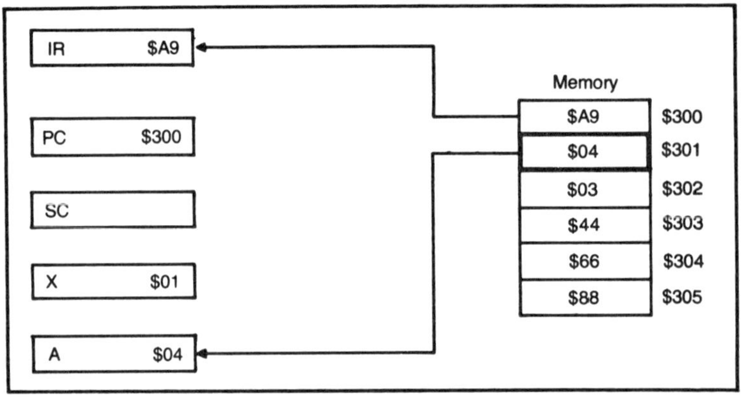

Fig. 13-1. Immediate LDA instruction.

for the A Register." Notice how that little ",Y" has changed things. Figures 13-1 through 13-3 show what is happening in a little more detail.

Here is a simple example to show what will happen:

```
$300:               LDA #$10       ; A = $10 (decimal 16)
$302:               LDY #$02       ; Y = 2
$304: $99 $20 $03   STA $320,Y     ; put A into $320 + Y = $322
$307:               DEY            ; Y = Y - 1
$308: $99 $20 $03   STA $320,Y     ; put A into $320 + Y = $321
$30B: $60           RTS            ; BASIC return
$30C:               BRK            ; QUIT!!!
```

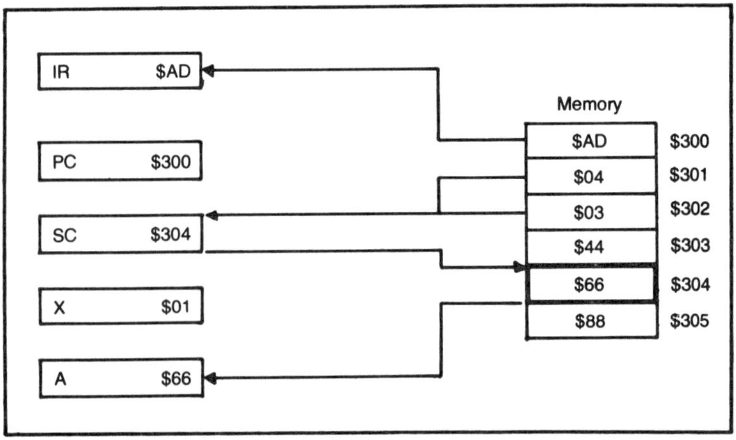

Fig. 13-2. Absolute LDA instruction.

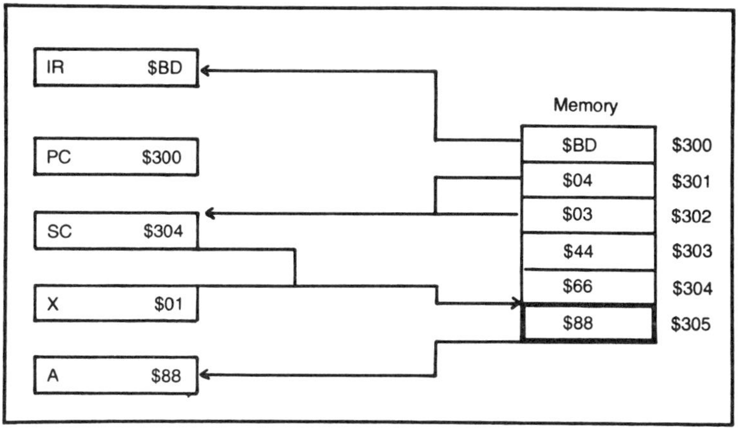

Fig. 13-3. Indexed absolute LDA instruction.

(For the C64 use location $C321.)

Notice how the instructions at location $304 and $308 are exactly the same, but they do different things. The instruction in $304 stores things in location $322. The instruction at $308 stores things in location $321. Clear the memory with the CL instruction and load the program with the A (assembler) command. Since the new indexed instructions have not been put into the TYPE% array, use the $ mode of the assembler to put them in. Use the GO instruction and see that it really does happen. The value of the A Register ($10) will be stored in both locations $321 and $322.

Using these new instructions this way is not really efficient, but put them into a loop and watch the efficiency. This is how Program 2 looks using our new instruction:

```
$300:                  CLD         ; clear decimal flag
$301:                  LDX #$20    ; X = $20 (decimal 30)
$303:                  LDA #$20    ; A = $20
$305: $99 $20 $03      STA $320,X  ; put A into location $320 + X
$308:                  SEC         ; Set Carry flag
$309:                  SBC #$01    ; A = A - 1
$30B:                  DEX         ; X = X - 1
$30C:                  BNE $305    ; Branch if x <> 0 (C64 use
                                               $C305)
$30E: $60              RTS         ; BASIC return
$30F:                  BRK
$320:              G   DS  $20     ; Leave room
```

Try that with the GO instruction. This only took 16 memory locations, not 150. You see how powerful the new instructions are.

But there is one problem you should be aware of: if you look carefully at what is stored in memory after using the GO instruction, then you will see that instead of what we wanted:

```
G(1) = 1
G(2) = 2
```

we have

```
G(2) = 1
G(3) = 2
```

since G starts at $320. See if you can change just one thing (one memory location) and get things to be stored in the right place. You need to change $306 to be one smaller ($1F). Try it and see.

The new instructions are as follows:

| ASSEMBLER MNEMONICS | HEX CODE | WHICH FLAGS CHANGE |
|---|---|---|
| ADC $####,X | $7D | N Z V C |
| ADC $####,Y | $79 | N Z V C |
| LDA $####,X | $BD | N Z |
| LDA $####,Y | $B9 | N Z |
| LDX $####,Y | $BE | N Z |
| LDY $####,X | $BC | N Z |
| SBC $####,X | $FD | N Z V C |
| SBC $####,Y | $F9 | N Z V C |
| STA $####,X | $9D | |
| STA $####,Y | $99 | |

The symbol $#### means some memory location. Notice that only the A Register can be stored using either the X or the Y Register, giving extra pointing direction. Also, although you can load X or the Y Registers by this method, you can't store the X and Y Registers this way.

Let us add the mnemonics of these instructions to our animation so that we can use the assembler and disassembler more easily.

```
60950 MN$(125) = "ADC" : TYPE%(125) = 9 : REM <<adc memory,x>>
60960 MN$(121) = "ADC" : TYPE%(121) = 10 : REM <<adc memory,y>>
60970 MN$(189) = "LDA" : TYPE%(189) = 9 : REM <<lda memory,x>>
```

Watch the line number change.

```
60515 MN$(185) = "LDA" : TYPE%(185) = 10 : REM <<lda memory,y>>
60525 MN$(190) = "LDX" : TYPE%(190) = 10 : REM <<ldx memory,y>>
60535 MN$(188) = "LDY" : TYPE%(188) = 9 : REM <<ldy memory,x>>
60545 MN$(253) = "SBC" : TYPE%(253) = 9 : REM <<sbc memory,x>>
60555 MN$(249) = "SBC" : TYPE%(249) = 10 : REM <<sbc memory,y>>
60565 MN$(157) = "STA" : TYPE%(157) = 9 : REM <<sta memory,x>>
60575 MN$(153) = "STA" : TYPE%(153) = 10 : REM <<sta memory,y>>
```

Notice that one small change in the addressing modes has given us 10 new instructions.

Test out the new assembler types by retyping the last machine code program without using the $ assembler instruction. You'll find a problem. The assembler will not accept the comma in the STA $31F,X instruction. BASIC can't use an INPUT statement to pick up something with a comma in it. We'll have to make a small change to the assembler program, so that instead of picking up ANS$ completely, it picks up ANS$ one character at a time.

```
47060 PRINT ":"; : BELL$; : ANS$ = "" : REM nothing in answer
47062 GET TEMP$ : IF TEMP$ = "" THEN 47062 : REM get character
47064 IF ASC(TEMP$) = 8 THEN PRINT "DELETED"; EH$ : GOTO 47040
47066 PRINT TEMP$; : IF ASC(TEMP$) = 13 THEN 47070
      : REM end of line
47068 ANS$ = ANS$ + TEMP$ : GOTO 47062
```

Line 47064 takes care of a problem that occurs when you pick up one character at a time. When you use the <– key, then that character also gets put into the ANS$ string. This line makes sure that if you make a typing mistake, then you get a chance to retype the assembler mnemonic. It is not the most friendly way of doing it, so why not rewrite this section to make it personalized?

There is one other small problem. We have not animated these instructions. If we attempt to run the machine code program using the animation, it would be nice if we put in some explanation.

```
30905 IF TYPE%(IR) <> 0 THEN PRINT : PRINT "NOT ANIMATED"
      : GOSUB 55500
30906 IR = 0 : REM change to BRK instruction
```

Note that we have changed the unanimated instruction into a BRK.

This will cause the animation to stop. After all, if an instruction is not recognized, then the rest of the machine language program which needs that instruction will not be animated properly.

## OTHER ADDRESSING MODES

The other major addressing modes are:

1) Zero page modes (3 kinds).
2) Indirect modes (3 kinds).
3) Accumulator modes (1 kind).

The *zero page* modes are special instructions that work only on the memory locations in the zero page. They behave like the absolute instructions, except they only need two bytes of memory rather than three. This means they take less storage space and can operate faster. If you are mixing BASIC and machine code, watch how you use these instructions if you add them. They can interfere with the operation of BASIC.

The *indirect* modes work rather like the indexed instructions. They operate like this:

1) Using the next part of the instruction, go and get two values from the zero page.
2) Now use these values from the zero page and the value stored in the X or Y Register to make an address.
3) Now use this address to go and get something.

The way that the indirect indexed instructions work with the X Register is different from the way they work with the Y Register; the exact things that happen are very complex and require an advanced textbook. This mode is used by the monitor a lot when it is using BASIC pointers.

The *accumulator* modes do things to the accumulator or A Register. For example the instruction LSR (Logical Shift Right) moves all the bits in the accumulator to the right. Suppose that there was $88 in the A Register; this is 10001000 in binary. If you use the LSR instruction, then all the bits in the register get shifted to the right. This means that the A Register becomes 01000100 or $44. This means that the LSR instruction acts like a divide-by-two instruction. The accumulator instructions are really an *inherent* instruction type where the address is known to be the accumulator.

## ANIMATING THE *ABSOLUTE,X* INSTRUCTIONS

The EXECUTE logic needed for the ABSOLUTE,X instruction is quite complex and interesting. Suppose we wanted to animate the LDA $####,X instruction. The EXECUTE logic in BASIC would go like this:

```
GOSUB 51000 : REM <<fetch-next-memory>>
GOSUB 51500 : REM <<use-pc-get-again>>
SC = SC + XREG
    : REM use the X register to get the TRUE address needed
ADJUST = PEEK(SC) : REM go get the value
GOSUB 52000 : REM <<set N and Z flags>>
AREG = ADJUST
RETURN
```

Except for line 3, where the X Register value is added to the value stored in the Scratch Register, this EXECUTE logic is *exactly* the same as for the LDA $#### instruction. If you want to, and have enough room in memory, implement the animation for these new instructions. The line numbers from 20000 to 29000 will not be used in the rest of the animation, so you can put the animation for these new instructions there.

# Chapter 14

# Turning Basic Into Machine Code

In the last couple of chapters, we have learned a lot about turning BASIC instructions into machine code. Let us take a look at a fairly complex BASIC program that uses arrays, numbers, additions, subtractions, and GOTOs. The program does not do very much, but it shows all but three of the most important types of instructions. We shall write an equivalent machine language program.

```
10 J = 20
20 FOR K = 1 TO J:        REM loop of variable size
30 A(K) = 0:              REM initialize an array
40 NEXT K
50 GOTO 80:               REM move around within the program
60 STOP
70 REM                        dummy statement
80 M = 5
90 FOR K = 1 TO J
100 A(K) = A(K) +  M - 2: REM showing storing and arithmetic
110 NEXT K:                 REM operations using an array
120 GOTO 60
```

That just about uses all the major BASIC instructions.

We shall design our equivalent machine language program so that it starts at memory location \$300, stores the variable J at \$338 and the variable M at $339, and begins the array A at $33A. We shall use the X Register for the loop counter K.

```
$300:        CLD             ; Clear D-flag
$301:        LDA #$14        ; Make a decimal 20
$303:        STA $338        ; J = 20          (C64 use $C338)
$306:        LDA #$0         ; Make a 0
$308:        LDX $338        ; Get the top of the
                               loop variable (C64 use $C338)
$30B:        STA $339,X      ; A(K) = 0, stored at $339 + X
                              (C64 use $C339)
$30E:        DEX
$30F:        BNE $30B        ; End of loop? (C64 use $C30B)
$310:        JMP $315        ; GOTO 80         (C64 use $C315)
$313:        RTS             ; STOP - BASIC RETURN
$314:        NOP             ; REM
$315:        LDA #$5         ; Make a 5
$317:        STA $339        ; M = 5            (C64 use $C339)
$31A:        LDX $338        ; Get the old top of the loop
                               (C64 use $C338)
$31D:        LDA $339,X      ; Get A(K) stored at $339 + X
                              (C64 use $C339)
$320:        CLC             ; Clear C flag so get ADD
$321:        ADC $339        ; A(K) + M         (C64 use $C339)
$324:        SEC             ; Set C flag so get SUB
$325:        SBC #$2         ; A(K) + M - 2
$327:        STA $339,X      ; A(K) = A(K) + M - 2
                              (C64 use $C339)
$32A:        DEX
$32B:        BNE $31D        ; End of loop?    (C64 use $C31D)
$32D:        JMP $313        ; Go to 60        (C64 use $C313)
$32E:        DS $B           ; Expansion room
$338:    J   DS 1            ; Room for J
$339:    M   DS 1            ; Room for M
$33A:    A   DS $16          ; DIM A(20)
```

Notice how we made room for all the variables and arrays at the end. We could have left room for these at the beginning of the program, but it just seems to be more convenient this way. Your screen should look either like Fig. 14-1 for the Apple or Fig. 14-2 for the Commodore 64.

Notice the instruction at $32E. This just leaves room at the end

```
                            ! IR $00 PC $00
                            ! DR $00 AR $00
C D I N V Z                 !        SC $0000
? ? ? ? ? ?                 ! X  $00 Y  $00
                            ! A  $00
                            !-----------------

MEMORY STARTING AT $0300
0300: D8 A9 14 8D 38 03 A9 00
0308: AE 38 03 9D 39 03 CA D0
0310: FA 4C 15 60 EA A9 05 8D
0318: 39 03 AE 38 03 BD 39 03
0320: 18 6D 39 03 38 E9 02 9D
0328: 39 03 CA D0 F0 4C 13 03
0330: 00 00 00 00 00 00 00 00
0338: 00 00 00 00 00 00 00 00



TYPE 'HELP' FOR COMMANDS
YOUR WISH, MASTER?
```

Fig. 14-1. A machine language program using equivalents of the most common BASIC statements.

of our program. If we find that we need to add something more, then here is the room to put it. Leaving spaces like this is a good technique when you are first writing a program that uses a large number of machine code subroutines. Once the routines are working, you have to go in and remove the empty areas if you find yourself short of memory. Otherwise leave them in and don't waste time by finding unnecessary work for yourself.

Suppose that you suddenly found that the instruction at $327 was not needed. What could you do to avoid having to rewrite the program? Simple! We replace the instructions at $327, $328, and $329 with NOPs ($EA). That removes the unwanted instruction without requiring any major rewriting. We might leave the NOPs in our final version of the program if it were not in a part of the program that needs speed. NOPs are instructions that do nothing except use up time.

There are three important BASIC commands for which we still don't have any equivalent machine language instructions. They are

```
                          ! IR $00 PC $00
                          ! DR $00 AR $00
C D I N V Z               !        SC $0000
? ? ? ? ? ?               ! X  $00 Y  $00
                          ! A  $00
                          !-----------------

MEMORY STARTING AT $C300
C300: D8 A9 14 8D 38 C3 A9 00
C308: AE 38 C3 9D 39 C3 CA D0
C310: FA 4C 15 60 EA A9 05 8D
C318: 39 C3 AE 38 C3 8D 39 C3
C320: 18 6D 39 C3 38 E9 02 9D
C328: 39 C3 CA D0 F0 4C 13 C3
C330: 00 00 00 00 00 00 00 00
C338: 00 00 00 00 00 00 00 00



TYPE 'HELP' FOR COMMANDS
YOUR WISH, MASTER?
```

Fig. 14-2. The BASIC-equivalent program on the Commodore 64.

1) IF K = 9 THEN GOTO . . .
2) GOSUB ####
3) RETURN

The subroutine call and its return need some special programming techniques. They deserve a chapter of their own (Chapter 15). The other instruction is what is called a *compare* instruction. Compare instructions come in four major kinds, just like SBC or subtract instructions. In fact a compare instruction is exactly the same as the subtract instruction except that the register does not change its value.

Suppose you want to subtract $5 from the A Register. You would use SBC #$5. If the A Register held $3 and the C flag were clear, then this is what would happen:

| | |
|---|---|
| N FLAG is set | since A is negative. |
| C FLAG is cleared | since we went past the marker ($00). |
| Z FLAG is cleared | since A is not zero. |

| | |
|---|---|
| V FLAG is cleared | since we did not go past the marker ($80). |
| A = $FE(−2) | at end. |

Suppose instead you want to compare A with $5 without changing what is stored in the A Register. You would use the CMP #$5 instruction, (with A starting at 3 and the C flag is clear *or* set), and this would be the result

| | |
|---|---|
| N FLAG is set | since (A − 5) is negative. |
| C FLAG is clear | since (A − 5) went past the marker. |
| Z FLAG is clear | since (A − 5) is not zero. |
| A = $3 | at end. |

You can see that the only real difference between the SBC and CMP instructions is what happens to the A Register. You can also do comparing with the X and the Y Registers. That is something you can't do with the SBC instructions. There is one other thing. The SBC instructions work with the C flag and set the V flag. The compare instructions work the same way whether the C flag starts set or clear and they don't change the V flag.

These are the new instructions:

| ASSEMBLY MNEMONICS | HEX CODE | WHAT THE INSTRUCTION DOES |
|---|---|---|
| CMP #$ZZ | $C9 | Compare A with the number $ZZ |
| CMP $ZZZZ | $CD | Compare A with what is stored in $ZZZZ |
| CMP $ZZZZ,X | $DD | Compare A with what is stored in ($ZZZZ + X) |
| CMP $ZZZZ,Y | $D9 | Compare A with what is stored in ($ZZZZ + Y) |
| CPX #$ZZ | $E0 | Compare X with the number $ZZ |
| CPX $ZZZZ | $EC | Compare X with what is stored in $ZZZZ |
| CPY #$ZZ | $C0 | Compare Y with the number $ZZ |
| CPY $ZZZZ | $CC | Compare Y with what is stored in $ZZZZ |

The compare instructions are always followed by a branch instruction in a machine language program. You make a comparison and then branch or don't branch, depending on whether the comparison is or is not what you expected.

Here is a simple BASIC program that shows how the compare instructions might be used. You will notice that it is part of the animation program. This part of the BASIC logic was from the decision logic of line 30000 and beyond.

```
30060 IF IR = 232 THEN 31300 : REM <<inx>>
30070 IF IR = 200 THEN 31400 : REM <<iny>>
30080 IF IR = 202 THEN 31500 : REM <<dex>>
30090 IF IR = 136 THEN 31600 : REM <<dey>>
```

Let us suppose that the new machine language <<inx>> part of the EXECUTE logic starts at $5000, that the new machine language <<iny>> starts at $5100, and so on. If we decided to turn that part of the BASIC program into machine code for speed, the program would look like this:

```
$300:          IR DS 1        ; Make room for IR
$301:             LDA $300    ; Get the value inside IR
$304:             CMP #$E8    ; is it <<inx>>?
$306:             BNE $30B
$308:             JMP $5000   ; yes
$30B:             CMP #$C8    ; is it <<iny>>?
$30D:             BNE $312
$30F:             JMP $5100   ; yes
$312:             CMP #$CA    ; is it <<dex>>?
$314:             BNE $319
$316:             JMP $5200   ; yes
$319:             CMP #$88    ; is it <<dey>>?
$31B:    and so on.....
```

Notice that the program starts at $301. We placed the storage location at $300 because it was more convenient in this case. (Arrays do tend to get put at the end of programs.) Single locations tend to get put where they are convenient to place. In this case, since we don't know now how long the program will be, we don't know where its end is. Commercial assembler programs do a more convenient job than this.

Notice also that we only loaded the A Register once. Unlike the SBC instructions, using the compare instruction does not change anything. After doing one compare that did not work, we do another without having to reload the A Register.

Finally, each comparision was followed by a branch and then a jump. If the compare showed that the Instruction Register was not the value expected, then the program branched to the next compare instruction. If the compare was the expected value then a jump happened.

This bit of code is not the most sophisticated way of doing the many decisions needed in replacing the BASIC statements with the equivalent machine code. However, it does the job in an understandable way.

Before leaving this chapter, we must add the new instructions so that the assembler and disassembler commands can do their work.

```
60565 MN$(201) = "CMP" : TYPE%(201) = 1 : REM <<cmp #$%%>>
60575 MN$(205) = "CMP" : TYPE%(205) = 2 : REM <<cmp $%%%%>>
60585 MN$(221) = "CMP" : TYPE%(221) = 9 : REM <<cmp $%%%%,x>>
60595 MN$(217) = "CMP" : TYPE%(217) = 10 : REM <<cmp $%%%%,y>>
60605 MN$(224) = "CPX" : TYPE%(224) = 1 : REM <<cpx #$%%>>
60615 MN$(236) = "CPX" : TYPE%(236) = 2 : REM <<cpx $%%%%>>
60625 MN$(192) = "CPY" : TYPE%(192) = 1 : REM <<cpy #$%%>>
60635 MN$(204) = "CPY" : TYPE%(204) = 2 : REM <<cpy $%%%%>>
```

Save this program as *CHAP.14*.

# Chapter 15

# Lots of Coming and Going: An Introduction to Subroutines

In the last chapter we used the X Register to allow us to put things into arrays. Using arrays is a very useful technique. It makes our programs more compact (shorter) and more understandable. When you make use of an array, you are saying to a person who needs to use your program, "Look, all these things belong together."

Using arrays is a way of grouping things such as variables together. Subroutines are a way of grouping a part of a program into an idea or mathematical "paragraph." We have made a great deal of use of this approach in the animation program. Here are examples of the advantages we have gained.

- The <<wait>> subroutine is all over the place. If we used the same statements again and again, instead of GOSUB 55500, our program would be much longer. In addition, we can quickly change the speed of wait loops all over the program by making one small change at one place in the program.
- We have the chance for increased speed. We have used GOSUB 57000 to allow us to <<print-hex-number>> from a number of places in our program. This is probably our slowest and most often used subroutine. It would be an excellent idea to turn lines 57000-58000 into machine code. If we decided to do this, then we need just one change to our program. Suppose that the new machine code for the hex

print was at $300. Then our new subroutine would be

```
57000 CALL 768 : RETURN
```

We have then made big changes to the way our program behaves. But look at how small the programming changes have been. Could you imagine trying to find all the changes and—more important—all the time that would be needed if we tried to correct all the times we used a hex print if they were not subroutines? We will actually be making this change in Chapter 17.

- We have provided easier understanding and changing. Look at our menu selection routine:

```
4520 IF TEMP$ = "CH" THEN GOSUB 43000 : GOTO 4000
4530 IF TEMP$ = "CL" THEN GOSUB 42000 : GOTO 4000
4540 IF TEMP$ = "ST" THEN GOSUB 41000 : GOTO 4000
4550 IF TEMP$ = "SA" THEN GOSUB 48000 : GOTO 4000
```

By using subroutines we were able to keep separate the part that *selected* the command and the part that *did* the command. It was easy to check each part independently, and easy to make changes that didn't affect other parts of the program.

## WHEN TO USE MACHINE CODE RATHER THAN BASIC

When you are writing a machine language program, you have to ask yourself the question, "Why am I doing this?" If you need speed you should ask yourself, "What parts need speed." There are two kinds of speed. The first kind, "I want my program to work quickly," is the kind most people think of. What most people forget is the other kind of speed. "I want my program working in a useful fashion in the shortest possible time."

Getting your program's mistakes removed as quickly as possible is the second important kind of speed. It is no good getting your program to run to completion in 1 minute instead of 3 mintues if it takes you 30 hours of programming to do so. You "save" time if you work with the slower program. You would have to run your program 900 times before the time saved in program speed would equal the time lost because of programming.

Okay, you have decided to go the machine language route but you want to keep you programming time to a minimum. What's the best way to go? The answer is to try your ideas out first using a high-level language; BASIC is as good as any for that. Once you have made sure that your program ideas work, then translate each BASIC statement into the equivalent machine code. You will not have the absolute fastest machine code in the world, but it will be working in the shortest time after you start. Once it is working, look for the *slow* sections that are used *often* and improve those for greater speed. If there is a slow section that you don't use often, then don't worry about it. Those sections don't give back in speed the time you spend in programming. You might even find that a mixture of BASIC and machine code might be useful and quick. In Chapter 17 we shall look at techniques for doing this.

## WHY IS BASIC SLOW?

Let's look at a very simple BASIC program

```
10 A = 1
20 STOP
```

In machine code it would be very simple, just three instructions:

```
LDA #$1
STA $320          ; Variable A is at $320
BRK
```

What would the monitor have to do getting the two-line BASIC program to run?

Using about eight machine language instructions, the monitor would find out where statement 10 was in memory. Then, using eight more instructions, it would look along the line and find an A. Again using eight instructions, it would find out where variables are stored in memory. Using about eight times as many instructions as the number of variables used, it would look to see if A was already stored in memory. If not, it would take more instructions to make room for this new variable.

Then using eight instructions, it would look along the line and find the next command, the assignment (=) operator. Using from 8 to 50 instructions, it would look into ROM to try and find out what to do when a "=" command has been found. Using eight instructions, it would look along the line and find the *character* 1. Then, using eight more instructions, it would keep looking along the line to see if there were any more letters before the next statement.

Using 10 to 50 more instructions, it would take the character 1, turn it into a number 1, and then put it into the place where the variable A was in memory. Using eight instructions, it would find out where line 20 was in memory. Now it *still* has to look along that line to see what to do and then look into memory to see how to do it.

Whereas our simple program in machine code takes three instructions to do, the BASIC one takes about 100 to 300. There is a lot of saving in going to machine code. However, is it worth it? Instructions are executed about 300,000 times a second. The machine code takes 1/100,000 of a second and the BASIC takes 1/1,000 of a second. Is it worth changing the BASIC to machine code?

If you have decided that your problem *is* worth all that extra effort, then you should approach machine code with a time saving approach. Such approach is as true for machine code as it is for BASIC. You should

1) Find out what you *really* want to do. How many times have you had problems with a program and, after spending time solving the problems, found out you were doing the wrong thing in the first place?
2) Break the program into parts that "hold together."
3) Get the parts working, a bit at a time.
4) Try to make sure that any changes in one part will not cause problems in another part.
5) Work hard and make sure that you have backup copies.

The biggest problem is breaking the ideas up and keeping them separate. Subroutines are a way of doing this. In this chapter, we shall look at machine language subroutines, how they are used and their problems and limitations. In order to better understand them, we shall also animate the instructions JSR and RTS.

## THE STACK AND THE STACK POINTER

An important part of the way that a microprocessor is able to handle subroutines is a special part of RAM called the *stack*. For a 6502 microprocessor, this special part of memory is fixed in the first page of memory ($100-$1FF). Its use is helped by a special register called the *Stack Pointer*, or *SP* for short.

You might ask, "What is the stack?" The answer is very simple. It is the "pencil and scrap paper pile" of the machine language programmer. The Stack is a place in memory that the machine language programmer can use to store things for a short while. Just like a pile of scrap paper, the programmer can write things down, which is called *pushing* something onto the Stack. The opposite of pushing is obviously *pulling* things from the Stack. When you pull something you read it from the Stack.

When you are programming, either in machine code or BASIC, you very often have to have a place to store a number. In order that the number can be stored, you have to make a place in memory for it using the DS instruction. This means that every small part of your program has a small area used for storage. That can end up being a lot of memory wasted. It is wasted because those storage areas are only used when that bit of the program is being run.

Why not have all the program parts use the same storage area? That's a valid question. If your program is fairly small, then you will have no problems in doing it. If you have a large program, however, watch out. In BASIC, most people like to call the thing that changes in a FOR..NEXT loop by the name I or J. They do this because there is no need for a special name. This can be nasty. You might just end up doing something like this:

```
Lots and
Lots of
program

30000 FOR I = 1 TO 100
30010 FOR J = 1 TO 100
30020 PAR = I + J : REM PAR is a parameter being
30030 GOSUB 60000 : REM passed to this subroutine
30040 PRINT PAR
30050 NEXT J
30060 NEXT I
30070 STOP

Lots and
Lots of
program

60000 SUM = 0 : REM this program adds all the numbers
60010 FOR I = PAR TO 100 : REM from PAR up to 100
60020 SUM = SUM + I
60030 NEXT I
60040 RETURN
```

Do you think that this program will behave correctly?

The problem here is that the main program is using the variable I and so is the subroutine. This is a very common problem when you are programming and are trying to keep the amount of memory you are using to a minimum. This is where the stack helps. As an example, suppose you have a value stored in the A Register that you want to use in two loops. The equivalent BASIC program would be this:

```
 10 A = 20
 20 FOR I = 1 TO A
 30 K = M + N
 40 .....
100 NEXT I
110 FOR I = 1 TO A
120 .....
200 NEXT I
```

As you can remember, loops can be done in machine code by putting values into the X Register and counting backwards. There are two problems. First how can you get a value from the A Register into the X Register? Second, where can you put the value in the A Register for a short while so that you can do the addition in line 30? After all, only the A Register can be used for an addition. Then you need to get back the old value of the A Register to use in the next loop. The answer is found in four new machine language instructions:

| ASSEMBLY LANGUAGE MNEMONIC | HEX CODE | WHAT THE INSTRUCTION DOES |
|---|---|---|
| TAX | $AA | Transfers (moves) the A register into the X |
| TXA | $8A | Transfers the X register into the A-register |
| PHA | $48 | PusHs the A-register onto the stack. |
| PLA | $68 | PuLls the A register (loads) from the stack |

To see what happens, we need to add these instructions to our assembler instructions.

```
60645 MN$(170) = "TAX" : TYPE%(170) = 5
60655 MN$(138) = "TXA" : TYPE%(138) = 5
```

```
60665 MN$(72) = "PHA" : TYPE%(72) = 5
60675 MN$(104) = "PLA" : TYPE%(104) = 5
```

Make the changes and store as CHAP.15.

Let us try a simple program. We shall load up the X Register and then, using the TXA instruction, move it into the A Register. To show that the transfer really happened, we shall store the contents of the A Register in location $320. The BASIC program would look like this:

```
10 X = 5 : REM load up X
20 A = X : REM do transfer
30 J = A : REM do store
40 STOP
```

In machine code this becomes:

```
$300:          LDX #$5        ; Load up X
$302:          TXA            ; Do transfer
$303:          STA $320       ; Store          (C64 use $C320)
$306:          RTS            ; BASIC return
$307:          BRK
$320:    J     DS 1           ; Make room
```

Try it with the GO command and see that you can do the transfer between the X and A Registers. You can also do transfers between the A and the Y Registers (TAY $A8) or between the Y and the A (TYA $98).

The PHA (push A Register onto the Stack) instruction works very much like the TAX instruction. Instead of moving the A Register into the X Register, they move the value stored in the A Register into the second page of memory. This is exactly the same as doing the instruction

```
STA $1FF
```

except for two things. First, it only takes one memory location for the instruction rather than three. The second is that the computer might not actually put the value in location $1FF. Instead the computer will automatically find the *next* empty space in the memory range $100 to $1FF. Where it goes does not worry us. The microprocessor will always find a space. We don't have to worry about whether that space is or isn't being used by another part of our program. There will never be unused memory bits scattered around our program.

The PLA (pull A Register from stack) instruction works the opposite way to the push instruction. It brings back a value stored on the stack and stores it in the A Register.

Imagine that you are in a cafeteria line with one of those spring-loaded plate stackers. You put plates on the spring and they sink out of view. Take a plate off the spring and the next plate pops up. You have a plate in your hand; write the number 5 on it and put into the spring (Stack). Now take another plate and write a 6 on it and put that onto the spring. Now do the same with the numbers 7 and 8. You now have four plates stacked on the spring. When you want the first one back to use it, you pull the plate off the stack of plates and look at the number. When you want the next number, you pull the next plate off. This is exactly how the stack in a computer works.

In this analogy to a simple program using a stack, you have stored four numbers but never had to set aside any special storage area. Let us write a simple program that puts things onto the Stack and then brings them back. To make sure that things come back correctly, we will need to store them in memory so we can look at them at the end of the program.

```
$300:        LDA #$5        ; Load A with 5
$302:        PHA            ; and store on stack
$303:        LDA #$6        ; Load A with 6
$305:        PHA            ; and store
$306:        LDA #$7        ; Load
$308:        PHA            ; and store
$309:        LDA #$8        ; Load
$30B:        PHA            ; and store
$30D:        NOP
$30E:        PLA            ; Recover
$30F:        STA $330       ; and store  (C64 use $C330)
$312:        PLA            ; Recover
$313:        STA $331       ; and store  (C64 use $C331)
$316:        PLA            ; Recover
$317:        STA $332       ; and store  (C64 use $C332)
$31A:        PLA            ; Recover
$31B:        STA $333       ; and store  (C64 use $C333)
$31E:        NOP
```

```
$31F:          NOP
$320:          NOP
$321:          NOP
$322:          RTS            ; BASIC return
$323:          BRK            ; QUIT
$330:          DS 4           ; Leave room for 4
```

Save this machine language program as DEMO 15.1.OBJ using the new SA (save) command and then use the GO instruction and see what you get.

If you look carefully at what has been stored, you will see that the last thing ($8) stored on the Stack is the first thing pulled off the Stack and placed into location $330.

Unlike storing things in memory, the PLA instruction will actually allow you to pull things off the Stack—even though you have not put things there. Try changing the NOPs into PLAs and see what happens. I can guarantee that you will crash your computer. You see, although you did not put those extra four things on the stack, the monitor did. The monitor program is also using the stack at the same time as you. When you use the GO instruction, the monitor pushes information about where you are in the BASIC program onto the Stack. When you did those extra PLAs, you took away some of the information that the monitor wanted to use. That caused the system crash. You can get exactly the same effect by turning all the PLAs into NOPs. Now you are leaving the monitor more information than it wants. Another crash. Reload DEMO15.1.OBJ and try it.

Remember, just like your parents would have moaned if you did not clean up your room, so will the computer complain (crash) if you don't clean up the Stack after you have used it. You must not leave things on the Stack that were not there when you started. You can't take more things from the Stack than you put there. That's like raiding the fridge. The monitor is bound to notice.

## STACK OPERATIONS: A CLOSER LOOK

To get a better understanding of what happens in the Stack operations, let us animate these instructions. To do this we need three things: an additional register in the register display, a new routine to handle putting things on the Stack, and new pieces of encoding logic. With these changes the internal architecture of the system looks something like Fig. 15-1. Here is the decision logic:

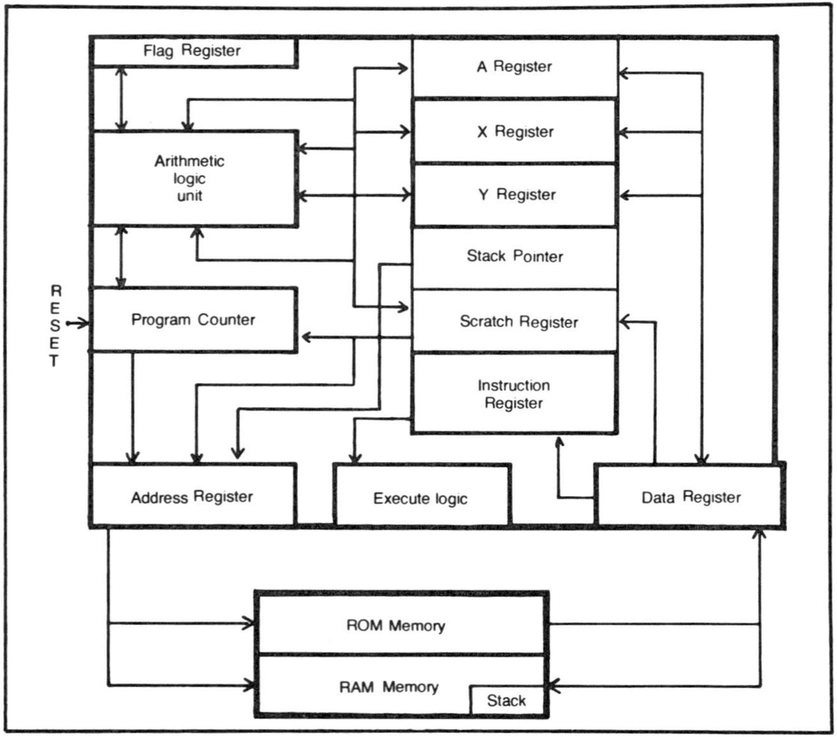


Fig. 15-1. The stack and Stack Pointer.

```
30360 IF IR = 170 THEN 34300 : REM <<tax>>
30370 IF IR = 138 THEN 34400 : REM <<txa>>
30380 IF IR = 72 THEN 34500 : REM <<pha>>
30390 IF IR = 104 THEN 34600 : REM <<pla>>
```

The execution logic:

```
34300 XREG = AREG
34310 ADJUST = XREG : GOSUB 52000: REM  set N and Z flags
34320 RETURN : REM <<end tax>>
34400 AREG = XEG
34410 ADJUST = AREG : GOSUB 52000: REM  set N and Z flags
34420 RETURN : REM <<end txa>>
34500 PUSH = AREG
34510 GOSUB 48000 : REM <<do-push>>
34520 ADJUST = AREG : GOSUB 52000: REM  set N and Z flags
34530 GOSUB 57500 : REM <<display-stack>>
34540 RETURN : REM <<end pha>>
34600 GOSUB 48100 : REM <<do-pull>>
34610 AREG = PULL
34620 ADJUST = AREG : GOSUB 52000: REM  set N and Z flags
34630 RETURN : REM <<end pla>>
```

Special Stack handling subroutines:

```
47990 REM <<add-to-stack>> <<do-push>>
48000 POKE (SP), PUSH : REM store on stack value in PUSH
48010 SP = SP - 1 : REM adjust and then
48020 IF SP < NSAFE - 7 THEN SP = NSAFE
      : REM check that haven't overflowed
48030 RETURN : REM <<end do-push>>
48090 REM  <<remove from stack>> <<do-pull>>
48100 SP = SP + 1 : REM adjust and then check that
48110 IF SP > NSAFE THEN SP = NSAFE - 7 : REM stack okay?
48120 PULL = PEEK (SP)
48130 RETURN : REM <<end do-pull>>
```

Changes to register display:

```
54430 PRINT " SP $";: REM show stack pointer
54440 HEX = SP : GOSUB 58000 : REM <<print-hex-number>>
54450 PRINT
```

We don't want to redisplay all memory in the safe area; that would be too slow. We just need to update the Stack to show the changes in that area. You may have to change the value of DOWN (line 57500) to make sure that the things are printed on the screen in the correct place.

```
57500 DOWN = 15 : GOSUB 61200 : REM <<move down>>
57510 OVER = 7 : GOSUB 61500 : REM <<move-over>>
57520 FOR NUM = (NSAFE - 7) TO NSAFE
57530 HEX = PEEK(NUM) : GOSUB 58000 : REM <<print-hex>>
57540 PRINT " ";
57550 NEXT NUM
57560 RETURN : REM <<end print-stack>>
```

Set the Stack Pointer to the top of the Stack. We shall use the last eight locations in our safe area as our Stack for the animation.

```
61015 SP = NSAFE
```

After saving this BASIC program as CHAP.15, let's look at what we have done:

1) We have set aside the last eight locations of the safe area for our Stack.
2) We have got the Stack Pointer pointing to the top of the stack.
3) We have made sure that if the Stack Pointer starts pointing outside the stack, then it is adjusted to point to the start of the stack. (Lines 53520 and 55010). This happens on the real stack which has the same "wraparound" feature.
4) Because putting something onto the stack is so important, we have redisplayed the memory used by the stack.

In "real life" the stack is 256 locations starting at $100 and ending at $1FF. We can't use the real stack, because BASIC is using it all the time. The wraparound feature of the real stack can cause real problems when we use machine language programs.

If you reload the machine language program you saved, DEMO15.1.OBJ then you will be able to see what happens as things get put on the stack. First the number is put onto the stack and the Stack Pointer is decreased. Then the next number is pushed onto the stack and the Stack Pointer is decreased. This means the

Stack Pointer is always pointing to the next empty space. To PULL something from the stack, the Stack Pointer is increased, and then the number is taken from that bit of memory. By watching the animation, you can see our small stack in action. As you might be expecting, the stack plays a very important part in subroutines.

## THE STACK AND SUBROUTINES

Let's take a look at some BASIC code that needs to be changed into subroutines.

```
 10 A = 2
 20 B = A + 2
 30 B = B + A * 3
 40 PRINT A, B
 50 A = 3
 60 B = A + 2
 70 B = B + A * 3
 80 PRINT A, B
 90 A = 4
100 B = A + 2
110 B = B + A * 3
120 PRINT A, B
130 STOP
```

In this program, A is changed in three places (10, 50, 90) and exactly the same things are done using A in the next three lines. We can see that there are three lines repeated three times.

Repeating lines is bad programming practice for two reasons: it wastes memory, and repeated code means extra places to make mistakes. The second reason is the most important; if you have three large pieces of repeated code, then you have two more places to make mistakes that you will have to debug.

We can improve things by moving the repeated lines to lines 100 on and use GOTO statements.

```
10 A = 2
20 GOTO 100
30 A = 3
40 GOTO 100
50 A = 4
60 GOTO 100
70 STOP
```

```
100 B = A + 2
110 B = B + A * 2
120 PRINT A, B
130 GOTO 30
```

Here's how this works. Line 10 sets A and then jumps to 100 for the calculation. Then line 130 jumps back to line 30 to reset A. Line 40 jumps to 100 for the calculation, and the process continues. If the calculation were longer, then we would really save space. You can see that the GOTO statement allows us to reuse the calculation.

Everything is wonderful except for one thing: the routine does not work. It works the first two times, but not the third. The line 130 always jumps back to line 30. What we want is a technique that changes line 130 so that it will jump back to line 30 the first time it is used and line 50 the next time it is used. To get this to work, somewhere in memory there must be a place used to remember where to jump back to. This remembering is done by the monitor when we use GOSUB and RETURN statements.

```
 10 A = 2
 20 GOSUB 100
 30 A = 3
 40 GOSUB 100
 50 A = 4
 60 GOSUB 100
 70 STOP
100 B = A + 2
110 B = B + A * 2
120 PRINT A, B
130 RETURN
```

This version of the program works the way we want.

We can now expand our machine language instruction set to encompass two new, useful instructions.

| ASSEMBLY LANGUAGE MNEMONIC | HEX CODE | WHAT THE INSTRUCTION DOES |
|---|---|---|
| JSR | $20 | Does the equivalent to a BASIC GOSUB |
| RTS | $60 | Does the equivalent to a BASIC RETURN |

In machine language programming there is the same need for

subroutines. The thing that does the equivalent to a BASIC GOSUB is called a JSR or *jump to subroutine* instruction. The RETURN statement in BASIC becomes RTS or *return from subroutine.* Reload the program CHAP.15 so we can add the JSR to our assembler.

```
60685 MN$(32) = "JSR" : TYPE%(32) = 2
```

Remember to resave the modified program.

Let us try out our instruction with a machine language program that does the same as this BASIC program:

```
 10 A = 0 : REM clear A
 20 GOSUB 100
 30 GOSUB 100
 40 GOSUB 100
 50 J = A : REM store A for examination
 60 STOP
100 A = A + 1
110 RETURN
```

It is not a very exciting program but it does demonstrate nicely the use of subroutines and returns. In our machine code, we will put the storage location J at $330 and our subroutine at $320.

Using the A (assemble) instruction, load this program:

```
$300:        LDA #$0        ; Clear A
$302:        JSR $320       ; GOSUB
$305:        JSR $320
$308:        JSR $320
$30B:        STA $330       ; Store A at $330
$30E:        RTS            ; BASIC return
$30F:        BRK            ; Quit
```

Use the A instruction again, to load the subroutine. We had to use the A instruction twice because the subroutine and the main program don't touch in memory.

```
$320:        CLC            ; Clear Carry
$321:        ADC #$1        ; A = A + 1
$324:        RTS            ; RETURN
```

Use the SA (save) instruction to save this program as

DEMO15.2.OBJ, using $300 as a starting address and $324 as an end address.

This is what will happen when you use the GO instruction. The A Register will be cleared and the program will jump to the subroutine, where 1 will be added to the A Register. When the RTS (RETURN) in location $324 is executed, then the program will jump back to the main program.

The JSR (GOSUB) will be done twice more before the A Register is saved so that we can examine it. When the RTS at $30E is reached, more values are taken from the stack. This causes the program to jump back into ROM. Once in ROM, instructions will be found that take more values from the stack, allowing us to jump properly back to our BASIC program.

Before using the GO instruction, check that you have entered the program correctly using the D (dissassemble) instruction. Your memory should look like Figs. 15-2 or 15-3.

When we are programming in machine language, we must take great care that we don't accidentally disturb the stack. If we do, our

```
                        ! IR $00 PC $00
                        ! DR $00 AR $00
C D I N V Z             !        SC $0000
? ? ? ? ? ?             ! X  $00 Y  $00
                        ! A  $00 SP $033F
                        !-----------------

MEMORY STARTING AT $0300
0300: A9 00 20 20 03 20 20 03
0308: 20 20 03 60 00 00 00 00
0310: 00 00 00 00 00 00 00 00
0318: 00 00 00 00 00 00 00 00
0320: 18 69 01 60 00 00 00 00
0328: 00 00 00 00 00 00 00 00
0330: 00 00 00 00 00 00 00 00
0338: 00 00 00 00 00 00 00 00



TYPE 'HELP FOR COMMANDS
YOUR WISH, MASTER?
```

Fig. 15-2. A machine language program demonstrating the use of the stack.

```
                              ! IR $00 PC $00
                              ! DR $00 AR $00
C D I N V Z                   !           SC $0000
? ? ? ? ? ?                   ! X  $00  Y  $00
                              ! A  $00  SP $C33F
                              !------------------------

MEMORY STARTING AT $C300
C300: A9 00 20 20 C3 20 20 C3
C308: 20 20 C3 60 00 00 00 00
C310: 00 00 00 00 00 00 00 00
C318: 00 00 00 00 00 00 00 00
C320: 18 69 01 60 00 00 00 00
C328: 00 00 00 00 00 00 00 00
C330: 00 00 00 00 00 00 00 00
C338: 00 00 00 00 00 00 00 00

TYPE 'HELP' FOR COMMANDS
YOUR WISH, MASTER?
```

Fig. 15-3. Using the stack with the Commodore 64.

program will behave very strangely when we use subroutines. To see why this happens, we must animate our two new instructions. The decision logic follows:

```
30400 IF IR = 32 THEN 34700 : REM <<jsr>>
30410 IF IR = 96 THEN 34800 : REM <<rts>>
```

The execution logic is coded thus:

```
34700 PUSH = INT (PC / 256) : REM find HIBYTE of PC
34710 GOSUB 48000 : REM <<push onto stack>>
34720 PUSH = PC - 256 * INT (PC/256) : REM find LOBYTE
34730 GOSUB 48000 : REM <<push-onto-stack>>
34740 SC = PEEK(PC) : REM get the next memory location
34750 PC = PC + 1
34760 SC = PEEK(PC) * 256 + SC : REM complete the address
34770 PC = SC : REM change the PROGRAMME COUNTER
34780 GOSUB 57500 : REM <<display memory changes in the stack>>
34790 RETURN : REM <<end jsr>>
```

```
34800 GOSUB 48100 : REM <<pull-from-stack>>
34810 SC = PULL : REM store value pulled in scratch register
34820 GOSUB 48100 : REM <<pull-from-stack>>
34830 SC = PULL * 256 + SC
      : REM last thing used BEFORE JSR happened
34840 PC = SC + 2 : REM PC now points to instruction AFTER jsr
34850 RETURN : REM <<end RTS>>
```

Save this program as CHAP15.

If you look carefully at both of these instructions you will see that they are almost exactly the same as a jump instruction. The jump instruction gets the place to which it will jump from the two locations in memory. The JSR instruction does that too. However, before the JSR instruction finds out where to jump, it stores (remembers) where it currently is on the stack. The RTS instruction also gets its jump target by using memory. However, in this case, the "memory" is in the stack.

To better understand what is happening, use the CL instruction, load up the machine language program DEMO15.2 OBJ, and use the W instruction. Notice how the values on the stack change. The reason for this is that the stored numbers are the place to which the program must jump back after doing the subroutine. The values that the JSR instruction puts on the stack are called the *return address*.

In the next chapter, we shall be using a lot of subroutine calls to enable us to use more of the ROM programs stored in the computer. With the JSR and RTS, we have added the last of the instructions for animation.

**Notes:**

1) There is the need for clearing the memory before loading the program because otherwise the RTS instruction at $30E will not work properly in our animation. Why? (Hint: think about what the RTS instruction at location $30E will do with the stack wraparound.)
2) In line 34430, 2 was added to the Program Counter to get it to go to the next instruction. In a 6502 microprocessor, the value stored on the stack happens to be 1 larger than what we store. When the real microprocessor does this EXECUTE logic, it only needs to add 1. The technique described here for JSR and RTS is, therefore, off by 1 from the real microprocessor. This was done in the animation to make things easier to program in BASIC.

# Chapter 16

# The UnBASIC Instructions

In the previous chapters we have looked at machine language instructions that were equivalent to BASIC statements. There are, however, a number of machine language instructions for which there are no simple equivalents. These additional functions are often used to help in the translation or encoding of things in memory. They also have a number of unexpected uses, which you will find when you read magazine articles. We shall examine six of these instructions.

1) AND and BIT instructions allow the machine language programmer to determine whether or not certain bits in the Accumulator or memory locations are set.
2) ORA instructions allow the setting of certain bits in the Accumulator or a memory location.
3) LSR and ASL are *shifting* instructions. The *logical shift right* (LSR) instruction is approximately the same as a "divide by 2" instruction, while the *arithmetic shift left* (ASL) is approximately the same as a "multiply by 2" instruction.
4) EOR is a rather difficult instruction to describe in a few words. The *exclusive OR* instruction is an instruction similar to the AND and ORA instructions. However, instead of determining whether certain bits in a word are set, it looks at the *differences* between things.

Here is our summary of the new machine language instructions:

| ASSEMBLY LANGUAGE MNEMONIC | HEX CODE | DESCRIPTION OF INSTRUCTION |
|---|---|---|
| AND #$%% | $29 | AND's number $%% with A Register |
| AND $%%%% | $2D | AND's location $%%%% with A Register |
| AND $%%%%X | $3D | AND's location ($%%%% +X) with A Register |
| AND $%%%%,Y | $39 | AND's location ($%%%% + Y) with A Register |
| BIT $%%%% | $2C | AND's location $%%%% with A Register without storing the result |
| ORA #$%% | $09 | OR's number $%% with A Register |
| ORA $%%%% | $0D | OR's location $%%%% with A Register |
| ORA $%%%%,X | $1D | OR's location ($%%%% +X) with A Register |
| ORA $%%%%,Y | $19 | OR's location ($%%%% + Y) with A Register |
| EOR #$%% | $49 | EOR's number $%% with A Register |
| EOR $%%%% | $4D | EOR's location $%%%% with A Register |
| EOR $%%%%,X | $59 | EOR's location ($%%%% + X) with A Register |
| EOR $%%%%,Y | $5D | EOR's location ($%%%% + Y) with A Register |
| ASL | $0A | Arithmetic Shift Left the A Register |
| ASL $%%%% | $0E | Arithmetic Shift Left location $%%%% |
| LSR | $4A | Logical Shift Right the A Register |
| LSR $%%%% | $4E | Logical Shift Right location $%%%% |

Before proceeding with these instructions, let us add them all to CHAP.15. These are the last things needed in our assembler/disassembler commands. We now have all the major instructions needed but one. This instruction RTI or *return from interrupt* is an instruction needed when you are trying to make the computer handle two or three things that happen at the same time. This is needed when you are trying to get data (numbers) quickly from a device attached to your computer. Enough said. If you need more information, then take a look at some of the books mentioned in the Appendix.

```
60695 MN$(41) = "AND" : TYPE%(41) = 1 : REM <<and #$%%>>
60705 MN$(45) = "AND" : TYPE%(45) = 2 : REM <<and $%%%%>>
60715 MN$(61) = "AND" : TYPE%(61) = 9 : REM <<and $%%%%,x>>
60725 MN$(39) = "AND" : TYPE%(39) = 10 : REM <<and $%%%%,y>>
60735 MN$(44) = "BIT" : TYPE%(44) = 2 : REM <<bit $%%%%>>

60745 MN$(9) = "ORA" : TYPE%(9) = 1 : REM <<ora #$%%>>
60755 MN$(13) = "ORA" : TYPE%(13) = 2 : REM <<ora $%%%%>>
60765 MN$(29) = "ORA" : TYPE%(29) = 9 : REM <<ora $%%%%,x>>
60775 MN$(25) = "ORA" : TYPE%(25) = 10 : REM <<ora $%%%%,y>>

60785 MN$(73) = "EOR" : TYPE%(73) = 1 : REM <<eor #$%%>>
60795 MN$(78) = "EOR" : TYPE%(78) = 2 : REM <<eor $%%%%>>
60805 MN$(89) = "EOR" : TYPE%(89) = 9 : REM <<eor $%%%%,x>>
60815 MN$(93) = "EOR" : TYPE%(93) = 10 : REM <<eor $%%%%,y>>

60825 MN$(74) = "LSR" : TYPE%(74) = 5 : REM <<lsr a-reg>>
60835 MN$(90) = "LSR" : TYPE%(90) = 2 : REM <<lsr $%%%%>>

60845 MN$(10) = "ASL" : TYPE%(10) = 5 : REM <<asl a-reg>>
60855 MN$(14) = "ASL" : TYPE%(14) = 2 : REM <<asl $%%%%>>
```

In the assembler program, if an instruction started with a B it was a branch instruction. The new instruction BIT starts with a B but is not a branch. We need to put in a patch to make sure that the BIT instruction is treated correctly.

```
47415 IF MID$(ANS$,1,3) = "BIT" THEN 47600
        : REM branch patch
```

Save this program as PROGRAM. It is now complete.

Although it has taken a lot of effort in getting all the animation and software tools loaded, I hope that you will have thought it worthwhile and that it has helped your understanding of what machine language instructions do. Now let's look at things in greater detail.

## THE *AND* AND *BIT* INSTRUCTIONS

These two instructions act as "windows" into a memory word.

Imagine there is a house where some rooms have windows and some rooms don't. If you are outside the house, how could you find out what is in a room? The obvious answer is to look into a window. Those rooms without a window remain a mystery.

Let's look at the instruction AND #$F. In computerese this means AND the A Register with the *mask* $F. In English, it is a bit simpler. Let us suppose that the A Register contains a $C8 (or %1100 1000). The instruction AND #$F says, "Look at what is in the A Register using the window $F or binary %00001111." Where there is a 1 in the window, the curtains are open and we can look into the computer house (word); where there is 0 in the window, the curtains are closed.

This is what will happen:

```
A - register      $C8   % 1 1 0 0 1 0 0 0
MASK (window)     $0F   % 0 0 0 0 1 1 1 1

Curtains open                   ^ ^ ^ ^

RESULT            $08   % 0 0 0 0 1 0 0 0
```

The result of AND #$F is $08 in the case and is stored back into the A Register.

You can see why it is called an AND instruction. The result is only a 1 if the window AND and the A Register have a 1 in them. The AND instruction is very useful when using the D flag. When the D flag is set, two decimal numbers are stored in each memory location. If we use the AND instruction we can separate out the two numbers and put them into separate memory locations. We can find the bottom number if we use a window of $0F, and the top number using a mask of $F0. Here's a simple program to demonstrate this. Use the CL instruction and load this program using the A command.

```
$300:       SED          ; Set the Decimal flag
$301:       LDA $320     ; Get a number stored in $320
$304:       AND #$F      ; MASK with %00001111
$306:       STA $321     ; Store LO-NYBBLE in $321
$309:       LDA $320     ; Re-get the number stored in $320
$30C:       AND #$F0     ; MASK with %11110000
$30F:       STA $322     ; Store HI-NYBBLE in $322
$312:       CLD          ; Clear decimal flag before
                           BASIC return
$313:       RTS          ; BASIC return
$320:       DS 1         ; Starting Number
```

```
$321:            DS 1            ; LO-NYBBLE storage
$322:            DS 1            ; HI-NYBBLE storage
```

Save this machine language program as DEMO16.1.0BJ, using $300 as a start address and $313 as the end address. Before using the GO instruction to get the program to execute, use the CH instruction to load $28 into location $320. When the program is complete, you should find that the low-nybble of $28, which is $08, will be stored in location $321, while the high nybble, $20 will be in location $322. Try using other numbers in location $320.

The instructions AND $300 and BIT $300 both "AND" the contents of the A Register with what is stored in location $300. The big difference is that the AND instruction stores the result back into the A Register, while the BIT instruction does not execute the store. This is exactly the difference between the CMP (compare) and the SBC (subtract with carry) instructions. To see what happens, suppose that the A Register contains $F0 (%11110000) and that location $300 contains $06 (%00000110)

```
Starting value in A-register  $F0      %11110000
Value in location $300        $06      %00000110

Result of window              $00      %00000000

A-register after AND $300     $00      %00000000
Flags set                                          N clear, Z set

A-register after BIT $300     $F0      %11110000
Flags set                                          N clear, Z set
```

There are two things to notice. First, the A Register is changed after the AND instruction but not after the BIT instruction. Second, the flags show the result of using the window and *not* what is left in the A Register. After the BIT instruction, the A Register contains a number that is negative and not zero. However, the flags show that the result of using the window was a number that was zero.

## ANOTHER USE OF *AND*

The AND and a mask can provide another sort of useful instruction. Our animation uses a display that has a carriage return every eight memory locations. In BASIC we could do something like this:

```
10 FOR J = 1 TO 63
20 IF J <> 8 * INT ( J / 8) THEN 40
30 PRINT
40 NEXT J
```

If J is 15 then the program calculates

8 * INT(J/8) = 8 * INT(1.875) = 8.

This means that line 30 does not get done. If, on the other hand, J = 16, then the program calculates

8 * INT(J/8) = 8 * INT(2) = 16

so that the PRINT in line 30 is done.

Using the mask $07 and the AND instruction, we can do something similar. All numbers that can be divided by 8 have no bits set in the last three bits of the word

```
CAN BE                    CAN'T BE
DIVIDED                   DIVIDED
BY 8                      BY 8
16  %00010000             15  %00001111
48  %00110000             50  %00110010
```

This means that if we use the AND instruction we can check to see if the A Register has a value that can be divided by 8. If the value in the A Register is like 16 or 48, the result of doing an instruction such as AND #$7 will be zero and the Z flag will be set.

```
A Register        A Register
Before AND        After AND

16 %00010000      00 %00000000
48 %00110000      00 %00000000
```

On the other hand, if the number is like 15 or 50, then after doing AND #$7, the answer will not be zero and the Z flag will be clear.

```
A Register        A Register
Before AND        After AND

15 %00001111      07 %00000111
50 %00110010      02 %00000010
```

We can use the BEQ instruction to cause a JSR to a <<print-a-carriage-return>> subroutine whenever the AND #$7 gave a zero answer. That would give us a carriage return every eighth number.

Unfortunately, this technique only works if you want to check that something is an even multiple of 2. Just the same, it is a useful technique. Write a program that loops 12 times and stores a number in memory, provided that the loop variable is an odd number. Make sure you use the AND instruction.

## THE *ORA* INSTRUCTION

The ORA (OR with A Register) instruction treats the bits inside a word just as if they were switches. The ORA instruction allows the machine language programmer to set any bit inside the word.

Consider the instruction ORA #$80. Suppose that the A Register contains a $4 or %00000100 pattern and we use the ORA #$80 instruction. This is what will happen. Any bit that is set in either the A Register *OR* in the mask pattern (the $80, %10000000) will be set in the final answer.

```
A-register before   $04    %000001000
Mask                $80    %100000000

Switches to set             ^    ^

A-register after    $84    %100001000
```

If the bit is set in both of them, then the answer will also have that bit set. For example, suppose that we use the ORA #$26 instruction when the A Register contains $35.

```
A-register before   $35    %00110101
Mask                $26    %00100110

Switches to set               ^^ ^^^

A-Register after    $37    %00110111
```

## THE *EOR* INSTRUCTION

This is a very useful command that is used a lot in graphics. The EOR instruction is very much like the ORA in the way it acts. However, the result is the *exclusive* OR between the A Register and something. The ORA instruction leaves a result with a bit set if either the A Register has a bit set and/or the other thing has a bit set. The EOR instruction leaves the result with a bit set if the A Register has a bit set or the other thing has a bit set—*but not both.* For example, suppose the A Register contains $35.

```
                              ORA #$26          EOR #$26

A-register before   $35      %00110101         %00110101
Mask                $26      %00100110         %00100110

                                ^^ ^^^             x^ x^^

A-Register after    $37      %00110111         %00010011  $13
```

The reason that the EOR instruction is used in graphics is that it has the special ability to change things in such a way that changing them a second time brings the old thing back. Many computers store graphics in RAM as a pattern. When you draw something on the screen, like an "invader" shape, it is very simple to draw it. However, what happens if you want to remove it so that you can draw it somewhere else? The steps in the way games make things move are

1) Undraw the image.
2) Work out what you have removed from the background by removing the image.
3) Redraw the background.

As you can imagine, if you have a complex background working out how to redraw can take a lot of time. If you take time in redrawing something, your game slows down. Not good. Let us see where the EOR instruction comes in. Suppose that the RAM in your computer from $800 to $900 is used for drawing graphics. If you use an instruction like STA $850, which stores something in the graphics RAM, then the screen changes. Now suppose you want to make a mark on the screen (for a cursor, say). Then a short while later you want to remove the cursor. This is what you could do.

```
1)      LDA $850        ; Get the screen value
2)      EOR #$FF        ; Make a mark
3)      STA $850        ; and show it

.....               ; many other things to be done
```

```
200)    LDA $850         ; Get the marked screen value
201)    EOR #$FF         ; and unmark it
202)    STA $850         ; and show it
```

In this program, we have applied an exclusive or (EOR) to the A Register with the mask $FF, which is %11111111 in binary. Suppose that, before the first instruction, location $850 had a value of $C8 (%11001000). Let's look at what happens:

```
before 1)     $C8        %11001000
Mask          $FF        %11111111

                          xx^^x^^^

after 3)      $37        %00110111
```

You can see that the screen was showing something that was stored as $C8 and it becomes $37. That means a change will appear. Now look what happens at instruction $200

```
before  200)    $37          %00110111
Mask            $FF          %11111111

                               ^^xx^xxx

after   202)    $C8          %11001000
```

We have changed back to the value we had to start with by using the EOR instruction a second time. Notice that we had no idea what caused the $C8 to be on the screen. It could be part of a complex picture of a battleship or part of a piece of snow. All that matters is that we marked the screen and then, with no calculation, unmarked it.

*Question: Can you write a small machine language program that loads the A Register with a number and then uses the AND, ORA, and EOR instructions on that number?* Store the result so that you can compare what happens with each of these different instructions.

## THE *LSR* and *ASL* INSTRUCTIONS

These two instructions cause the bits in a word to be moved or shifted. The LSR or *logical shift right* moves the bits to the right; the ASL or *arithmetic shift left* moves the bits to the left. The effect of the LSR instruction is the same as dividing the contents of memory or the A Register by 2. The remainder is stored in the C flag. The ASL instruction is the same as multiplying by 2, with the carry being stored in the C flag. Each of the instructions acts on the A Registers. You can see the effect of these instructions below.

| A-register before | After LSR | C-flag | After ASL | C-flag |
|---|---|---|---|---|
| $80 %10000000 | $40 %01000000 | (clear) | $00 %00000000 | (set) |
| $35 %00110101 | $1A %00011010 | (set) | $6A %01101010 | (clear) |
| $CD %11001101 | $66 %01100110 | (set) | $9A %10011010 | (set) |

Because these instructions set the C flag, they can be used in checking (with the BCC and the BCS instructions) that things are transmitted between computers correctly. When you are using a *modem,* you are sending letters between computers. The letters are encoded using the numbers $00 to $7F (0-127 decimal). This means that only seven bits of the word are used. When the word is transmitted, noise on the telephone line might change what bits are set in word. This means that one computer might send the letter A which is (%01000001) and one bit gets set by noise to give %01010001. This is the letter Q. How can the receiving computer know whether it has or has not received the correct thing?

The answer is *parity.* The sending computer puts something in the high bit (the unused 7th one) to help the receiving computer determine whether or not an error has occurred. The simplest check is to add up all the bits that are set in the word to be transmitted. Then the extra, 8th bit is set to make the total number of bits be an even number. The receiving computer can check how many bits are set in the received word. If the total number is even, then the word has been received correctly. This is called *even parity.*

| Original Letter | Bits set | Parity bit needs setting? | Final word |
|---|---|---|---|
| A %01000001 | 2 | no | %01000001 |
| B %01000010 | 2 | no | %01000010 |
| C %01000011 | 3 | yes | %11000011 |
| D %01000100 | 2 | no | %01000100 |
| E %01000110 | 3 | yes | %11000110 |
| F %01000111 | 4 | no | %01000111 |
| G %01001000 | 2 | no | %01001000 |

Suppose that the receiving computer receives the following message:

```
$42 $41 $C4
```

Was it correctly received? To check, the computer has to look at the total number of bits set in each word.

| Byte received | Bits set | Okay? |
|---|---|---|
| $42 %01000010 | 2 | very likely |
| $41 %01000001 | 2 | very likely |
| $C4 %11000100 | 3 | DEFINITLY wrong |

The third byte received is definitely wrong. Either an extra bit has been set *or* a bit that was set has been cleared. We know this because the sending computer made sure that an even number of bits were set before transmitting the word. Notice that the other two things received are "very likely" to be correct. We are not absolutely sure. It is possible that *two* things have been changed such that the errors they produce cancel out.

Suppose that the chance of a bit being changed is 1 in 10,000. Then the chances of two bits being changed is (1 in 10,000) times (1 in 10,000), or 1 in 100,000,000. The chance that two things have changed to cancel out is 1 in 200,000,000. You can see that the chances of receiving something wrong is quite small. If you transmit a large amount of data, however, this check is not enough. Other checks have to be added.

## SETTING AND CHECKING PARITY

To show the use of the LSR instruction, we need to write two machine language programs for parity. The first one is the program inside the sending computer. It adds the parity bit. The second program is inside the receiving computer. It checks the parity and then removes it, so that things are back to the way that a computer normally stores letters, using seven bits.

Suppose that the character to be sent is already stored in location $330.

```
$300:   LDA $330        ; Get the letter   (C64 use $C330)
$303:   PHA             ; Store letter on the STACK
$304:   LDY #$7         ; Need to check 7 bits
```

```
$306:   LDX #$0        ; Clear the X-register. Used for
                         counting
$308:   LSR            ; Use LSR to shift low bit into
                         the C-flag
$309:   BCC $30C       ; BRANCH if C-flag clear (C64 use $C30C)
$30B:   INX            ; Add 1 to X-register (low bit was set)
$30C:   DEY            ; Do more?
$30D:   BNE $308       ;  (C64 use $C308)
$30E:   TXA            ; Need to look at number of bits set
$30F:   AND #$1        ; is low bit set ?
$311:   BEQ $317       ; NO!! no need to add parity then
                        (C64 use $C317)
$313:   PUL            ; get back letter from STACK
$314:   ORA #$80       ; set the hi-bit
$316:   PHA            ; put back onto STACK
$317:   PUL            ; word on STACK has the correct parity
$318:   JSR $????      ; go send the word
$31B:   RTS            ; do return
```

Notice that we have used a large number of instructions here. We have used LSR to allow checking of the low bit ($308), and to check if there is an odd number of bits set ($30F), and ORA to force the high bit to be set ($314).

If you want to check that this program actually does set the parity correctly, change $318 to read

```
$318:   STA $331                 (C64 use $C331)
```

That will store the fixed (parity-correct) number in location $331. Use the CH instruction and load a number into location $330. Now use GO instruction and see if it works.

The checking routine is very similar, but we will introduce a new technique: passing parameters in machine code. When we use subroutines, we often need to pass things and bring things out of the subroutine. The most convenient way of doing this is by placing things in the A, X, and Y Registers. That way we can pass things very easily. Many of the ROM subroutines used by BASIC do just this. If you want to put a letter on the screen, you load up the A Register with the thing you want displayed and then jump to the <<display-screen>> ROM routine. The A Register is used here for passing the parameter. There is no guarantee that, when you return from the <<display-screen>> ROM routine, the A Register will have the same thing in it you first put there. You must be careful about this if you make use of the ROM routines in your machine language programs.

Let's suppose that the ROM routine at $XXXX is a <<get-letter-from-modem>> routine that puts the letter it gets from the modem into the A Register. Our checking program will look something like this:

```
$300:  JSR $XXXX    ; <<get-letter-from-modem>>
$303:  PHA          ; store letter on the stack
$304:  LDY #$8      ; Need to check 8 bits (not 7)
$306:  LDX #$0      ; Clear the X-register.
$308:  LSR          ; LSR to shift low bit into the C-flag
$309:  BCC $30C     ; BRANCH if C-flag clear (C64 use $C30C)
$30B:  INX          ; Add 1 to X-register (low bit was set)
$30C:  DEY          ; Do more?
$30D:  BNE $308     ; (C64 use $C308)
$30E:  TXA          ; Need to look at number of bits set
$30F:  AND #$1      ; is low bit set ?
$311:  BEQ $317     ; If no the parity okay (C64 use $C317)
$313:  PUL          ; get back letter from STACK
$314:  JSR $????    ; Go do error
$316:  RTS          ; do return back to calling routine
$317:  PUL          ; word on STACK has the correct parity
$318:  AND #$7F     ; remove parity bit
$31A:  STA $331     ; store valid thing (C64 use $C331)
$31D:  RTS          ; do return
```

In this program we have assumed a subroutine at $XXXX that fetches a number, as well as a routine at $???? that handles things when they are received incorrectly. What happens in this subroutine depends on the programmer.

To test the program using the GO instruction, we need to make a couple of changes. Using the CH instruction, load location $330 with a number whose parity you want to check. Now change these instructions:

```
$300:  LDA $330     ; get the thing to check  (C64 use $C330)
$314:  STA $332     ; store bad thing         (C64 use $C332)
```

With this version of the program, the machine code will pick up a number from location $330. If the number has valid parity, it will be stored in location $331 with the parity bit removed. If the number has invalid parity, it will be stored in location $332.

Once again we have made use of a number of the new instructions. LSR was used to load the C flag with the low bit of the word. This enables checking to occur ($308). We used AND in two ways. At location $30F, we used it to check if the last bit of the A Register was set. At location $318, we used it to remove or *mask off* the parity bit. Notice, we did not check to see if it needed removing, that would take extra steps. Instead we used the AND instruction to remove the high bit—whether it was there or not.

### PASSING PARAMETERS TO BASIC ROM ROUTINES

The ROM routines stored in your computer are very useful if you can find out exactly what they need in order to be used. You will need to search magazines and books for information. The manuals that come with your computer are probably designed for people interested in BASIC and not for the machine code specialist you have become. The magazines listed in the Appendix can provide very useful information and machine code programs.

When you are using a ROM routine, this is the sort of information you will need to know:

1) Where does the routine start?
2) Does it need registers with special numbers in them?
3) What special memory locations need special things stored in them?
4) After the routine, do the registers and memory locations have the old values left in them, so that the values can be used again?
5) Does anything need to be done to the stack or is it left in a correct state?
6) How can you get back to BASIC?

These are the major things that you need to ask yourself. If the author of the program has provided enough documentation, you should not have too many problems.

# Chapter 17
# Faster and Faster

In previous chapters we have talked about getting a program to work in the shortest possible time and to GO or operate as quickly as possible. The animation program is probably the biggest BASIC program that many of us have ever written. Some parts of it work far too slowly. Let us try out some techniques to see if they really make the program operate more quickly.

## TIMING STANDARDS

If we are going to see if the techniques really make for better speed, we need something to compare against. There are three major areas that look suitable for speeding up and testing.

1) Timing 1, the time from typing RUN until the program is ready to accept a command. This covers making up all the variables.
2) Timing 2, the time to rewrite the memory display. This can be easily timed if we enter the command ST (stop) and then type *NO*.
3) Timing 3, the time taken to assemble 6 NOPs typed in as fast as possible.

The times given in the rest of the chapter are the times my program needs on an Apple II+. You can use the time given to compare to what your machine takes.

**Timing 1.** Load the program but don't run it. Now type RUN and time how long it takes before the menu selection question appears. My time is 11 seconds.

**Timing 2.** Probably the slowest thing of our program is how fast the memory display appears. Type the command ST. Then enter the letter N for no. This will cause the memory display to be remade. Time how long that takes. Mine generally takes 5 seconds.

**Timing 3.** Type the A (assembler) command and type 6 NOPs as fast as the program will accept them. If possible, don't wait for the program to finish the previous one. This way you cut out the time needed to type things in. My usual time is 21 seconds.

## PREPLANNING

We have already applied some "go-fast" techniques to get a program working in the shortest possible time. We have done the following things:

1) Made the program into modules or subroutines that could be easily tested.
2) Made sure that the subroutines did not affect each other by keeping different variables for the subroutines.
3) Got all the variables together at the start of the program to make sure that we did not get into problems by having two variables with the names accidentally the same. Remember that in most BASICs only the first two letters count.
4) Used plenty of REM statements so that we could follow and better understand what each program part was trying to do. Then, when it did not do what it was supposed to, we could more easily find out why.
5) Made use of software tools. In the animation program we developed software tools to allow us to make machine language programming easier. However there are software tools designed especially for entering BASIC programs.

When I enter the program I use a *Global Program Line Editor* (GPLE). The global program line editor works like a word processor on my BASIC program. A lot of the lines were almost repeats of other lines. I didn't retype them. Instead I used my GPLE to make extra copies of the lines and then made the small changes necessary. On a CBM machine, you can achieve the same effect by using screen editing. Using the GPLE program, I could also change the names of variables easily. The command

```
EDIT 0,60000,"START","BEGIN"/R
```

allowed me to change all occurrences of "START" into "BEGIN".

Even if you start with BASIC line numbers far apart, you can find that errors in your thoughts can make the line numbers get too close together. A renumbering program helps by automatically changing the line numbers to larger numbers. It does this by moving the lines around and changing all the GOTO and GOSUB statements to point to the new lines.

## INITIALIZATION

In Chapter 1 I made the comment that it was important to make room for all the variables you use before making room for the arrays like TYPE%( ). I said that although the monitor program would automatically make room, the program runs faster if *you* do it. Here's proof. Type in the following simple program and time how long it takes between the start and the end.

```
20 PRINT "START"
30 DIM A(400) : REM make first array
40 J = 1 : PRINT J
50 DIM B(400) : REM make second array
60 K = 2 : PRINT K
70 DIM C(400)
80 L = 3 : PRINT L
90 M = 4 : PRINT M
100 DIM D(400) : REM make last array
110 N = 5 : PRINT N
120 PRINT "END"
130 STOP
```

This is a typical program where you use arrays and numbers as you need them, with no preplanning. Write down the time needed for it to execute. Now add this one line, which makes room for all the variables.

```
10 J = 0 : K = 0 : L = 0 : M =0 : N = 0
```

Time it again, after making room.

Makes quite a difference, doesn't it? Although this technique of making room speeds things up, it is only important at the start of a program. Once the program has used all the variables once, no further increases in speed occur.

Why the change in speed? It is the way the monitor has to handle BASIC. In memory, the monitor stores things as shown in Fig. 17-1. Notice how everything is in layers, like a chocolate cake.

To see why things get slow when you don't make all the room for variables, let us suppose that the monitor has made room for variables J and K from our program, and is about to make room for C(400). Where will it put it? Well, all new things go at the end. At

| | |
|---|---|
| ------------- | start of memory |
| ZERO PAGE | special pointers |
| FIRST PAGE | stack |
| POINTERS | |
| BASIC PROGRAM | our program |
| VARIABLE STORAGE | I, J, K |
| NUMBER ARRAY STORAGE | C(100) etc. |
| AVAILABLE FOR USE | |
| CHARACTER ARRAY STORAGE | C$(100) |
| ROM | interpreter and monitor |
| ---------- | top of memory |

Fig. 17-1. A typical microprocessor memory map when using BASIC.

the end of the place for arrays, there is unused space. The monitor can add the C(400) array easily.

Now, what happens when the monitor needs to add the variable L? This has to go at the end of the variable section of memory. But there is no room there. The monitor makes room by moving the C array up, then the B array up, and finally the A array up so that there is a gap. In this gap, the monitor puts L. Now the monitor needs to add the variable M. What happens? Well there is no room again. So, the monitor has to spend the time moving up C, then B, and then A again. Each time it does the moving it takes up time. The more arrays to be moved and the more variables to be added, then the slower your program runs.

If we tell the monitor about all the variables *before* it has any arrays to move, any new variables can be added to the end of the variable section. Since there are no arrays present, there is no need to spend time moving them. That makes things faster.

To see what effect this has on the animation, load the PROGRAM and add the lines

```
60480 DIM T1(100) : DIM T2(100) : DIM T3(100) : DIM T4(100)
60485 DIM T5(100) : DIM T6(100) : DIM T7(100) : DIM T8(100)
```

Now find the time it takes from RUN to until the menu appears. Mine takes 12 seconds. We can remove the initialization statements by typing

```
DEL 60010, 60160
```

Time the execution with extra arrays but no initialization. My Apple takes 14 seconds. There is not much improvement in this case. It all depends on how many arrays you are using.

## PLACING FREQUENTLY USED VARIABLES

When you want to use a variable like HEX in a BASIC statement, what does the monitor have to do? The answer is that the monitor has to look through all the variables it has made until it finds HEX. If HEX is used often, and is near the end of the variables, this looking can take a lot of time. If we put variables we use frequently at the start of the initialization, then they will be placed at the start of the variable section. The monitor will (we hope) find things more quickly.

Reload the program. At the moment we make room for HEX in

line 60030. Delete that line and make room for HEX at line 60190, which makes HEX the last variable in our variable list.

```
DEL 60030
60190 HEX = 0
```

Now redo Timing 1 to see if it makes any difference. Now move HEX to the front and see what happens.

```
DEL 60190
60001 HEX = 0
```

My Timing 1 took 12 seconds the first time and 10 the second. You should also see some small improvement. Try the same thing with Timing 3, which uses the variable TYPE. On my computer it took 21 seconds regardless of where TYPE was declared.

## USE VARIABLES NOT NUMBERS

Suppose you have a number of statements like those listed from the HEX display subroutine.

```
58000 HITEMP = INT(HEX /256)
58010 IF HEX > 255 THEN PRINT HEX$(HITEMP);
58020 LOTEMP = HEX - 256 * HITEMP
58030 PRINT HEX$(LOTEMP)
58040 RETURN
```

What do you think makes this slow? The answer is in the numbers 255 and 256.

It is slow because these numbers are not read as numbers, but as letters (characters). Before the BASIC interpreter can use the letters "256" as the number 256 in line 58010, it must do these things:

1) Find the letter "2" and turn it into the number 2.
2) Find the letter "5" and turn it into the number 5.
3) Multiply 2 by 10 and add the 5.
4) Find the character "6" and turn it into the number 6.
5) Multiply 25 by 10 and add 6.

Those conversions are slow, but the two multiplications are *very* slow. Remember, every time our program has to do <<print-hex-

number>> it has to do all five of these things for each hex number it has to print.

Let's make the following changes to our program:

```
58000 HITEMP = INT(HEX /N6)
58010 IF HEX > N5 THEN PRINT HEX$(HITEMP);
58020 LOTEMP = HEX - N6 * HITEMP
58030 PRINT HEX$(LOTEMP)
58040 RETURN

60002 N6 = 256 : N5 = 255
```

Now things are different. When our program gets to line 60002, it must do the same five slow steps as before. The big difference is when the program does <<print-hex-number>>; at line 58010 it has to find N6 and look it up.

That is only one step. The looking-up process probably takes about the same time as turning one character into a number. But there are no multiplications. That makes for speed. Try Timing 1 with this new approach. My computer required 11 seconds for numbers as characters, but only 10 when I changed them to variables. With Timing 2 I also saved 1 second, from 5 seconds to 4. Try it yourself.

Changing numbers into variables is very important in loops and other routines that are done often. Most people don't realize how important this can be. The book on Applesoft BASIC puts it as the number one "go-fast" technique. If you want, you can change all the letters into variables. However, I would suggest that you only change the letters in loops that the program uses often. It is not worth doing more.

## REDUCING IN-LINE OVERHEAD

Type in the following two programs and compare the speeds at which they execute:

PROGRAM 1

```
1 FOR J = 1 TO 10000
2 X = X
3 NEXT J
4 STOP
```

PROGRAM 2

```
1 FORJ=1TO10000:X=X:NEXTJ
2 STOP
```

Program 2 is quite a bit faster. The monitor has to spend time looking for the next statement when it is doing loops and this is slow. Program 2 has only one statement, so the monitor can work more quickly. The monitor also has to look at each blank character in a line and then ignore it. This is also slow. This slowness is only important when you have large loops or a bit of a program that is used often. Let us modify our routine at 5800 and use Timing 2.

With no changes my computer took 5 seconds. Now make these changes to the program:

```
DEL 58000, 58040

58000 HITEMP=INT(HEX/256):IFHEX>255THENPRINTHEX$(HITEMP)
58010 LOTEMP=HEX-256*HITEMP:PRINTHEX$(LOTEMP);:RETURN
```

After minimizing the number of lines and blanks it required 5 seconds once again, but execution did seem faster by an increment too small to time accurately.

Removing the spaces to get things on the smallest number of lines, however, makes very difficult reading and correcting the program. It is something you should do *only* after you have your program running. Apple users will find that if they take away the spaces, the Apple seems to put them back in when you use LIST. The Apple actually never stores blanks even when you put them in. This means that for a given readability, the Apple goes faster than most other microcomputers.

The technique of removing all the blanks in a line also makes programs difficult to debug. Only after you have got your program working should you do this. Then, because it would take so long to do it on ALL the programs, only change it for pieces of code your program uses often.

## REM REMOVERS

The time that the monitor takes looking for the next line can be very important in long loops. We saw how important this was in Chapter 12, when we were doing the A (assemble) software tool. When we changed our program to remove the GOTOs from the loop, our program became four times faster in assembling.

Any program using GOTO statements causes the monitor to jump to the beginning of the program and then look at every line number to find the one it wants. Each time there is a REM, the monitor has to check that line number before moving on. Now that the program is working, we can afford to have a second version that has all the REMs removed. We also keep a copy of a version with the REMs to make changes to.

Removing the REMs takes forever unless you have a software tool called a *REM remover.* I bought one of these, although many of the computing magazines tell you how to build your own. With the knowledge you now have about machine language programs, you should not have too much trouble entering and using such programs. My REM remover also joins together all lines that can be joined together, and works like this:

Old program

```
1 I = 1
2 REM an example
3 J = 2
4 REM an another example
5 K = 3 : REM third example
```

DeREMMED program

```
1 I = 1 : J = 2
5 K = 3 : REM
```

Lines 1 and 3 have been joined together. This means that in a GOTO the monitor will not have to look at line 3 to see if it is the line wanted. The REMs on lines 2 and 4 are completely removed. The REM on line 5 is only partly removed. This means that the monitor will still have to look at that REM statement when it actually does line 5. It will not have to look at any REM when doing GOTOs.

My REM-free version of the animation program is just about completely unintelligible. All the subroutines have new line numbers and it would be difficult to add new parts to the program or make changes to this version. Since it is so difficult, I don't do it. Instead I make changes to the version with the REMs in it, and then use the REM remover again. It only takes about 30 seconds to remove the REMs, so it is no problem. The REM remover bleeps every time it makes the program smaller. It sounds just like a Geiger counter. You can hear the program getting smaller . . . and it makes you feel good.

Since you probably don't have a REM remover and it is not Christmas, you could go down to your local computer shop and ask them to remove the REMs for you "just this once." Offer to sweep the shop or something. Before you do so, I should give you my results. Before REM removal, the size of the program on my disk was 103 sectors; after removal, the size was 59 sectors—which is quite a change in size. However, with REMs in or with them out and the lines crunched, Timing 2 was the same, 5 seconds. I was very disappointed. I have built some programs that go twice as fast when the REMs are removed. However, this was with all the REMs on separate lines rather than on the same line as I have done in the animation program.

## BELIEVE THIS ONE OR NOT

According to some magazine articles, the monitor can find lines faster if each line is a multiple of 256. This means that instead of using line numbers that go up 10, 20, 30, etc., you make your line numbers go up 256, 512, 768, 1024, etc. If you have a software tool that renumbers lines automatically, you can give it a try in a program. Our animation program is a bit too big to change all the numbers. If you number lines this way, you can only have 64 times 4 lines. We have many more than that. Perhaps, this program would work faster if all the subroutines and other important lines had line numbers that were multiplies of 256. I don't think that it is really worth trying. Let me know if it is.

## COMPILING

In Chapter 15 I explained why BASIC is slow. Let's look at a very simple BASIC program:

```
10 A = 1
20 STOP
```

In machine code it would be very simple, just three instructions:

```
LDA #$1
STA $320        ; Variable A is at $320
BRK
```

But what would the monitor do for BASIC? It would do the whole elaborate sequence of operations listed in Chapter 15.

All the "looking for this, looking for that" I outlined is very slow. The reason that machine code is so much faster is that it does not have to do the looking while the program is working. When we wrote the machine code, we did the looking in our head. There is one problem. Changing a program like this animation program into machine code takes a long time. What we need is a software tool that turns BASIC into machine code. Then we can turn a working BASIC program straight into a working machine language program.

Such software tools do exist and are, in fact, fairly common. They are called *compilers*. (In Appendix F is an explanation of the difference between a compiler and an interpreter.) You take a BASIC program and then compile it or turn it into machine code. On a big machine this takes 1 or 2 seconds; on my Apple it takes a long time, around 30 minutes for the 6502 animation program. It is next to impossible to make changes to the compiled program so you have to recompile each time you make changes.

It takes time to compile, but it is worth it. The new compiled versions go fast. I have a BASIC version of one of those "bash the walls down" games. Using BASIC version, I can clear all the bricks most times. After I compiled it, I have managed to score 4 points—and that was only luck because the ball hit my bat accidentally. The game is so fast that it is normally finished before I can even move the paddle once.

Compilers come in various sorts. The cheaper ones do a fairly good job of changing things to machine code, but the more expensive ones do a much better job and get tighter code, meaning that they use the smallest number of machine code lines for each BASIC command. This means they should run faster.

If you can't afford a compiler, go down to the local computer shop and clean a few more windows. You can always ask, "Please, just this once?" if you go into a different shop from the one that let you use the REM remover. Here are my results for you to decide if it is worth it. Timing 1 on the animation program took 11 seconds to execute while interpreting, but only 3 seconds after compilation. Timing 2 dropped from 5 to 1.5 seconds, and Timing 3 decreased from 21 seconds to 5—and that last figure is artificially high because the program was working faster than I could type in the six NOP instructions. Now that IS a big change and shows you how much faster things run.

Compiling a large, complex program, however, normally takes so long that I start it and go to bed. In the morning, it is all done. I don't like doing it twice, so I make sure that my BASIC program does exactly what I want *before* I compile. There is also another possible disadvantage of compiling. The final program is often a lot bigger than the BASIC program. For a very large BASIC program, the compiled program might not fit into the memory.

### MACHINE CODE PROPER

Compilers do a nice job of turning BASIC into machine code, but they don't always do the best job. They work automatically and don't think of clever ways of making things happen fast. It takes a compiler on a bigger machine to do a better job—and even those don't always do as good a job as a clever human. However, a compiler never gets tired, does not make frequent mistakes, and can help many people at once. This means that in most cases they do a faster and better job than a human.

Turning our whole program into machine code is a very large task. Instead of changing everything, we shall just take the subroutine that displays a range of memory and change that into machine code. The rest of the program will still run in BASIC. If you want, you can make the changes to other parts of program.

What we are going to do, in the end, is to change line 57000 to call the machine language program in our safe area.

```
57000 CALL (SAFE+1) : RETURN : REM Apple
57000 SYS (SAFE+1) : RETURN : REM CBM
```

But don't do it now! If you don't have a 6502 machine, you should read through the following section so you can do the equivalent for your machine.

Now we need to write a machine code program that prints a range of memory. We shall have to use the built-in ROM routine that prints a letter. This is where that routine hides in the various machines.

```
JSR $FDED    ; Apple
JSR $E202    ; CBM
JSR $FFD2    ; C64
```

Before doing the program in machine code, let's try and write it in BASIC to see what needs to be done. The program would look something like this:

```
10000 REM BASIC version of machine code to <<print-hex>>
10010 PLACE = START : REM START contains place where to start
10020 COUNT = 0 : REM  going to do 64 locations
```

Print the value stored in memory:

```
10030 VALUE = PEEK(COUNT + PLACE) : REM get the value
10040 GOSUB 10500 : REM print number
```

Print blanks after each value:

```
10050 A = 32 : REM this is a blank
10060 GOSUB 10800 : REM print a blank
10070 COUNT = COUNT + 1
```

Print a new line after every eighth memory location:

```
10080 IF COUNT <> 8 * INT (COUNT / 8) THEN 10200
10090 A = 13 : REM print carriage return every 8 numbers
10100 GOSUB 10800 : REM print carriage return
```

Stop at the end of the safe area:

```
10200 IF COUNT <> 64 THEN 10030
10210 RETURN : REM done all we want
```

Subroutine to split up the number to be printed into two hex characters:

```
10500 V1 = INT (VALUE / 16) : REM first part of HEX number
10510 V2 = VALUE - 16 * V1 : REM second part
10520 PAR = V1
10530 GOSUB 10600 : REM print
10540 PAR = V2
10550 GOSUB 10600 : REM print
10560 RETURN
```

Turn numbers 0 to 9 into characters "0" to "9:"

```
10600 IF PAR > 9 THEN 10700
   : REM  this needs a letter from 'A' to 'F'
10610 A = PAR + 48 : REM make into letter '0' to '9'
10620 GOTO 10750
```

Turn number $A to $F into letters "A" through "F:"

```
10700 A = PAR - 10 + 65  : REM made into 'A' to 'F'
10750 GOSUB 10800: REM  go and print the character
10760 RETURN
```

This subroutine has the same effect as the ROM <<print>> routine:

```
10800 PRINT CHR$(A);
10810 RETURN
```

You can test to see what will happen by changing line 57000 to:

```
57000 GOSUB 10000 : RETURN
```

As mentioned in the last chapter, we must be careful when we use the ROM routines. The ROM routines very often change values stored in the registers. We must make sure then that when we use the registers after using a ROM routine, things are correct.

There is a second problem. In the CBM machines, letters are stored starting as the numbers 65 and on. In the Apple, however, this gives the inverse or flashing version of the letter. For the Apple, letters are stored as the number (128 + 65) and on. The machine code for the displays are therefore a little different.

### Apple Version

```
$300:   COUNT   DS 1            ; Place for count
$301:           LDA #$0
$303:           STA $300        ; Count = 0
$306:           LDX $300        ; Load array pointer
$309:           LDA $300,X      ; Get the memory location.
                                  PLACE = $300
$30C:           JSR $32E        ; Go print the number
$30F:           LDA #$A0        ; Load a BLANK
$311:           JSR $FDED       ; Print a character
$314:           CLC             ; Get ready for ADD
$315:           LDA $300        ; Get count
$318:           ADC #$1         ; count = count + 1
$31A:           STA $300        ; store count
$31D:           AND #$7         ; get last three bits
$31F:           BNE $326        ; same as
                                  COUNT <> 8 * INT (COUNT /8)
$321:           LDA #$8D        ; Load carriage return
$323:           JSR $FDED       ; Print a character
$326:           LDA #$40        ; Have we done 64?
$328:           CMP $300        ; Check againest Count
$32B:           BNE $306
```

```
$32D:          RTS              ; BASIC leave
$32E:          PHA              ; Remember value in A
$32F:          LSR
$330:          LSR
$331:          LSR
$332:          LSR              ; Divide by 16
$333:          JSR $33D         ; Print number
$336:          PLA              ; Get back value of A
$337:          AND #$F          ; same as V2 = VALUE - 16 * V1
$339:          JSR $33D         ; Print number
$33C:          RTS              ; Leave subroutine
$33D:          CLC              ; Get ready for ADD
$33E:          CMP #$A          ; >= 10?
$340:          BPL $346
$342:          ADC #$B0         ; + 48 + 128
$344:          BNE $348         ; Always branches since <> 0
$346:          ADC #$B6         ; - 10 + 64 + 128
$348:          JSR $FDED        ; Print the character
$34B:          RTS              ; Leave subroutine
```

## Commodore 64 Version

```
$C300:  COUNT  DS 1             ; Place for count
$C301:         LDA #$0
$C303:         STA $C300        ; Count = 0
$C306:         LDX $C300        ; Load array pointer
$C309:         LDA $C300,X      ; Get the memory location.
                                  PLACE = $C300
$C30C:         JSR $C32E        ; Go print the number
$C30F:         LDA #$20         ; Load a BLANK
$C311:         JSR $FFD2        ; Print a character
$C314:         CLC              ; Get ready for ADD
$C315:         LDA $C300        ; Get count
$C318:         ADC #$1          ; count = count + 1
$C31A:         STA $C300        ; store count
$C31D:         AND.#$7          ; get last three bits
$C31F:         BNE $C326        ; same as
                                  COUNT <> 8 * INT (COUNT /8)
$C321:         LDA #$0D         ; Load carriage return
$C323:         JSR $FFD2        ; Print a character
$C326:         LDA #$40         ; Have we done 64?
$C328:         CMP $C300        ; Check againest Count
```

```
$C32B:          BNE $C306
$C32D:          RTS             ; BASIC leave
$C32E:          PHA             ; Remember value in A
$C32F:          LSR
$C330:          LSR
$C331:          LSR
$C332:          LSR             ; Divide by 16
$C333:          JSR $C33D       ; Print number
$C336:          PLA             ; Get back value of A
$C337:          AND #$F         ; same as V2 = VALUE - 16 * V1
$C339:          JSR $C33D       ; Print number
$C33C:          RTS             ; Leave subroutine
$C33D:          CLC             ; Get ready for ADD
$C33E:          CMP #$A         ; >= 10?
$C340:          BPL $C346
$C342:          ADC #$30        ; + 48
$C344:          BNE $C348       ; Always branches since <> 0
$C346:          ADC #$36        ; - 10 + 64
$C348:          JSR $FFD2       ; Print the character
$C34B:          RTS             ; Leave subroutine
```

### Other Commodore Machines Version

```
$300:   COUNT   DS 1            ; Place for count
$301:           LDA #$0
$303:           STA $300        ; Count = 0
$306:           LDX $300        ; Load array pointer
$309:           LDA $300,X      ; Get the memory location.
                                  PLACE = $300
$30C:           JSR $32E        ; Go print the number
$30F:           LDA #$20        ; Load a BLANK
$311:           JSR $E202       ; Print a character
$314:           CLC             ; Get ready for ADD
$315:           LDA $300        ; Get count
$318:           ADC #$1         ; count = count + 1
$31A:           STA $300        ; store count
$31D:           AND #$7         ; get last three bits
$31F:           BNE $326        ; same as
                                  COUNT <> 8 * INT (COUNT /8)
$321:           LDA #$0D        ; Load carriage return
$323:           JSR $E202       ; Print a character
$326:           LDA #$40        ; Have we done 64?
```

```
$328:          CMP $300        ; Check againest Count
$32B:          BNE $306
$32D:          RTS             ; BASIC leave
$32E:          PHA             ; Remember value in A
$32F:          LSR
$330:          LSR
$331:          LSR
$332:          LSR             ; Divide by 16
$333:          JSR $33D        ; Print number
$336:          PLA             ; Get back value of A
$337:          AND #$F         ; same as V2 = VALUE - 16 * V1
$339:          JSR $33D        ; Print number
$33C:          RTS             ; Leave subroutine
$33D:          CLC             ; Get ready for ADD
$33E:          CMP #$A         ; >= 10?
$340:          BPL $346
$342:          ADC #$30        ; + 48
$344:          BNE $348        ; Always branches since <> 0
$346:          ADC #$36        ; - 10 + 64
$348:          JSR $E202       ; Print the character
$34B:          RTS             ; Leave subroutine
```

This is a little bit bigger than the safe area we have displayed. Use the D (disassembler) command to check that it is entered correctly; use the SA (save) command to save it as FAST.OBJ.

Now we need to make some changes to program in order to get this new display to work, but all we need to do is:

```
57000 SYS(769) : RETURN : REM CBM VERSION

57000 SYS(49821) : RETURN : REM C64 version
```

Now type RUN and do your timing. With the normal display method my Apple took 5 seconds, but with the machine code display it was too fast to time. I think you will like the change!

Notice also that this is much faster than the compiled version. The reason for this is that the compiled version is doing a machine code version of BASIC program logic. It is still doing BASIC-like things to print out and find things from arrays. Our version is completely customized to do *exactly* the job we want and nothing else. In the time we took to customize just one part of the program, however, the compiler did improve every part a bit. You have to decide if you need to convert all the programs to machine code.

# Chapter 18

# Other Things to Do

Throughout the book, we have slowly added things to our animation program. We have dveloped assemblers/disassemblers and other software tools. The final version of PROGRAM will be sufficient for testing out small machine language programs. For much larger programs, I would suggest that you purchase a good commercial assembler. I think that you will find that having macros, excellent checking and editing features, labels, helpful pseudo instructions, etc., will quickly convince you that it was money well spent. Though you might feel that what you have here is sufficient, there are a couple of things that you might like to add.

## DISASSEMBLER IMPROVEMENTS

**Speed Improvements.** The only way for greater speed is to go to machine code. In the book *Beyond Games: System Software for Your 6502 Personal Computer* mentioned in the Appendix, there is a 6502 disassembler. I would suggest using that. There is no point in reinventing the wheel.

**Display Features.** It would be useful if you could dump the disassembled program to a printer for hard copy, or to a disk file so that you can make changes. With the mnemonics on disk, you could use an editor to make changes. Then change the assembler so that it can read these files.

**Adding Unmentioned Instructions.** Appendix F details what instructions have already been animated and discussed.

**File Handling.** The checking for nonexistent files needs improving.

## ASSEMBLER IMPROVEMENTS

**Speed Improvements.** It is not really worthwhile putting this into machine code. You are better off buying an inexpensive commercial assembler.

**Loading from Disk.** It would be useful if you could use a text file from the disk rather than having to retype in a file from the keyboard. How you do this depends on your machine. The *EXEC* feature of the Apple makes it easy. If you build a text file called DOIT that had in it the following set of commands:

| | |
|---|---|
| RUN | (or if you wanted to LOAD and then RUN - RUN PROGRAM) |
| ASS | (automatically call the ASSEMBLER) |
| $300 | |
| LDA #$3 | |
| | |
| ASL | |
| etc. . . . . | |
| END | (quit the assembler) |
| SAVE | (Save the assembled code) |
| NAMEFILE | |
| $300 | |
| $338 | |
| YES | |
| STOP | |
| YES | |

You can automate the entry. After making the file DOIT, return to BASIC and type.

```
EXEC DOIT
```

and PROGRAM will be automatically run, the *A* command selected, the program will be assembled, and, finally, the save and stop commands will be chosen. The CBM does not have the same feature, unless you want to write a program that uses the dynamic keyboard we used in Chapter 12.

**Adding Other Instructions.** Appendix F will help you here.

**File Handling.** This command will be used in conjunction

with the *SA* command on most occasions. The save command needs to have checks built in so that the program does not bomb if the drive malfunctions of if the object program already exists.

**Pseudo-assembly Instructions.** If you are entering a lot of programs from magazines, you might find it convenient to allow the following pseudo-commands:

- **DS $num,** a command to allow $num spaces. This could be implemented by recognizing the character string DS with

  ```
  IF MID$(ANS$,1,2)="DS" THEN . . .
  ```

  and then increase the variable BEGIN by the amount NUM worked out using the subroutine at line 56010 <<get-hex>>.
- **ASCII LETTERS,** a command to allow entry of ASCII characters into memory. This would be useful where the magazine article uses machine code to issue instructions. This could be implemented by
  1) Looking for the string "ASCII."
  2) Looking for the double quote, CHR$(34).
  3) Storing the character with POKE(BEGIN), ASC(LETTER).
  4) Stopping when you reach the closing quote.

Apple users will have to make certain that step 3 correctly sets the high bit when stored.

## ANIMATION IMPROVEMENTS

**Adding Other Instructions.** If you are using this animation as a teaching tool, you might find it useful to add the *zero page* instructions. This will have to be done in a couple of steps:

1) Use an advanced text to make sure you understand what the zero page instructions do.
2) Find out from your user's manual what zero page locations are not used by BASIC. You will probably find that locations $00 through $03 are probably safe for the Apple and CBM machines (but not the Commodore 64, which uses these locations for memory management).
3) Add a display routine to show that area of memory.

**Faster Display.** It would make sense to use the machine code program to display the safe area of memory. You will have to move the machine code for the display out of the safe area. See Appendix B for locations to do this. It would be of some advantage to redisplay the screen each time the registers are redisplayed. This would show the changes occurring in memory.

## CONCLUSION

I hope you have enjoyed the book. In it, you have started off using BASIC to understand what goes on inside a microprocessor. You have been introduced to hexadecimal numbers, registers, flags, ROM, and RAM. By now you should be a fairly accomplished machine language programmer. Perhaps you are not the best in the world, but you can hold your own with anybody.

# Appendix A

# Machine-Dependent Program Lines

Throughout our development of a 6502 machine language simulator program, the lines given in the text have been for the Apple and, where appropriate, the Commodore 64 and other CBM machines (except the VIC-20, which we'll deal with in a few moments). Changes in the lines noted in this Appendix will allow our simulator to run on any machine that supports BASIC. Since the animation has been written in modules, very little is needed in the way of changes.

- Line 41740 needs the machine-specific command to save machine language programs.
- Line 61000 needs a hex description of the safe working area to load machine code.

This area (approximately 80 bytes) must remain untouched by BASIC.

- Line 61100 needs the appropriate code to clear the screen.
- Line 61200 needs the code to TAB down the screen.
- Line 61340 needs the command to run a machine language program from BASIC. Replace by a RETURN if your microcomputer doesn't use a 6500-series processor (6502, 6510, etc.).
- Line 61400 needs the code to move the cursor to the top of the screen.
- Line 61500 needs the code to move the cursor across the screen.

- Line 61600 needs a command to catalog the disk drive directory.
- Line 61900 needs a command to load a machine language program.

I believe that the rest of the program is completely compatible with all microprocessors that can run a version of BASIC. The only obvious exception is the BASIC command GET when it is used to take a single character from the keyboard. In some machines, the GET command must be replaced by INKEY$ or some such similiar command. A problem can occur when one of the variables used in the animation is a *reserved word* for your machine. For example, the variable HEX is not permitted on an Osborne and should be replaced by the equivalent variable HE.

### Changes for the VIC-20

Although this is a 6502-like machine, there are a number of problems in getting a large program such as we described in this book to fit into the VIC-20. The first problem is the very small amount of memory available in the standard VIC-20 (The following pages assume you have this machine with one or more of the RAM extender cards.) A second problem is the much smaller screen size on the VIC.

**Screen Size Changes.** To make the display fit into the 23-character by 18-line VIC-20 screen, we must make a number of programming compromises. Basically, the compromises mean moving things around on the screen until they fit, removing all unnecessary lines and putting up with a crowded screen.

In Chapter 2 change line 57060 to read

```
57060 HEX = D2TEMP : GOSUB 58000
Delete lines 57020, 57030, 57040, 57100
```

This will make the screen more compact because all the numbers from the memory display will be scrunched together. Although the numbers now fit on the screen, they are effectively unreadable. The following line causes alternate bytes to be printed in inverse. If you don't like a partially inverse screen, then change colors.

```
57075 PRINT CHR$(18);
      : IF D3TEMP <> (2 * INT(D3TEMP / 2)) THEN PRINT CHR$(46);
```

In Chapter 4 through 8, you might like to change the value of DOWN in line 55010 to control the position of the memory display on the screen. In line 54010, the value of 20 for OVER is too large for the VIC-20 screen. Try a value of 4 and delete line 54810, so that there is no box around the register display. In Chapter 8, the positioning of the FLAG display overwrites everything else. Delete line 54920, in line 54910 change DOWN to 6, and add:

```
54930 PRINT "C";C$;"I";I$;"N";N$;"V";V$;"Z";Z$
```

The final problem is where to put the information about which instruction is being executed. You can add the following lines that move that information around the screen:

```
30005 DOWN = 7 : GOSUB 61200
39025 DOWN = 7 : GOSUB 61200
39125 DOWN = 7 : GOSUB 61200
39225 DOWN = 7 : GOSUB 61200
```

Chapter 12 is the last area where extra spaces need to be removed:

```
DELETE 46130
46170 OVER = 6 : GOSUB 61500
46230 HEX = M2 : GOSUB 58000
46400 OVER = 12 : GOSUB 61500
```

**Memory Saving Techniques.** The small standard size of the VIC-20 memory is a major obstacle. The animation has been run on a VIC with 28K of additional memory (one 16K and one 12K RAM cartridge added). To get the animation to run with just one of these additional cartridges requires a number of special techniques. All these techniques will compromise the readability and debugging of the animation. Try the easiest solutions first and then progress to the more difficult ones if you still run out of memory.

First, remove unnecessary blank spaces from *BASIC* statements. Instead of writing

```
47070 IF ANS$ = "END" THEN RETURN
```

write

```
47070IFANS$="END"THENRETURN
```

This example shows the saving of six bytes of memory, but shows how the line becomes very difficult to read.

Then double up the lines. Instead of the lines

```
57140 NEXT D3TEMP
57150 PRINT
57160 NEXT D2TEMP
57170 RETURN
```

use the colon to have several statements for each line number:

```
57140 NEXT D3TEMP : PRINT : NEXT D2TEMP : RETURN
```

For ease of reading, compress the shorter lines. Watch out that you don't remove a line number needed by a GOTO statement.

You can also remove unnecessary commands. For example, the HELP, GET, and SAVE commands can be removed. Deleting lines 45000 to 45220 and replacing line 45000 with a RETURN would remove the HELP command completely. With the A (assembler) command working the L (load) and CH (change) commands can be removed.

Removing the less important REM statements will also free up memory space. REM statements are very important in the debugging of a section of a program. However, once the section is working, we need to have an approach that would allow us to find easily and remove automatically all unnecessary REM statements. A simple approach is to write all REMs on a separate line with a special line number. For example, instead of writing

```
57100 HEX = PEEK(D2TEMP + D3TEMP): REM GET MEMORY VALUE
57110 GOSUB 58000 : REM USE THAT ROUTINE AGAIN
57120 PRINT " "; : REM ADD A SPACE
57130 NEXT D3TEMP
57140 PRINT : REM PUT OUT A NEW LINE
```

we could write

```
57100 HEX = PEEK(D2TEMP + D3TEMP)
57101 REM GET MEMORY VALUE
57110 GOSUB 58000
57111 REM USE THAT ROUTINE AGAIN
57120 PRINT " ";
57121 REM ADD A SPACE
```

```
57130 NEXT D3TEMP
57140 PRINT
57141 REM PUT OUT A NEW LINE
```

Notice that all REM lines end in the number 1 (57101, 57111, etc.) We can now easily find the REM statements and remove them by hand or by using that dynamic keyboard discussed in Chapter 12. An alternate approach that might be used (since all the modules are kept small) is not to put the unimportant REMs in at all. Just keep the section headings. If you decide to use the dynamic keyboard, these are the important locations to remember.

The keyboard buffer starts at location 631. The address to POKE to make the dynamic keyboard start is 198. The following program shows how to put nine carriage returns into the buffer.

```
FOR J = 0 TO 8 : POKE (J + 631), 13 : NEXT J : POKE 198, 9
```

If the above methods still don't give you enough room with your extra RAM card, there is only one resort. Split the program into two parts and have each part call the other as necessary. The program is already ready to be split. The first part of the program is the software tools, which need lines 10 to 4900 and 40000 to 62020; the second part is the animation, which needs lines 10 to 4210, 4250, 4890 to 40000, and 48100 to 62020. If you save each part separately onto disk or tape, you will have nearly halved the amount of memory needed for each section. To run the program, call in the software tools to load your program into the safe area. Now call in the animation part.

This is not the easiest thing to do, but it certainly would allow the program to operate in a small amount of memory. Each VIC-20 has a safe area that depends on the amount of extra RAM you are using. Look in the back of the user manual to find the correct safe area for your particular machine.

Finally, if you are feeling particularly adventuresome, you could try using the standard (unenhanced) VIC-20. You could split the program up into very small sections and load each part or command as you needed to. The program would be very slow and there is no guarantee that it would work.

# Appendix B

# Making More Room

If you are not using BASIC, then the whole of memory is available to you for large machine language programs. However, this appendix assumes that you are going to mix BASIC and machine code programs. The major problem here is to ensure that BASIC, its program, and its variables don't go tromping all over the area you want to use. There are two easy ways of making sure this doesn't happen.

**Raising the Bottom of Memory.** This technique is very satisfactory for the Apple; it causes problems with the CBM machines if you keep on deciding to increase the amount of space needed, after you have started to write a BASIC program. (Try it and see if you can understand why problems occur.)

The normal Apple "start of BASIC location" is $801 (2049). We can get $100 memory locations by using the following set of instructions:

```
X = PEEK(104) + 1 : REM change 1 to 2 for $200 locations
POKE 104, X
POKE (X * 256 + 1), 0
NEW
```

The new safe area starts at $803. These instructions could be included in your HELLO program and will safeguard things until you power down.

**Lowering the Top of Memory.** The main disadvantage of

this method is that different machines have different tops of memory. This may mean that machine code written for one machine may not work on another. The normal top of memory is given by the pointers 115, 116 (Apple) and 52, 53 (CBM). The following commands give a safe area at the top of memory.

APPLE

```
PRINT(PEEK(116) * 256 + PEEK(115) - 1):REM top of 'SAFE' area
X = PEEK(116) - 1 :                    REM change 1 for more
POKE 116,X
PRINT(PEEK(116) * 256 + PEEK(115)) : REM bottom of 'SAFE' area
NEW
```

CBM

```
PRINT(PEEK(53) * 256 + PEEK(52) - 1) : REM top of 'SAFE' area
X = PEEK(53) - 1 :                     REM change 1 for more
POKE 53,X
PRINT(PEEK(53) * 256 + PEEK(52))     : REM bottom of 'SAFE' area
NEW
```

Commodore 64

There is plenty of room $C000 to $CFFF for most programs.

# Appendix C
# Additional Reading

Apple Computer, Inc. *Apple II Reference Manual.* Cupertino, Calif.: Apple Computer, Inc., 1979.

Camp, R.C.; Smay, T.A.; and Triska, C.J. *Microprocessor Systems Engineering,* Portland, Oreg.: Matrix, 1979.

Hallgren, Richard. *Interface Projects for the Apple II.* Englewood Cliffs, N.J.: Prentice-Hall, 1982.

----------. *Interface Projects for the TRS-80.* Englewood Cliffs, N.J., Prentice-Hall, 1982.

Harltey, Michael G., and Healey, Martin. *A first Course in Computer Technology.* New York: McGraw-Hill, 1978.

Inman, Don, and Inman, Kurt. *Apple Machine Language.* Reston, Va.: Reston Publishing Co., Inc., 1981.

Kidder, Tracy. *The Soul of a New Machine.* New York: Avon Books,

Leventhal, Lance A. *6502 Assembly Language Programming,* New York: Osborne/McGraw-Hill, 1979.

Osborne, Adam. *An Introduction to Microcomputers, Vol. 1.* New York: Osborne/McGraw-Hill, 1980.

Skier, Ken. *Beyond Games: Systems Software for Your 6502 Personal Computer.* New York: BYTE/McGraw-Hill, 1981.

West, Raeto. *Programming the PET/CBM: The Reference Encyclopedia For Commodore PET and CBM Users.* Greensboro, N.C.: Compute! Books, 1982.

White, Donnamaie E. *Bit-Slice Design: Controllers and ALUs.* New York: Garland Publishing, Inc., 1981.

Zaks, Rodnay. *Programming the 6502*. Berkeley, Calif.: Sybex, Inc., 1978.

PET users in the U.K. should also investigate Nick Hampshire's *The PET Revealed,* available through Computabits Ltd.

# Appendix D
# Useful Magazines

### *COMPUTE!*

Mainly CBM BASIC, with a good sprinkling of Apple and Atari material, can be found in this magazine, which frequently has machine language programs included in articles. However, the editor does not always provide the machine language listings you need to make best use of the programs. Frequent machine language tutorials are also featured. Subscribe care of:

Circulation Department
Box 5406
Greensboro, NC 27403

### *CALL-A.P.P.L.E*

This is a magazine put out by an Apple users group. They provide good insight into what goes on inside the BASIC interpreter, machine language programs, and tutorials on both BASIC and machine code. In addition, they manufacture inexpensive software tools that are well written, well documented, and less than half the price of commercial versions. The group also runs a hot-line to answer questions. The magazine is included in the cost of membership. For more information write:

CALL-A.P.P.L.E.
304 Main Avenue S., Suite 300
Renton, WA 98055

### *NIBBLE*

This magazine goes in for heavy (i.e., large) programs for the Apple that are very useful if you want them. They are not for the fainthearted or the person beginning machine language programming— although there are occasional tutorials. Many programs are long and complicated enough that it is well worthwhile buying the programs mentioned in the magazine on a disk (around $20 per issue). Personally, I have found that this magazine is not set out in an easily readable fashion. Some of the articles and programs, however, are really tremendous. This magazine often has articles on how to use machine code to add commands to your BASIC. With changes in the ROM addresses used, the ideas can be tried out on the Commodore machines.

NIBBLE
PO Box 235
Lincoln MA 01773

### *CREATIVE COMPUTING*

This is a general, all-round magazine with articles on many different machines and languages. The articles range from game reviews, BASIC, machine code, and an occasional FORTAN program, to legal issues concerning computers. It has a number of interesting (fairly regular) specialized sections for Apple, CBM, Atari and TRS-80 users. A good magazine to start with, although the reader must expect that in some months there will be very little of particular interest.

Creative Computing
P.O. Box 789-M
Morristown NJ 07976

# Appendix E
# Useful Software Tools

This Appendix contains information on software tools that are helpful in developing BASIC and machine language programs. The author can't comment on the suitability of the non-Apple tools because he has not used them. The operating principle here is *caveat emptor* or "Let the buyer beware."

**GLOBAL PROGRAM LINE EDITOR**
**Apple**
**copyable**

Developed and sold by the people of *CALL-A.P.P.L.E.* magazine, this software tool is able to do a "word processing" job on BASIC programs stored in memory. For example, the command

EDIT 1000,3000,"this","that"/R

will change "this" into "that" in lines 1000 to 3000. The /R on the end of the command means that the program will ask if you want to change each particular "this" into a "that." Using /F does an automatic change. This tool allows the easy insertion and deletion of normal and control characters, and allows the use of 40- or 80-column cards.

**BIG MAC.LC**
**Apple**
**copyable**

Also developed and sold by the people of *CALL-A.P.P.L.E.*

this is a good assembler/disassembler package that is very fast. It allows the use of MACROs in the machine language program. For example, you can use the word

LOADPUSH

which has the same meaning as the following group of machine language instructions:

```
LDA $300
PHA
JSR SHOW       ;show what has been stored
JSR BELL       ;Now ring a bell
```

This means you can describe complex sequences of machine code in a simple way. It makes assembly language programming like using a high-level language. Although not a necessity, MACROs are nice when you can get them.

**APPLESOFT TOOL KIT**
**Apple**
**copyable**

Developed by the Apple people, this is a collection of software tools. It contains a good, medium-speed assembler without MACROs. For BASIC users, it contains a renumbering program a high-resolution character generator for use with programs, and a tool called a *relocating loader.* This last thing is very useful when you start to use a large number of machine language programs.

**MICROSOFT TASC**
**Apple**
**copyable**

Developed by Microsoft, this is an Applesoft compiler. It compiles a BASIC program at about the same speed that a slow printer would list it, and has a number of "go-fast" features for doing things at a greater speed in the final program. Although compiled, the final programs are not (and should not be expected to be) as fast as straight machine code programming.

**BEYOND GAMES**
**ATARI—Pet-Apple**

This book, referenced in Appendix C, is a collection of machine language software tools for 6502 microprocessors.

# Appendix F
# Interpreters vs Compilers

The following discussion is reprinted from the *Microsoft Applesoft Compiler* manual by kind permission of Microsoft Corporation.

Since the microprocessor in the Apple can execute only its own machine instructions, it does not execute Applesoft program statements directly. Instead, statements must be simulated by machine language routines that perform the operations specified by each BASIC statement.

Compilers and interpreters provide two different methods of approaching this translation problem. This difference in method is demonstrated in the following analogy.

Suppose you wish to build a stereo from a kit. Unfortunately, you find that the provided instructions are written in Japanese, a language that you do not know.

One way of approaching this problem is to use a Japanese-English dictionary to translate and perform each instruction one by one. This process parallels the interpretation of Applesoft statements by the Applesoft interpreter. Your construction of a stereo kit is analogous to the Apple's execution of a program.

Inefficiencies can arise in this process, especially if you fail to write down the translated instructions as they are carried out. Suppose, for example, that halfway through the construction process you translate an instruction that says:

> Go back to instruction fourteen. Then repeat the preceding steps for the second speaker.

One problem becomes immediately apparent: you can't even find instruction fourteen without scanning the instructions from the start for the Japanese characters for fourteen. You then face the time-consuming task of re-translating each instruction so that the second speaker can be assembled precisely like the first; likewise, the Applesoft interpreter must repeatedly translate each statement executed inside a FOR/NEXT loop.

A faster, alternative approach to constructing the stereo is to sit down at a table with pencil and paper, away from the stereo kit, and translate the entire instruction sheet into English. When you are done, you have a new set of instructions written in English. These English instructions correspond to the object file created by the Microsoft Applesoft Compiler.

The actual assembly of the kit can then proceed without any further translation, and even without any further need for the original Japanese text. When you finally sit down to build your speakers, you construct them very quickly. Similarly, a compiled BASIC program does not require the original BASIC source and runs very quickly in comparison to the interpreted version of the same program.

This analogy gives you a feel for the difference between interpretation and compilation. The following paragraphs discuss interpretation and compilation more technically, but also more directly.

### Interpretation

The interpreter translates Applesoft source statements line by line at runtime. Each time the interpreter executes an Applesoft statement, it must analyze the statement, check for errors, and call machine language routines that perform the desired function.

When statements must be executed repeatedly, as must those within a FOR/NEXT loop, the translation process must be repeated each time the statement is executed.

In addition, BASIC line numbers are stored in a list. GOTOs and GOSUBs force the interpreter to search this list to find the desired line. This search is quite slow when the needed line is near the end of a long program.

The interpreter keeps track of variables using a list, too. When it encounters a reference to a variable, the interpreter searches from the beginning of the list to find the desired variable. If the variable is not present in the list, the interpreter must create a new entry for it. This procedure also slows interpreted programs.

## Compilation

A compiler, on the other hand, takes a source program and translates it into a machine-language object file. This object file consists of a large number of machine language CALLs to routines in the runtime library and to routines in the Applesoft interpreter. By calling routines in the Applesoft interpreter, the Microsoft Applesoft Compiler assures close language compatibility with the interpreter.

In contrast to the interpreter, the compiler analyzes all statements before runtime. In addition, absolute memory addresses are provided for variables and program lines. These addresses eliminate the list searching that occurs while an interpreted program executes.

The Microsoft Applesoft Compiler, unlike the interpreter, implements true integer arithmetic and integer loop variables in FOR/NEXT loops. In comparison, the Applesoft interpreter converts all integers to real numbers before operating on them. These conversions make interpreted integer arithmetic relatively inefficient. In addition, the interpreter forbids use of integers as loop control variables in FOR/NEXT loops.

These factors all combine to make compiled programs considerably faster. In most cases, execution of compiled programs is two to twenty times faster than execution of the same program under the interpreter.

# Appendix G

# Instructions Animated and Discussed

## Animated

ADC (immediate/absolute)
BCC
BCS
BEQ
BMI
BNE
BPL
BRK
BVC
BVS
CLC
CLD
CLV
DEX
DEY
INX
INY
JSR
JMP
LDA (immediate/absolute)
LDX (immediate/absolute
LDY (immediate/absolute)
NOP
PHA
PLA
RTS
SBC (immediate/absolute)
SEC
SED
STA (absolute)
STX (absolute)
STY (absolute)
TAX
TXA

## Discussed

ADC (indexed)
AND (absolute/immediate/indexed)
ASL (implied/absolute)
LDA (indexed)
LDX (indexed)
LDY (indexed)

BIT (absolute)

CMP (absolute/immediate/indexed)

CPX (immediate/absolute)
CPY (immediate/absolute)
EOR (absolute/immediate/indexed)

LSR (implied/absolute)

ORA (absolute/immediate/indexed)

SBC (indexed)
STA (indexed)

# Appendix H

# Final Animation Program Listing

This is a complete listing of the program given in the text of the book. Appendix A lists all program lines that need to be changed for different microprocessors

```
10  GOSUB 60000: REM  <<SET-UP-VARIABLES>>
20  PRINT "SETTING UP HEX": REM   EXPLAIN WAIT
30  GOSUB 59000: GOSUB 59100
40  GOSUB 61000: REM  <<MAKE-SAFE-AREA>>
50  GOTO 4000
4000  GOSUB 55000: REM  <<DISPLAY-SAFE-AREA>>
4005  GOSUB 54000: REM  <<DISPLAY-REGISTERS>>
4010 DOWN = 20: GOSUB 61200: REM      <<MOVE-DOWN-THE-SCREEN>>

4100  PRINT "TYPE 'HELP' FOR COMMANDS ";BELL$
4110  INPUT "YOUR WISH, MASTER? ";ANS$
4120  IF  LEN (ANS$) < 1 THEN  PRINT EH$: GOTO 4010: REM

4190  REM  CHECK 'ONE' LETTER COMMANDS
4200  REM  EACH COMMAND JUMPS TO A SUBROUTINE
4210 TEMP$ =  MID$ (ANS$,1,1): REM   GET FIRST LETTER

4220  IF TEMP$ = "L" THEN  GOSUB 40000: GOTO 4000: REM <<LOAD>>
4230  IF TEMP$ = "H" THEN  GOSUB 45000: GOTO 4000
     : REM    <<HELP>>
```

```
4240  IF TEMP$ = "D" THEN  GOSUB 46000: GOTO 4000
     : REM <<DISASSEMBLE>>

4250  IF TEMP$ = "W" THEN  GOSUB 5100: GOTO 4000
     : REM   <<WORKING-MODEL>>
4260  IF TEMP$ = "A" THEN  GOSUB 47000: GOTO 4000
     : REM  <<ASSEMBLER>>
4490  REM  CHECK FOR 'TWO' LETTER COMMANDS
4500  IF  LEN (ANS$) < 2 THEN  PRINT EH$: GOTO 4010
     : REM   INVALID!!
4510 TEMP$ =  MID$ (ANS$,1,2): REM   GET FIRST TWO LETTERS

4520  IF TEMP$ = "CH" THEN  GOSUB 43000: GOTO 4000
     : REM  <<CHANGE>>
4530  IF TEMP$ = "CL" THEN  GOSUB 42000: GOTO 4000
     : REM   <<CLEAR>>

4540  IF TEMP$ = "ST" THEN  GOSUB 41000: GOTO 4000
     : REM   <<STOP>>
4550  IF TEMP$ = "GO" THEN  GOSUB 44000: GOTO 4000
     : REM    <<GO>>
4560  IF TEMP$ = "CA" THEN  GOSUB 61600: GOTO 4000
     : REM   <<CATALOG>>
4570  IF TEMP$ = "GE" THEN  GOSUB 61700: GOTO 4000: REM <<GET>>
4580  IF TEMP$ = "SA" THEN  GOSUB 41500: GOTO 4000
     : REM   <<SAVE>>
4890  PRINT EH$: GOTO 4010: REM   EVERYTHING ELSE IS WRONG
4900  STOP : REM  <<END CHAPTER 4>>

5000 DISP = SAFE: GOSUB 55000: REM  <<DISPLAY-SAFE-MEMORY>>
5010  GOSUB 54000: REM  <<DISPLAY-REGISTERS>>
5100 DOWN = 22: GOSUB 61200: REM    <<MOVE-DOWN-THE-SCREEN>>
5110  PRINT "WHAT STARTING ADDRESS $";
5120  GOSUB 56000:START = HEX: REM  <<GET-HEX-NUMBER>> FOR START
5130  IF (START < SAFE) OR (START > NSAFE) THEN  PRINT EH$
     : GOTO 5100
5140 PC = START: REM   'REST' PROGRAM COUNTER:REM

5150  GOSUB 39000: REM  'FETCH' AN INSTRUCTION
5170  GOSUB 30000: REM   'EXECUTE' AN INSTRUCTION
5180  GOSUB 54000: REM  <<DISPLAY-REGISTERS>>
5185  IF IR = 0 THEN  RETURN : REM  STOP 'W'ORK COMMAND
```

```
5190  GOSUB 55500: REM   <<WAIT>

5200  IF (PC >  = SAFE) AND (PC <  = NSAFE) THEN 5150
5210  REM  DO NEXT 'FETCH' AND 'EXECUTE'
5300  RETURN : REM  <<END CHAPTER 6>>

29995  REM

       <<EXECUTION OF INSTRUCTIONS>>
30000  GOSUB 61400: REM  <<HOME-CURSOR>>
30010  PRINT "EXECUTING ";BELL$;
30015  IF MN$(IR) = "" THEN MN$(IR) = "???"
       : REM  INCASE NOT KNOWN
30020  PRINT MN$(IR): REM   EXPLAIN

30030  IF IR = 0 THEN 31000
       : REM   IR SAYS WHAT INSTRUCTION TO DO <<BRK>>
30040  IF IR = 234 THEN 31100: REM   <<NOP>>
30050  IF IR = 76 THEN 31200: REM   <<JMP>>

30060  IF IR = 232 THEN 31300: REM <<INX>>
30070  IF IR = 200 THEN 31400: REM   <<INY>>
30080  IF IR = 202 THEN 31500: REM   <<DEX>>
30090  IF IR = 136 THEN 31600: REM     <<DEY>>

30100  IF IR = 240 THEN 31700: REM <<BEQ>>
30110  IF IR = 208 THEN 31800: REM <<BNE>>
30120  IF IR = 16 THEN 31900: REM <<BPL>>
30130  IF IR = 48 THEN 32000: REM  <<BMI>>

30140  IF IR = 162 THEN 32100: REM  <<LDX #>>
30150  IF IR = 160 THEN 32200: REM  <<LDY #>>
30160  IF IR = 142 THEN 32300: REM  <<STX-MEMORY>>
30170  IF IR = 140 THEN 32400: REM <<STY-MEMORY>>
30180  IF IR = 174 THEN 32500: REM   <<LDX-MEMORY>>
30190  IF IR = 172 THEN 32600: REM  <<LDY-MEMORY>>
30200  IF IR = 24 THEN 32700: REM <<CLC>>
30210  IF IR = 184 THEN 32800: REM <<CLV>>
30220  IF IR = 56 THEN 32900: REM <<SEC>>
30230  IF IR = 169 THEN 33000: REM <<LDA #>>
30240  IF IR = 173 THEN 33100: REM   <<LDA-MEMORY>>
30250  IF IR = 141 THEN 33200: REM  <<STA-MEMORY>>
```

```
30260  IF IR = 105 THEN 33300: REM  <<ADC #>>
30270  IF IR = 109 THEN 33400: REM    <<ADC-MEMORY>>
30280  IF IR = 233 THEN 33500: REM <<SBC#>>
30290  IF IR = 237 THEN 33600: REM <<SBC-MEMORY>>
30300  IF IR = 216 THEN 33700: REM <<CLD>>
30310  IF IR = 248 THEN 33800: REM <<SED>>
30320  IF IR = 144 THEN 33900: REM <<BCC>
30330  IF IR = 176 THEN 34000: REM <BCS>>
30340  IF IR = 80 THEN 34100: REM <<BVC>>
30350  IF IR = 112 THEN 34200: REM  <<BVS>>

30360  IF IR = 170 THEN 34300: REM <<TAX>>
30370  IF IR = 138 THEN 34400: REM  <<TXA>>
30380  IF IR = 72 THEN 34500: REM  <<PHA>
30390  IF IR = 104 THEN 34600: REM <<PLA>>
30400  IF IR = 32 THEN 34700: REM  <<JSR>>
30410  IF IR = 96 THEN 34800: REM <<RTS>>
30900  PRINT EH$: REM    DON'T UNDERSTAND
30905  IF TYPE%(IR) <  > 0 THEN  PRINT "NOT ANIMATED"
30910 IR = 0
      : REM  FORCE ANIMATION TO STOP ON THIS UNKNOWN INSTRUCTION
30920  RETURN : REM   <<END EXECUTE>>

31000  RETURN : REM    <<BRK>>
31100  RETURN : REM    <<NOP>>

31200 SC =  PEEK (PC)
31210  GOSUB 54000: REM   <<DISPLAY-REGISTERS>>
31220 PC = PC + 1: REM  INCREMENT THE PROGRAMME COUNTER
31230  GOSUB 55500: REM  <<WAIT>>
31240 SC =  PEEK (PC) * 256 + SC: REM  USE NEW VALUE
31250 PC = PC + 1: REM  INCREMENT
31260  GOSUB 55500: REM  <<WAIT>>
31270 PC = SC: REM  PUSH SCRATCH REGISTER INTO PROGRAMME COUNTER
31280  RETURN : REM  <<END JMP>>

31300 ADJUST = XREG + 1: REM  <<INX>
31310  GOSUB 52000: REM  <<GO-ADJUST>>
31320 XREG = ADJUST
31330  RETURN : REM    <<END INX>>

31400 ADJUST = YREG + 1: REM   <<INY>
```

```
31410  GOSUB 52000: REM   <<GO-ADJUST>>
31420 YREG = ADJUST
31430  RETURN : REM     <<END INY>>

31500 ADJUST = XREG - 1: REM   <<DEX>
31510  GOSUB 52000: REM   <<GO-ADJUST>>
31520 XREG = ADJUST
31530  RETURN : REM   <<END DEX>>

31600 ADJUST = YREG - 1: REM     <<DEY>
31610  GOSUB 52000: REM    <<GO-ADJUST>>
31620 YREG = ADJUST
31630  RETURN : REM  <<END DEY>>

31700  GOSUB 51000: REM  <<GET-NEXT-MEMORY-LOCATION>>
31710  IF Z$ < > "S" THEN  RETURN
31720  GOSUB 50000: REM  <<CHANGE-PROGRAMME-COUNTER>>
31730  RETURN : REM   <<END BEQ>>

31800  GOSUB 51000: REM    <<GET-NEXT-MEMORY-LOCATION>>
31810  IF Z$ < > "C" THEN  RETURN
31820  GOSUB 50000: REM    <<CHANGE-PROGRAMME-COUNTER>>
31830  RETURN : REM    <<END BNE>>

31900  GOSUB 51000: REM     <<GET-NEXT-MEMORY-LOCATION>>
31910  IF N$ < > "C" THEN  RETURN
31920  GOSUB 50000: REM     <<CHANGE-PROGRAMME-COUNTER>>
31930  RETURN : REM     <<END BPL>>

32000  GOSUB 51000: REM      <<GET-NEXT-MEMORY-LOCATION>>
32010  IF N$ < > "S" THEN  RETURN
32020  GOSUB 50000: REM      <<CHANGE-PROGRAMME-COUNTER>>
32030  RETURN : REM <<END BMI>>

32100  GOSUB 51000: REM  <<FETCH-ANOTHER>>
32110 ADJUST = SC: GOSUB 52000: REM     <<GO ADJUST>>
32120 XREG = ADJUST: REM   LOAD X-REGISTER
32130  RETURN : REM   <<END LDX #>>

32200  GOSUB 51000: REM   <<FETCH-ANOTHER>>
32210 ADJUST = SC: GOSUB 52000: REM    <<GO ADJUST>>
32220 YREG = ADJUST: REM    LOAD Y-REGISTER
```

```
32230  RETURN : REM    <<END LDY #>>

32300  GOSUB 51000: REM  <<FETCH-ANOTHER>>
32310  GOSUB 51500: REM  <<USE-PC-YET-AGAIN>>
32320  POKE (SC),XREG: REM    STORE THE X-REGISTER
32330  RETURN : REM <<END STX-MEMORY>>

32400  GOSUB 51000: REM  <<FETCH-ANOTHER>>
32410  GOSUB 51500: REM  <<USE-PC-YET-AGAIN>>
32420  POKE (SC),YREG: REM    STORE THE Y-REGISTER
32430  RETURN : REM <<END STY-MEMORY>>

32500  GOSUB 51000: REM  <<FETCH-NEXT-MEMORY>>
32510  GOSUB 51500: REM  <<USE-PC-AGAIN>>
32520 SC =  PEEK (SC): REM   USE 'SCRATCH' REGISTER TO FETCH
32530 ADJUST = SC: GOSUB 52000: REM   <<ADJUST-N-Z-FLAGS>>
32540 XREG = ADJUST: REM  LOAD THE X-REGISTER
32550  RETURN : REM <<END LDX-MEMORY>>

32600  GOSUB 51000: REM   <<FETCH-NEXT-MEMORY>>
32610  GOSUB 51500: REM   <<USE-PC-AGAIN>>
32620 SC =  PEEK (SC): REM    USE 'SCRATCH' REGISTER TO FETCH
32630 ADJUST = SC: GOSUB 52000: REM    <<ADJUST-N-Z-FLAGS>>
32640 YREG = ADJUST: REM   LOAD THE Y-REGISTER
32650  RETURN : REM  <<END LDY-MEMORY>>

32700 C$ = "C"
32710  RETURN : REM <<END CLV>>
32800 V$ = "C"
32810  RETURN : REM  <<END CLV>>
32900 C$ = "S"
32910  RETURN : REM <<END SEC>>

33000  GOSUB 51000: REM  <<FETCH-ANOTHER>>
33010 ADJUST = SC: GOSUB 52000: REM  <<SET-N-Z-FLAGS>>
33020 AREG = ADJUST: REM  LOAD A-REGISTER
33030  RETURN : REM <<END LDA #>>

33100  GOSUB 51000: REM <<FETCH-NEXT-MEMORY>>
33110  GOSUB 51500: REM <<USE-PC-YET-AGAIN>>
```

```
33120 SC =  PEEK (SC): REM  USE 'SCRATCH' REGISTER TO FETCH
33130 ADJUST = SC: GOSUB 52000: REM  <<SET-N-Z-FLAGS>>
33140 AREG = ADJUST: REM  SET A-REGISTER
33150  RETURN : REM <<END LDA-MEMORY>>

33200  GOSUB 51000: REM <<FETCH-ANOTHER>>
33210  GOSUB 51500: REM  <<USE-PC-YET-AGAIN>>
33220  POKE (SC),AREG: REM  STORE A-REGISTER
33230  RETURN : REM <<END STA-MEMORY>>
33300  GOSUB 51000: REM <<FETCH-ANOTHER>
33305 P1 = AREG:P2 = SC

33310 AREG = AREG + SC: IF C$ = "S" THEN AREG = AREG + 1
      : REM  ADD
33320 ADJUST = AREG: GOSUB 52500: REM  <<SET-N-V-Z-C>>
33330 AREG = ADJUST: REM  BECAUSE OF THE EXTRA 1
33340  RETURN : REM <<END ADC #>>

33400  GOSUB 51000: REM <<FETCH-ANOTHER-MEMORY>>
33410  GOSUB 51500: REM  <<USE-PC-YET-AGAIN>>
33420 SC =  PEEK (SC): REM  USE 'SCRATCH' REGISTER TO FETCH
33425 P1 = AREG:P2 = SC
33430 AREG = AREG + SC: IF C$ = "S" THEN AREG = AREG + 1
      : REM  ADD
33440 ADJUST = AREG: GOSUB 52500: REM  <<SET-N-Z-V-C-FLAGS>>
33450 AREG = ADJUST
33460  RETURN : REM  <<END ADC-MEMORY>>

33500  GOSUB 51000: REM <<FETCH-ANOTHER>>
33505 P1 = AREG:P2 = SC
33510 AREG = AREG - SC - 1: IF C$ = "S" THEN AREG = AREG + 1:
      REM SUBTRACT
33520 ADJUST = AREG: GOSUB 52500: REM   <<SET-N-Z-V-C-FLAGS>>
33530 AREG = ADJUST: REM  BECUASE OF THE EXTRA 1
33540  RETURN : REM <<END SBC #>>

33600  GOSUB 51000: REM <<FETCH-NEXT-MEMORY>>
33610  GOSUB 51500: REM ,,USE-PC-YET-AGAIN>>
33620 SC =  PEEK (SC): REM  USE 'SCRATCH' REGISTER TO FETCH
33625 P1 = AREG:P2 = SC
33630 AREG = AREG - SC - 1: IF C$ = "S" THEN AREG = AREG + 1:
      REM SUBTRACT
```

```
33640 ADJUST = AREG: GOSUB 52500: REM  <<SET-N-Z-V-C>>
33650 AREG = ADJUST
33660  RETURN : REM <<END SBC-MEMORY>>

33700 D$ = "C"
33710  RETURN : REM <<CLD>>
33800 D$ = "S"
33810  RETURN : REM  <<SED>>

33900  GOSUB 51000: REM <<FETCH-ANOTHER-BYTE>>
33910  IF C$ <  > "C" THEN  RETURN
33920  GOSUB 50000: REM <<CHANGE-PC>>
33930  RETURN : REM <<END BCC>>
34000  GOSUB 51000: REM  <<FETCH-ANOTHER-BYTE>>
34010  IF C$ <  > "S" THEN  RETURN
34020  GOSUB 50000: REM  <<CHANGE-PC>>
34030  RETURN : REM   <<END BCS>>

34100  GOSUB 51000: REM   <<FETCH-ANOTHER-BYTE>>
34110  IF V$ <  > "S" THEN  RETURN
34120  GOSUB 50000: REM   <<CHANGE-PC>>
34130  RETURN : REM    <<END BVC>>

34200  GOSUB 51000: REM    <<FETCH-ANOTHER-BYTE>>
34210  IF V$ <  > "C" THEN  RETURN
34220  GOSUB 50000: REM    <<CHANGE-PC>>
34230  RETURN : REM    <<END BVS>>
34300 XREG = AREG
34310 ADJUST = XREG: GOSUB 52000: REM  SET N AND Z FLAGS
34320  RETURN : REM   <<END TAX>>

34400 AREG = XREG
34410 ADJUST = AREG: GOSUB 52000: REM   SET N AND Z FLAGS
34420  RETURN : REM   <<END TXA>>

34500 PUSH = AREG
34510  GOSUB 48000: REM <<DO-PUSH>>
34520 ADJUST = AREG: GOSUB 52000: REM  SET ^N
34530  GOSUB 57500: REM  <<DISPLAY-STACK>>
34540  RETURN : REM  <<END PHA>>

34600  GOSUB 48100: REM  <<DO-PULL>>
```

```
34610 AREG = PULL
34620 ADJUST = AREG: GOSUB 52000: REM  SET N AND Z FLAGS
34630  RETURN : REM  <<END PLA>>

34700 PUSH =  INT (PC / 256): REM  GET HI-BYTE OF PC
34710  GOSUB 48000: REM <<PUSH-ONTO-STACK>>
34720 PUSH = PC - 256 * PUSH: REM  FIND LO-BYTE
34730  GOSUB 48000: REM  <<PUSH-ONTO-STACK>>
34740 SC =  PEEK (PC): REM  GET THE SUBROUTINE ADDRESS
34750 PC = PC + 1
34760 SC =  PEEK (PC) * 256 + SC: REM  COMPLETE THE ADDRESS
34770 PC = SC: REM  CAUSE THE JUMP
34780  GOSUB 57500: REM  DISPLAY THE CHANGES
34790  RETURN : REM  <<END JSR>>

34800  GOSUB 48100: REM  <<PULL-FROM-STACK>>
34810 SC = PULL: REM  STORE VALUE
34820  GOSUB 48100: REM <<PULL-FROM-STACK>>
34830 SC = PULL * 256 + SC
34840 PC = SC + 2: REM   PC NOW POINTS TO INSTRUCTION AFTER JSR
34850  RETURN : REM   <<END RTS>>

38990  REM
        <<FETCH-NEXT-INSTRUCTION>>
39000 ADDREG = PC: REM  GATE OPENED
39010  GOSUB 54000: REM  <<DISPLAY-REGISTERS>>
39020  GOSUB 61400
39030  PRINT "FETCH PART 1 ": REM   EXPLAIN
39040  GOSUB 55500: REM  <<WAIT>>
39100 DREG =  PEEK (ADDRESS): REM  GET THE INFORMATION INTO THE
       DATA REGISTER
39110  GOSUB 54000: REM  <<DISPLAY-THE-REGISTERS.
39120  GOSUB 61400: REM  <<HOME-CURSOR>>
39130  PRINT "FETCH PART 2 "
39140  GOSUB 55500: REM  <<WAIT>>
39200 IRREG = DREG: REM  MOVE INFO OVER
39210  GOSUB 54000: REM  <<DISPLAY-REGISTERS>>
39220  GOSUB 61400: REM  <<HOME-CURSOR>>
39230  PRINT "FETCH PART 3 "
39240  GOSUB 55500: REM  <<WAIT>>
39250 PC = PC + 1: REM  GET READY FOR THE NEXT INSTRUCTION
39260  RETURN : REM    <<END FETCH>>
```

```
39990  REM
     <<LOAD>>
40000  PRINT : PRINT "WHAT STARTING ADDRESS? $";
40010  GOSUB 56000:START = HEX: REM   <<GET-A-HEX-NUMBER>>
40020  IF (START >  = SAFE) AND (START <  = NSAFE) THEN 40100
       : REM  CHECK!

40030  PRINT "UNSAFE";EH$
40040  GOSUB 55500: REM  <<WAIT>>
40050  RETURN : REM  BAD ADDRESS

40100  PRINT : PRINT "TYPE 'END' TO QUIT"
40110  FOR I = START TO NSAFE: REM  DO ALLOWED THINGS
40120 HEX = I: GOSUB 58000: REM  <<PRINT-HEX-NUMBER>>
40130  PRINT ": ";
40140  INPUT ANS$: REM  GET THE ANSWER
40150  IF ANS$ = "END" THEN  RETURN : REM  DONE ENOUGH?
40160  GOSUB 56010: REM  USE PART OF <<GET-HEX-NUMBER>>
40170  POKE (I),HEX: REM  STORE IN MEMORY
40180  NEXT I: REM

40190  PRINT : PRINT "CAN'T ADD ANY MORE ";EH$
40200  GOSUB 55500: REM  <<WAIT>>
40210  RETURN : REM  <<END LOAD>>
40990  REM

     <<STOP>>
41000  GOSUB 61100: REM   <<CLEAR-THE-SCREEN>>
41010 DOWN = 10: GOSUB 61200: REM  <<MOVE-DOWN-THE-SCREEN>>
41020  PRINT "PROGRAM STOPPING ";EH$;EH$
41030  INPUT "ARE YOU SURE? Y/N ";ANS$
41040  IF  LEN (ANS$) < 1 THEN  PRINT EH$: GOTO 41020
41050  IF  MID$ (ANS$,1,1) = "Y" THEN  STOP
41060  IF  MID$ (ANS$,1,1) <  > "N" THEN  PRINT EH$: GOTO 41020
41070  RETURN : REM  <<END STOP>>

41490  REM

       <<SAVE-MACHINE-CODE>>
41500  PRINT
41510  PRINT "SAVING"
41520  PRINT "TYPE 'END' TO QUIT  'CAT' FOR CATALOG": PRINT
```

```
41530  INPUT "SAVE AS WHAT NAME? ";NAME$
41540  IF NAME$ = "CAT" THEN  GOSUB 61600: GOTO 41500
41550  IF NAME$ = "END" THEN  RETURN
41560  IF  LEN (NAME$) < 5 THEN 41580: REM   CHECK ON '.OBJ'
41570  IF  MID$ (NAME$, LEN (NAME$) - 3,4) = ".OBJ" THEN 41590
41580 NAME$ = NAME$ + ".OBJ"
41590  PRINT "TYPE 'ERR' WHEN ERROR HAPPENS"
41600  INPUT "STARTING ADDRESS $";ANS$
41610  IF ANS$ = "ERR" THEN 41500
41620  GOSUB 56010: REM  JUMP INTO <<GET-HEX>>
41630 START = HEX
41640  INPUT "END ADDRESS $";ANS$
41650  IF ANS$ = "ERR" THEN 41500
41660  GOSUB 56010
41670 LAST = HEX
41680  PRINT : PRINT "SAVING AS ";NAME$

41690  PRINT "START ";:HEX = START: GOSUB 58000
       : REM  <<HEX-PRINT>>
41700  PRINT "  LAST ";:HEX = LAST: GOSUB 58000
41710  PRINT : INPUT "OKAY? ";ANS$
41720  IF  MID$ (ANS$,1,1) = "N" THEN 41500
41730  IF  MID$ (ANS$,1,1) <  > "Y" THEN  PRINT EH$: GOTO 41680
41740  PRINT  CHR$ (4);"BSAVE ";NAME$;",A";START;
       " ,L";LAST - START + 1
41780  REM  xxxCHANGE 41740 FOR YOUR MACHINE xxx
41790  PRINT "SAVED ";NAME$
41800  GOSUB 55500: REM   <<WAIT>>
41810  RETURN : REM <<END SAVE>>
41990  REM

     <<CLEAR>>
42000  GOSUB 61100: REM  <<CLEAR-THE-SCREEN>>
42010 DOWN = 10: GOSUB 61200: REM  <<MOVE-DOWN-THE-SCREEN>>
42020  PRINT "CLEARING MEMORY";EH$;EH$
42030  INPUT "ARE YOU SURE? Y/N ";ANS$
42040  IF  MID$ (ANS$,1,1) = "N" THEN  RETURN
       : REM  MISTAKES HAPPEN
42050  IF  MID$ (ANS$,1,1) <  > "Y" THEN  PRINT EH$: GOTO 42020
       : REM

42100  FOR G1TEMP = SAFE TO NSAFE
```

```
42110  POKE (G1TEMP),0: REM  CLEAR A LOCATION
42120  NEXT G1TEMP
42130  RETURN : REM  <<END CLEAR>>

42990  REM

     <<CHANGE>>
43000  PRINT "WHAT LOCATION $";
43001  INPUT ANS$: IF ANS$ = "END" THEN  RETURN
43010  GOSUB 56010:I = HEX: REM   <<GET-A-HEX-NUMBER>>
43020  IF (I >  = SAFE) AND (I <  = NSAFE) THEN 43100
43030  PRINT "UNSAFE";EH$: REM  BAD LOCATION
43040  GOSUB 55500: REM  <<WAIT>>
43050  RETURN : REM

43100  PRINT "WHAT VALUE $";
43110  GOSUB 56000:J = HEX: REM  <<GET-A-HEX-NUMBER>>
43120  IF (J < 0) OR (J > 255) THEN  PRINT EH$: GOTO 43100
43130  POKE (I),J
43140  GOTO 43000: REM   << CHANGE>>

43990  REM

     <<GO>>
44000  PRINT : PRINT "RUNNING MACHINE LANGUAGE PROGRAMS"
44010  PRINT "IS DANGEROUS FOR YOUR BASIC";EH$;EH$
44020  INPUT "ARE YOU SURE? ";ANS$
44030  IF  MID$ (ANS$,1,1) = "N" THEN  RETURN : REM  MISTAKE
44040  IF  MID$ (ANS$,1,1) <  > "Y" THEN  PRINT EH$: GOTO 44020
       : REM

44050  GOSUB 61300: REM  <<GO-RUN-A-MACHINE-LANGUAGE-PROGRAM>>
44060  RETURN : REM  <<END GO>>

44990  REM

     <<HELP>>
45000  GOSUB 61100: REM  <<CLEAR-THE-SCREEN>>
45010  PRINT "VALID COMMANDS"
45020  PRINT "xxxxxxxxxxxxxx"
45030  PRINT
45032  PRINT "A  - ASSEMBLER FOR MACHINE CODE"
```

```
45035  PRINT "CA - CATALOG FILES ON DRIVE"
45040  PRINT "CH - CHANGE ONE MEMORY LOCATION"
45050  PRINT "CL - CLEAR THE SAFE MEMORY AREA"
45055  PRINT "D  - DISASSEMBLE A MACHINE PROGRAM"
45058  PRINT "GE - GET MACHINE LANGUAGE PROGRAM": PRINT
45060  PRINT "GO - GO DO MACHINE PROGRAM"
45070  PRINT "L  - LOAD MACHINE PROGRAM"
45075  PRINT "SA - SAVE MACHINE LANGUAGE PROGRAM"
45080  PRINT "ST - STOP THIS PROGRAM": REM

45090  PRINT "W  - WORKING MODEL OF MICRO-PROCESSOR"
45200 DOWN = 20: GOSUB 61200: REM  <<MOVE-DOWN-THE-SCREEN>>
45210  INPUT "PRESS RETURN TO CONTINUE ";ANS$
45220  RETURN : REM  <<END HELP>>
45795  REM

     <<DISASSEMBLE>> ***APPLE VERSION***
45800 DISASSEMBLE = 65121: REM     ***ONLY WORKS ON AN APPLE***
45810  PRINT : PRINT "STARTING AT WHAT ADDRESS $";
45820  GOSUB 56000:START = HEX: REM    <<GET-HEX-NUMBER>>
45830 SPECIAL = 58: REM    SPECIAL ZERO PAGE ADDRESS
45840  POKE (SPECIAL),START - 256 *  INT (START / 256)
45850  POKE (SPECIAL + 1),START / 256: REM

45860  GOSUB 61100: REM    <<CLEAR-THE-SCREEN>>
45870  CALL DISASSEMBLE
45880  PRINT : PRINT "PRESS RETURN FOR MORE"
45890  INPUT "ANYTHING ELSE STOPS ";ANS$
45900  IF  LEN (ANS$) = 0 THEN 45860
45910  RETURN : REM       <<END DISASSEMBLE>>
45995  REM

     <<DISASSEMBLE>>
46000  PRINT : PRINT "STARTING AT WHAT ADDRESS? ";
46040  GOSUB 56000:START = HEX: REM   <<GET-HEX-NUMBR>>
46050  GOSUB 46100: REM   GO DO IT
46060  PRINT : PRINT "PRESS RETURN TO QUIT": PRINT "ANYTHING
       ELSE CONTINUES ";
46070  GET ANS$: IF ANS$ = "" THEN 46070
46080  PRINT ANS$: IF ANS$ < > CHR$ (13) THEN 46050
46090  RETURN
46100  GOSUB 61100: REM <<CLEAR-THE-PAGE>>
```

```
46110  FOR NUM = 1 TO 18: REM  MAX 18 ON A PAGE
46120 HEX = START: GOSUB 58000: REM <<PRINT:START-ADDRESS>
46130  PRINT ": ";
46140 M1 =  PEEK (START): REM  VALUES WE 'MIGHT'NEED
46150 M2 =  PEEK (START + 1)
46160 M3 =  PEEK (START + 2)
46170 OVER = 7: GOSUB 61500: REM  <<MOVE-OVER>>
46180 HEX = M1: GOSUB 58000: REM  <<HEX-PRINT>>
46190  PRINT " ";: REM  INSTRUCTION PRINTED
46200 TYPE = TYPE%(M1): REM  FIND TYPE

46210 START = START + 1: REM   KEEP TRACK
46220  IF (TYPE = 0) OR (TYPE = 5) THEN 46400
      : REM  NO MORE PRINTING
46230 HEX = M2: GOSUB 58000: PRINT " ";: REM  <<HEX-PRINT>>
46240 START = START + 1
46250  IF (TYPE = 1) OR (TYPE = 11) THEN 46400
46260 HEX = M3: GOSUB 58000: REM  THIRD <<HEX-PRINT>>
46270 START = START + 1
46280  IF (TYPE = 2) OR (TYPE = 9) OR (TYPE = 10) THEN 46400
46290 TYPE = 0: REM  MUST BE A MISTAKE
46300  PRINT EH$;EH$;: REM  WARNING
46400 OVER = 20: GOSUB 61500: REM    <<MOVE-OVER>>
46410  IF TYPE = 0 THEN  PRINT "EH?";: GOTO 46900
46420  PRINT MN$(M1);" ";: REM  PRINT INSTRUCTION
46430  IF TYPE = 5 THEN 46900: REM   DONE IMPLIED
46440  IF TYPE <  > 1 THEN 46470
46450  PRINT "#$";:HEX = M2: GOSUB 58000: REM  IMMEDIATE
46460  GOTO 46900
46470  IF (TYPE <  > 2) AND (TYPE <  > 9) AND (TYPE <  > 10)
      THEN 46550
46480  PRINT "$";:HEX = M3 * 256 + M2: GOSUB 58000
      : REM   <<HEX-PRINT>>
46490  IF TYPE = 2 THEN 46900: REM     ABSOLUTE
46500  IF TYPE = 9 THEN  PRINT ",X";: GOTO 46900
      : REM  ABSOLUTE,X
46510  IF TYPE = 10 THEN  PRINT ",Y";: GOTO 46900
      : REM  ABSOLUTE,Y
46550  IF TYPE <  > 11 THEN 46600
46560  IF M2 > 127 THEN M2 = M2 - 256: REM  BRANCH INSTRUCTION
46570  PRINT "$";:HEX = START + M2: GOSUB 58000
46580  GOTO 46900: REM  DONE BRANCH
```

```
46600  REM  LEAVE ROOM FOR BRANCH
46900  IF NUM = 0 THEN  RETURN : REM SPECIAL DISASSEMBLE 1 LINE
46905  PRINT
46910  NEXT NUM: REM  END OF LOOP
46920  RETURN : REM  <<END DISASSEMBLER>>
47000  PRINT : PRINT "ASSEMBLER STARTING ADDRESS ";
47010  GOSUB 56000
47020 START = HEX
47030  PRINT "TYPE 'END' TO QUIT": PRINT
47040  GOSUB 62000: PRINT : REM  GOTO PAGE BOTTOM
47045  PRINT "$";:HEX = START: GOSUB 58000: REM  <<PRINT-HEX>>
47050  PRINT ": ";BELL$;
47052 ANS$ = "": REM  GET AROUND COMMAS
47054  GET TEMP$: IF TEMP$ = "" THEN 47054
47055  IF TEMP$ =  CHR$ (8) THEN  PRINT " <<DELETED>>";EH$
       : GOTO 47040
47056  PRINT TEMP$;: IF TEMP$ =  CHR$ (13) THEN 47060
47058 ANS$ = ANS$ + TEMP$: GOTO 47054
47060  IF ANS$ = "END" THEN  RETURN
47070  IF ANS$ = "ERR" THEN 47000: REM

47100  IF  LEN (ANS$) < 2 THEN  PRINT EH$: GOTO 47850
       : REM  ERROR!!
47110  IF  MID$ (ANS$,1,1) <  > "$" THEN 47200
       : REM  HANDLE '$' COMMANDS
47120  GOSUB 56010: IF HEX > 255 THEN 47850
       : REM  JUMP INTO <<GET-HEX>>
47130  POKE (START),HEX
47140 START = START + 1
47150  GOTO 47040
47200  IF  LEN (ANS$) <  > 3 THEN 47300
47210 TYPE = 5: GOSUB 47900: REM  <<GO-LOOK>>
47220  IF FOUND = 0 THEN  GOSUB 47850: REM  ERROR!!!
47230  POKE (START),FOUND: GOTO 47800: REM   <<END IMPLIED>>

47300 TYPE = 0: REM  SO FAR NOT RECOGNIZED
47310  IF  MID$ (ANS$, LEN (ANS$) - 1,1) <  > "," THEN 47410:
       REM     NO ,  X OR ,Y
47320  IF  MID$ (ANS$, LEN (ANS$),1) = "X" THEN TYPE = 9
47330  IF  MID$ (ANS$, LEN (ANS$),1) = "Y" THEN TYPE = 10
47340 ANS$ =  MID$ (ANS$,1, LEN (ANS$) - 2): REM  REMOVE THE ,X
47350  GOSUB 47900: IF FOUND = 0 THEN 47850: REM ERROR!
```

```
47360  POKE (START),FOUND
47370 ANS$ =  MID$ (ANS$.5, LEN (ANS$) - 4)
      : REM     JUST WANT NUMBER PART

47380  GOSUB 56010: POKE (START + 2), INT (HEX / 256)
       : REM HIBYTE
47390  POKE (START + 1),HEX - 256 * ( PEEK (START + 2))
       : REM  LOBYTE
47400  GOTO 47800: REM   <<END ABSOLUTE X AND Y>>

47410  IF  MID$ (ANS$,1,1) < > "B" THEN 47500
47415  IF  MID$ (ANS$,1,3) = "BIT" THEN 47600
       : REM   PATCH FOR 'BIT'
47420 TYPE = 11: GOSUB 47900: IF FOUND = 0 THEN 47850
47430  POKE (START),FOUND: REM  LOAD INSTRUCTION
47440 ANS$ =  MID$ (ANS$,5, LEN (ANS$) - 4)
      : REM      GET JUST THE NUMBER
47450  GOSUB 56010:HEX = HEX - START - 2
47460  IF (HEX > 127) OR (HEX <  - 128) THEN  PRINT "TOO FAR"
       : GOTO 47850
47470  IF HEX < 0 THEN HEX = HEX + 256
47480  POKE (START + 1),HEX: GOTO 47800: REM   <<END BRANCH>>
47500  IF  MID$ (ANS$,5,1) < > "#" THEN 47600
       : REM  NOT IMMEDIATE
47510 TYPE = 1: GOSUB 47900: IF FOUND = 0 THEN 47850
47520  POKE START,FOUND: REM  LOAD INSTRUCTION
47530 ANS$ =  MID$ (ANS$,6, LEN (ANS$) - 5)
      : REM    JUST THE NUMBER PART
47540  GOSUB 56010: IF HEX > 255 THEN 47850
47550  POKE (START + 1),HEX: GOTO 47800: REM  <<END IMMEDIATE>>
47600 TYPE = 2: GOTO 47350: REM  ABSOLUTE IS LIKE ABSOLUTE,X
47790  GOTO 47850: REM  SHOULD NOT GET HERE
47800  GOSUB 62000: REM  <<MOVE-TO-BOTTOM-1>>
47810  PRINT "                                  "
47820  GOSUB 62000: PRINT "$";
47830 NUM = 0: GOSUB 46120: GOTO 47040: REM   DO MORE

47850  PRINT EH$;: INPUT "ERROR - TRY AGAIN?";ANS$
47855  IF  MID$ (ANS$,1,1) = "Y" THEN 47040
       : REM     REALLY START AGAIN
47860  IF  MID$ (ANS$,1,1) < > "N" THEN  PRINT EH$: GOTO 47850
47870  FOR NUM = 1 TO 3: REM DO ERROR
```

```
47880  POKE (START),0: REM   ERROR!!PUR IN 3 BRK'S
47890 START = START + 1: NEXT NUM: GOTO 47040: REM  DO MORE
47895  REM

       <<LOOK FOR INSTRUCTION>>
47900 FOUND = 0: REM   NOT FOUND YET
47910 LOOK$ =  MID$ (ANS$,1,3)
      : REM  LOOK AT FIRST 3 LETTERS ONLY
47920  FOR NUM = 0 TO 255
47930  IF TYPE <  > TYPE%(NUM) THEN  NEXT NUM: RETURN
       : REM   WRONG TYPE
47940  IF LOOK$ <  > MN$(NUM) THEN  NEXT NUM: RETURN
       : REM  WRONG CODE
47950 FOUND = NUM
47960  RETURN
47990  REM

       <<ADD-TO-STACK>> <<DO-PUSH>>
48000  POKE (SP),PUSH: REM  STORE VALUE INTO STACK
48010 SP = SP - 1: REM  ADJUST
48020  IF SP < NSAFE - 7 THEN SP = NSAFE
       : REM   CHECK FOR OVERFLOW
48030  RETURN : REM  <<END DO-PUSH>>

48090  REM

       <<REMOVE FROM STACK>> <<DO-PULL>>
48100 SP = SP + 1: REM   ADJUST AND THEN CHECK
48110  IF SP > NSAFE THEN SP = NSAFE - 7
48120 PULL =  PEEK (SP)
48130  RETURN : REM  <<END DO-PULL>>
49990  REM

<<RELATIVE-ADJUST-PROGRAM-COUNTER>>
50000  IF SC > 127 THEN SC = SC - 256: REM  ADJUST TO DECIMAL
50010 PC = PC + SC: REM  PROGRAMME COUNTER ADJUSTMENT
50020  RETURN : REM  <<END ADJUST-PC>>
50990  REM

        <<FETCH-ANOTHER-MEMORY>>
51000 SC =  PEEK (PC): REM  GET ANOTHER LOCATION
51010 PC = PC + 1: REM  UPDATE PROGRAMME COUNTER
```

```
51020  RETURN : REM <<END FETCH-ANOTHER>>
51500 SC = SC + 256 *  PEEK (PC): REM  GET NEW VALUE FROM
       MEMORY
51510 PC = PC + 1: REM  GET PROGRAMME COUNTER READY
51520  RETURN : REM  <<END USE-PC-YET-AGAIN>>
51990  REM

        <<ADJUST>> ALSO SET N AND Z FLAGS
52000  IF ADJUST < 0 THEN ADJUST = ADJUST + 256: GOTO 52000
52010  IF ADJUST > 255 THEN ADJUST = ADJUST - 256: GOTO 52010
       : REM

52020 Z$ = "C": REM  CLEAR THE 'Z' FLAG
52030  IF ADJUST = 0 THEN Z$ = "S": REM  SET IF NECESSARY

52040 N$ = "C": REM  CLEAR 'N' FLAG
52050  IF ADJUST > 127 THEN N$ = "S": REM  SET IF NECESSARY

52060  RETURN : REM  <<END ADJUST>>

52490  REM <<ADJUST-V-C-FLAGS>>
52500  C$ = "C" : REM CLEAR THE C FLAG
52510  IF (ADJUST > 255) AND ((IR = 105) OR
        (IR = 109)) THEN C$ = "S"
52520  IF (ADJUST > 0) AND ((IR = 233) OR
        (IR = 237)) THEN C$= "S"

52530  REM <<ADJUST-V-FLAG>>
52540  IF (ADJUST > 255) THEN ADJUST = ADJUST - 256
52550  IF (ADJUST < 0) THEN ADJUST = ADJUST + 256
52560  IF (IR = 105) OR (IR = 109) THEN V$ = "C" : GOSUB 52700
52565  REM ADD INSTRUCTIONS
52570  IF (IR = 233) OR (IR = 237) THEN V$ = "C" : GOSUB 52800
52575  REM SUB INSTRUCTIONS
52580  GOTO 52000 : REM <<go-adjust-the-N-and-Z-flags>>
52700  IF (ADJUST >  = 128) OR (ADJUST < 0) THEN 52750
       : REM  ADJUST NEG
52710  IF (P1 >  = 128) AND (P2 >  = 128) THEN V$ = "S"
52720  RETURN : REM  NEG + NEG <> POS
52750  IF (P1 <  = 127) AND (P2 <  = 127) THEN V$ = "S"
52760  RETURN : REM  POS + POS <> NEG
52800  IF (ADJUST >  = 128) OR (ADJUST < 0) THEN 52850: REM
```

```
      ADJUST NEGATIVE
52810  IF (P1 >  = 128) AND (P2 <  = 127) THEN V$ = "S"
52820  RETURN : REM  NEG - POS <> POS
52850  IF (P1 <  = 127) AND (P2 >  = 128) THEN V$ = "S"
52860  RETURN : REM  POS - NEG <> NEG
53990  REM
       <<DISPLAY-REGISTERS>>
54000  GOSUB 61400: REM  <<HOME-THE-CURSOR>>
54010 OVER = 20
54020  GOSUB 61500: REM   <<TAB-OVER>>
54030  PRINT "! IR $";: REM  DISPLAY THE INSTRUCTION REGISTER
54040 HEX = IR: GOSUB 58000: REM   <<DISPLAY-HEX-VALUE>>
54050  PRINT " PC $";: REM  DISPLAY THE PROGRAM COUNTER
54060 HEX = PC: GOSUB 58000: REM  <<DISPLAY-HEX-VALUE>>
54070  PRINT
54080  GOSUB 61500: REM  <<MOVE-OVER>>
54090  PRINT "! DR $";
54100 HEX = DREG: GOSUB 58000: REM   <<DISPLAY-HEX-VALUE>>
54110  PRINT " AR $";
54120 HEX = ADDREG: GOSUB 58000: REM <<PRINT-HEX-NUMBER>>
54130  PRINT
54200  GOSUB 61500: REM  <<MOVE-OVER>>
54210  PRINT "!         SC $";: REM SHOW SCRATCH PAD REGISTER
54220  IF SC < 256 THEN  PRINT "00";
54230 HEX = SC: GOSUB 58000: REM   <<PRINT-HEX-NUMBER>>
54240  PRINT
54300  GOSUB 61500: REM  <<MOVE-OVER>>
54310  PRINT "! X  $";: REM  SHOW X-REGISTER
54320 HEX = XREG: GOSUB 58000: REM <<PRINT-HEX-NUMBER>>
54330  PRINT " Y  $";: REM  SHOW Y REGISTER
54340 HEX = YREG: GOSUB 58000: REM  <<PRINT-HEX-NUMBER>>
54350  PRINT
54400  GOSUB 61500: REM  <<MOVE-OVER>>
54410  PRINT "! A  $";: REM  SHOW A-RGISTER
54420 HEX = AREG: GOSUB 58000: REM  <<PRINT-HEX-NUMBER>>
54430  PRINT " SP $";: REM  SHOW STACK POINTER
54440 HEX = SP: GOSUB 58000: REM  <<PRINT-HEX-NUMBER>>
54450  PRINT
54800  GOSUB 61500: REM  <<TAB-OVER>>
54810  PRINT "!----------------"
       : REM  PUTS BOX AROUND REGISTERS
```

```
54820  IF (SC > NSAFE) OR (SC < SAFE) THEN 54900: REM
       NO CHANGE IN DISPLAY
54830 TSC = SC - SAFE: REM     FIND OUT WHERE IN THE SAFE AREA
54840 DOWN = 9 +  INT (TSC / 8): GOSUB 61200: REM <<MOVE DOWN>>
54850 OVER = 7 + 3 * (TSC - 8 *  INT (TSC / 8)): GOSUB 61500:
      REM  <<MOVE OVER>>
54860  PRINT HEX$( PEEK (SC))
54900  GOSUB 61400: REM  <<HOME-CURSOR>>
54910 DOWN = 3: GOSUB 61200: REM  <<MOVE-DOWN>>
54920  PRINT "C D I N V Z "
54930  PRINT C$;" ";D$;" ";I$;" ";N$;" ";V$;" ";Z$
54940  RETURN : REM  <<END DISPLAY-REGISTER>>

54990  RETURN : REM  <<END REG-DISPLAY>>

54995  REM

     <<DISPLAY-THE-SAFE-AREA>>
55000  GOSUB 61100: REM  <<CLEAR-THE-SCREEN>>
55010 DOWN = 8: GOSUB 61200: REM    <<MOVE-DOWN-THE-SCREEN>>
55020 DISP = SAFE: GOSUB 57000: REM <<DISPLAY-ANY-MEMORY>>
55030  RETURN : REM  <<END DISPLAY-SAFE>>

55490  REM

     <<WAIT>>
55500  FOR WTEMP = 1 TO 30
55510  NEXT WTEMP
55520  RETURN : REM  <<END WAIT>>

55990  REM

     <<GET-A-HEX-NUMBER>>
56000  INPUT ANS$: REM  GET AN INPUT OF NUMBERS AND/OR LETTERS
56010  IF  LEN (ANS$) < 1 THEN  PRINT EH$: GOTO 56000
56020  REM  CHECK INCASE THERE IS NOTHING THERE
56030  IF  MID$ (ANS$,1,1) <  > "$" THEN 56100: REM  NO EXTRA
       '$'
56040  REM  REMOVE THE EXTRA '$'
56050  IF  LEN (ANS$) < 2 THEN  PRINT EH$: GOTO 56000
56060  REM  MAKE SURE THAT THERE WASN'T JUST '$'
56070 ANS$ =  MID$ (ANS$,2, LEN (ANS$) - 1)
```

```
56080  REM   REMOVES '$' AT BEGINNING

56100 HEX = 0: REM  RETURN THE PARAMTER 'HEX'
56110  FOR G1TEMP = 1 TO  LEN (ANS$): REM  CHECK ALL SYMBOLS
56120 TEMP$ =  MID$ (ANS$,G1TEMP,1): REM   GET A SYMBOLS
56130  IF (TEMP$ < "0") OR (TEMP$ > "9") THEN 56150
       : REM  NOT A NUMBER
56140 HEX = HEX * 16 +  VAL (TEMP$): GOTO 56200
      : REM  IS A NUMBER

56150  IF (TEMP$ < "A") OR (TEMP$ > "F") THEN  PRINT EH$
       : GOTO 56000
56160 G2TEMP =  ASC (TEMP$) -  ASC ("A") + 10: REM  TURN LETTER
      INTO NUMBER
56170 HEX = HEX * 16 + G2TEMP: REM

56200  NEXT G1TEMP
56210  IF HEX > 65535 THEN  PRINT EH$: GOTO 56000: REM  TOO BIG
56220  RETURN : REM   <<END HEX-INPUT>>

56990  REM

     <<DISPLAY-ANY-RANGE-OF-MEMORY>>
57000 D1TEMP = DISP + 63
57010  IF D1TEMP > 65535 THEN D1TEMP = 65535
       : REM  DON'T GO TOO HIGH

57020  PRINT "MEMORY STARTING AT $";
57030 HEX = DISP: GOSUB 58000: REM  USE OUR NEW ROUTINE AGAIN
57040  PRINT : REM

57050  FOR D2TEMP = DISP TO D1TEMP STEP 8
       : REM  DISPLAY 8 AT A TIME
57060 HEX = D2TEMP: GOSUB 58000: PRINT ": ";:
57070  FOR D3TEMP = 0 TO 7
57080 HEX =  PEEK (D2TEMP + D3TEMP): REM   GET MEMORY VALUE
57090  GOSUB 58000: REM  <<DISPLAY-LARGE-HEX-NUMBER>>
57100  PRINT " ";: REM  PUT SPACE BETWEEN NUMBERS
57110  NEXT D3TEMP
57120  PRINT
57130  NEXT D2TEMP
57140  RETURN : REM  <<END DUMP-ANY-RANGE-MEMORY>>
```

```
57490  REM

       <<DISPLAY-STACK>>
57500 DOWN = 8 +  INT ((NSAFE + 1 - SAFE) / 8): GOSUB 61200:
      REM <<MOVE-DOWN>>
57510 OVER = 7: GOSUB 61500: REM  MOVE OVER
57520  FOR NUM = (NSAFE - 7) TO NSAFE
57530 HEX =  PEEK (NUM): GOSUB 58000
57540  PRINT " ";
57550  NEXT NUM
57560  PRINT
57570  RETURN : REM   <<END DISPLAY-STACK>>
57990  REM

     <<PRINT-HEX-NUMBERS>>
58000 HITEMP =  INT (HEX / 256): REM  GET PAGE NUMBER
58010  IF HEX > 255 THEN  PRINT HEX$(HITEMP);
      : REM   PRINT IF NEEDED
58020 LOTEMP = HEX - 256 * HITEMP: REM  GET LO-BYTE
58030  PRINT HEX$(LOTEMP);
58040  RETURN : REM   <<END LARGE-HEX-PRINT>>

58995  REM

     <<SET UP HEX SYMBOLS>>
59000  FOR J = 0 TO 9:SYMBOL$(J) =  STR$ (J): NEXT J
59010  FOR J = 10 TO 15
59020 TEMP = J - 10: REM  WORK OUT HOW MUCH BIGGER THAN 10
59030 TEMP =  ASC ("A") + TEMP
      : REM  'ASC' TURNS A LETTER INTO A NUMBER
59040 SYMBOL$(J) =  CHR$ (TEMO): REM   'CHR$' TURNS A NUMBER
      BACK TO A LETTER
59050  NEXT J
59060  RETURN
59095  REM

     <<MAKE-HEX-FROM-DECIMAL-0-TO-255>>
59100 K = 0: REM  NUMBER WE SHALL CHANGE
59110  FOR I = 0 TO 15: REM  THE 'TENS' HEX DIGIT
59120  FOR J = 0 TO 15: REM  THE 'UNITS' HEX DIGIT'
59130 HEX$(K) = SYMBOL$(I) + SYMBOLS$(J)
59140 K = K + 1: REM  MAKE NEXT NUMBER
```

```
59150  NEXT J
59160  NEXT I
59170  RETURN : REM  <<END MAKE-HEX>>
59990  REM

     <<SET-UP-VARIABLES>>
60000 J = 0
60010 SPECIAL = 0
60020 I = 0:K = 0
60030 HEX = 0
60040 HITEMP = 0:LOTEMP = 0
60050 DISP = 0
60060 SAFE = 0:NSAFE = 0
60070 G1TEMP = 0:G2TEMP = 0
60080 START = 0
60090 WTEMP = 0
60100 DISASSEMBLE = 0:SPECIAL = 0
60110 OVER = 0:IR = 0:PC = 0
60120 DREG = 0:ADDREG = 0
60130 SC = 0
60140 XREG = 0:YREG = 0
60150 M1 = 0:M2 = 0:M3 = 0:TYPE = 0
60160 LAST = 0
60490  DIM TYPE%(255)
60500  DIM SYMBOL$(15): DIM MN$(255)
60505 MN$(185) = "LDA":TYPE%(185) = 10: REM  <<LDA-MEM,Y>>
60510  DIM HEX$(255)
60515 MN$(190) = "LDX":TYPE%(190) = 10: REM <<LDX-MEM,Y>>
60520 BELL$ =  CHR$ (7): REM   RINGS THE BELL
60525 MN$(188) = "LDY":TYPE%(188) = 9: REM <<LDY-MEM,X>>
60530 EH$ = BELL$ + BELL$
      : REM  THE COMPUTER DOESN'T 'UNDERSTAND'
60535 MN$(253) = "SBC":TYPE%(253) = 9: REM  <<SBC-MEM,X>>
60545 MN$(157) = "STA":TYPE%(157) = 9: REM <<STA-MEM,X>>
60550 TEMP$ = ""
60555 MN$(153) = "STA":TYPE%(153) = 10: REM <<STA-MEM,Y>>
60565 MN$(201) = "CMP":TYPE%(201) = 1: REM  <<CMP #>>
60570 MN$(0) = "BRK":TYPE%(0) = 5
60575 MN$(205) = "CMP":TYPE%(205) = 2: REM  <<CMP MEM>>
60580 MN$(234) = "NOP":TYPE%(234) = 5
60585 MN$(221) = "CMP":TYPE%(221) = 9: REM <<CMP MEM,X>>
60590 MN$(76) = "JMP":TYPE%(76) = 2
```

```
60595 MN$(217) = "CMP":TYPE%(217) = 10: REM <<CMP MEM,Y>>
60600 N$ = "?":Z$ = "?":D$ = "?"
60605 MN$(224) = "CPX":TYPE%(224) = 1: REM <<CPX #>>
60610 C$ = "?":I$ = "?":V$ = "?"
60615 MN$(236) = "CPX":TYPE%(236) = 2: REM <<CPX MEM>>
60620 MN$(232) = "INX":TYPE%(232) = 5
60625 MN$(192) = "CPY":TYPE%(192) = 1: REM   <<CPY #>>
60630 MN$(200) = "INY":TYPE%(200) = 5
60635 MN$(204) = "CPY":TYPE%(204) = 2: REM   <<CPY MEM>>
60640 MN$(202) = "DEX":TYPE%(202) = 5
60645 MN$(170) = "TAX":TYPE%(170) = 5
60650 MN$(136) = "DEY":TYPE%(136) = 5
60655 MN$(138) = "TXA":TYPE%(138) = 5
60660 MN$(240) = "BEQ":TYPE%(240) = 11
60665 MN$(72) = "PHA":TYPE%(72) = 5
60670 MN$(208) = "BNE":TYPE%(208) = 11
60675 MN$(104) = "PLA":TYPE%(104) = 5
60680 MN$(16) = "BPL":TYPE%(16) = 11
60685 MN$(32) = "JSR":TYPE%(32) = 2
60690 MN$(48) = "BMI":TYPE%(48) = 11
60695 MN$(41) = "AND":TYPE%(41) = 1: REM    <<AND #>>
60700 MN$(162) = "LDX":TYPE%(162) = 1
60705 MN$(45) = "AND":TYPE%(45) = 2: REM   <<AND MEM>>
60710 MN$(160) = "LDY":TYPE%(160) = 1
60715 MN$(61) = "AND":TYPE%(61) = 9: REM  <<AND MEM,X>>
60720 MN$(142) = "STX":TYPE%(142) = 2
60725 MN$(57) = "AND":TYPE%(57) = 10: REM <<AND MEM,Y>>
60730 MN$(140) = "STY":TYPE%(140) = 2
60735 MN$(9) = "ORA":TYPE%(9) = 1: REM <<ORA #>>
60740 MN$(174) = "LDX":TYPE%(174) = 2
60745 MN$(13) = "ORA":TYPE%(13) = 2: REM <<ORA MEM>>
60750 MN$(172) = "LDY":TYPE%(172) = 2
60755 MN$(29) = "ORA":TYPE%(29) = 9: REM <<ORA MEM,X>>
60760 MN$(24) = "CLC":TYPE%(24) = 5
60765 MN$(25) = "ORA":TYPE%(25) = 10: REM  <<ORA MEM,Y>>
60770 MN$(184) = "CLV":TYPE%(184) = 5
60775 MN$(78) = "LSR":TYPE%(78) = 2: REM  <<LSR MEM>>
60780 MN$(56) = "SEC":TYPE%(56) = 5
60785 MN$(74) = "LSR":TYPE%(74) = 5: REM  <<LSR>>
60790 MN$(169) = "LDA":TYPE%(169) = 1
60795 MN$(10) = "ASL":TYPE%(10) = 5: REM <<ASL>>
60800 MN$(173) = "LDA":TYPE%(173) = 2
```

```
60805 MN$(14) = "ASL":TYPE%(14) = 2: REM  <<ASL MEM>>
60810 MN$(141) = "STA":TYPE%(141) = 2
60815 MN$(44) = "BIT":TYPE%(44) = 2: REM     <<BIT MEM>>
60820 MN$(105) = "ADC":TYPE%(105) = 1
60830 MN$(109) = "ADC":TYPE%(109) = 2
60840 MN$(96) = "RTS":TYPE%(96) = 5
60850 MN$(233) = "SBC":TYPE%(233) = 1
60860 MN$(237) = "SBC":TYPE%(237) = 2
60870 MN$(216) = "CLD":TYPE%(216) = 5
60880 MN$(248) = "SED":TYPE%(248) = 5
60890 MN$(144) = "BCC":TYPE%(144) = 11
60900 MN$(176) = "BCS":TYPE%(176) = 11
60910 MN$(80) = "BVC":TYPE%(80) = 11
60930 MN$(112) = "BVS":TYPE%(112) = 11
60940 NAME$ = ""
60950 MN$(125) = "ADC":TYPE%(125) = 9: REM  <<ADC-MEM,X>>
60960 MN$(121) = "ADC":TYPE%(121) = 10: REM <<ADC-MEM,Y>>
60970 MN$(189) = "LDA":TYPE%(189) = 9: REM <<LDA-MEM,X>>
60980  RETURN : REM   <<END SET-UP>>
60990  REM

     <<MAKE-SAFE-AREA>>
61000 SAFE = 0 * 4096 + 3 * 256 + 0 * 16 + 0: REM  ***CHANGE
      FOR YOUR MACHINE***
61010 NSAFE = SAFE + 63: REM  END OF SAFE AREA
61015 SP = NSAFE
61020  RETURN : REM   <<END MAKE-SAFE>>
61095  REM

     <<CLEAR-THE-SCREEN>>
61100  HOME : PRINT  CHR$ (12): REM ***CHANGE FOR YOUR MACHINE***
61110  RETURN
61195  REM

     <<MOVEDOWN-THE-SCREEN>>
61196  REM  PARAMTER <<DOWN>> TELLS HOW FAR TO MOVE
61200  VTAB (DOWN): REM  ***CHANGE FOR YOUR MACHINE***
61210  RETURN
61295  REM

      <<RUN-A-MACHINE-LANGUAGE-PROGRAM>>
61300  PRINT "START ADDRESS $";: REM GET A HEX NUMBER FOR STARTING
61310  GOSUB 56000:START = HEX: REM  <<GO-GET-HEX-NUMBER>>
61320  IF (START < SAFE) OR (START > NSAFE) THEN  PRINT EH$:
```

```
      GOTO 61300: REM CHECK!!!
61340  CALL START: REM  xxxCHANGE FOR YOUR MACHINExxx
61350  RETURN : REM   <<END RUN-MACHINE>>
61390  REM
       <<HOME-THE-CURSOR-TO-THE-TOP-OF-THE-SCREEN>>
61400  VTAB (1): REM  xxxCHANGE FOR YOUR MACHINExxx
61410  RETURN : REM    MAKE SURE YOU DON'T CLEAR THE SCREEN!!!!
61490  REM
       <<TAB-OVER>> MOVE ACROSS TO THE 'OVER' COLUMN
61500  HTAB (OVER): REM  xxxCHANGE FOR YOUR MACHINExxx
61510  RETURN : REM

61590  REM <<CATALOG>>
61600  GOSUB 61100: REM <<CLEAR-SCREEN>>
61610  PRINT  CHR$ (4);"CATALOG "
       : REM   xxxCHANGE FOR YOUR MACHINExxx
61620  PRINT : INPUT "PRESS RETURN TO CONTINUE ";ANS$
61630  RETURN : REM  <<END CATALOG>>
61690  REM
       <<GET-MACHINE-PROGRAM>>
61700  GOSUB 61100: REM  <<CLEAR-SCREEN>>
61710  PRINT "TYPE 'END' IF NO FILE WANTED"
61720  PRINT "TYPE 'CAT' FOR CATALOG"
61730  INPUT "WHAT FILE NAME? ";NAME$
61740  IF NAME$ = "END" THEN  RETURN
61750  IF NAME$ = "CAT" THEN  GOSUB 61600: GOTO 61700
61800  IF  LEN (NAME$) < 5 THEN 61820: REM   CHCK FOR .OBJ
61810  IF  MID$ (NAME$, LEN (NAME$) - 3,4) = ".OBJ" THEN 61830
61820 NAME$ = NAME$ + ".OBJ"
61830  PRINT : PRINT "FETCHING ";NAME$
61840  INPUT "THIS OKAY? ";ANS$
61850  IF  MID$ (ANS$,1,1) = "N" THEN 61700
61860  IF  MID$ (ANS$,1,1) < > "Y" THEN 61830
61900  PRINT  CHR$ (4);"BLOAD ";NAME$
       : REM xxxCHANGE FOR YOUR MACHINExxx
61910  PRINT : PRINT "GOT ";NAME$;BELL$
61920  GOSUB 55500: REM  <<WAIT>>
61930  RETURN : REM  <<END GET>>
61990  REM
      <<MOVE TO BOTTOM OF THE SCREEN - 1>>
```

```
62000 DOWN = 23: REM  xxx CHANGE FOR YOUR MACHINE
62010  GOSUB 61200: REM  <<MOVE-DOWN-THE SCREEN>>
62020  RETURN
```

# Index

Edited by Stephen Moore